VOTES
FOR
WOMEN

CELEBRATING

VOTES

NEW YORK'S

FOR

SUFFRAGE

WOMEN

CENTENNIAL

JENNIFER A. LEMAK
ASHLEY HOPKINS-BENTON

excelsior editions

Published by
STATE UNIVERSITY OF NEW YORK PRESS, ALBANY

© 2017 New York State Education Department, Albany, NY 12230

EXCELSIOR EDITIONS is an imprint of STATE UNIVERSITY OF NEW YORK PRESS
For information, contact State University of New York Press, Albany, NY
www.sunypress.edu

Production and book design, Laurie D. Searl
Marketing, Kate R. Seburyamo

Library of Congress Cataloging-in-Publication Data

Names: Lemak, Jennifer A., author. | Hopkins-Benton, Ashley, author.
Title: Votes for women : celebrating New York's suffrage centennial /
Jennifer A. Lemak and Ashley Hopkins-Benton, New York State Museum.
Description: Albany : State University of New York Press, [2017] | Series:
Excelsior editions | Includes bibliographical references and index.
Identifiers: LCCN 2016056706 (print) | LCCN 2017001024 (ebook) | ISBN
9781438467306 (pbk. : alk. paper) | ISBN 9781438467320 (e-book)
Subjects: LCSH: Women—Suffrage—New York (State)—History. |
Suffragists—New York (State)—Biography.
Classification: LCC JK1911.N7 L46 2017 (print) | LCC JK1911.N7 (ebook) | DDC
324.6/2309747—dc23
LC record available at https://lccn.loc.gov/2016056706

10 9 8 7 6 5 4 3 2 1

CONTENTS

ACKNOWLEDGMENTS

"All men and women are created equal" seems fundamental to a nation founded on the ideals of liberty and democracy, yet this statement created a revolution that continues today. The women who devoted their lives to slowly chipping away at the forces keeping America from realizing this statement deserve our heartfelt thanks and gratitude. We hope the *Votes for Women* exhibition and catalog highlight the bravery and perseverance of the women who fought, and continue to fight, insurmountable odds and strong opposing forces for equal rights. If this exhibition and catalog are successful, it is because we have had a lot of help and support—and a fascinating history to work with.

This exhibition would not have been possible without artifacts, documents, photographs, and information from our lenders. We are grateful for the access to their collections over the last three years and, most importantly, for the friendships we have formed as a result of this project. In addition to our sister institutions, the New York State Library and New York State Archives, over thirty-six lenders are listed here. Without these lenders, there would be no exhibition. Several of the folks we have worked with went above and beyond to help us with this project—Andrew Arpey, Fran Barbieri, Laura Bierman, Travis Bowman, Shannon Butler, Cara Delatte, Yvonne Deligato, Ronna Dixson, Pam Elam, Frank Futral, Noemi Ghazala, Susan Goodier, Diana Mara Henry, Deborah Hughes, Thomas Hunter, Kay Irland, Coline Jenkins, Marguerite Kearns, Monica Mercado, Karen Osburn, Ronnie Lapinski Sax, Diane Shewchuk, Ann Tobey, Sally Roesch Wagner, Judith Wellman, Patricia White, and Carolyn Zogg.

As we began creating this catalog, we were one year away from the opening of the exhibition. The design process for the exhibition had just begun. However, based on past experiences, the New York State Museum exhibition and production staff, Nancy Kelley (director of exhibitions), Mehna Harders Reach (exhibition planner), Ford Bailey (designer), Karen Glaz (graphic designer and responsible for the striking catalog cover image), and Kathryn Weller (director of education and public programs), are top rate and make this exhibition outstanding. Supporting the project as well is the entire NYSM History Department including: John Abeel, Kara Chambers, Matthew DeLaMater, Emily Finelli, Cornelia Frisbee Houde, Robyn Gibson, Devin Lander, Stephen Loughman, Aaron Noble, Karen Quinn, Candace Sanders, Anne Tyrrell, and Brad Utter. Lastly, additional thanks are owed to Nancy Berns, Janet Braga, Marie Culver, Kelley Feranec, Antonia Giuliano, Albert Gnidica, Ethan Hacklin, Scott Heydrick, Chris Kobuskie, Nicole LaFountain, Koren Lazarou, Tom Link, Nicholas Lue, Dawn Mankowski, Bernard Margolis, Andrew Meier, Steve Michalek, Stephanie Miller, Alan Noble, Raissa Robinson, Tom Ruller, Michael Sgambellone, Kathi Stanley, Tamara Zavinski, and a host of others.

There are a few individuals who have spent months working on this catalog. Without them, it would not have become a reality. Shannon Risk served as our content advisor on both the exhibition and catalog. We are also grateful to the scholars who wrote articles for the catalog. Their scholarship broadens its scope and pays tribute to the women and men they researched. Amanda Lanne-Camilli, acquisitions editor at State University of New York Press, has enthusiastically supported this project since the beginning. John Yost, NYSM photographer, lent his artistic talents and photographed each of the artifacts. Vicki Weiss, senior librarian of Manuscripts and Special Collections at the NYSL, made the library's vast collections available to us at a moment's notice, offered her personal research and insights on the suffrage movement, and has been a loyal colleague. Special thanks go to Bridget Enderle, NYSM collections technician. Bridget organized each artifact and image, met every ridiculous deadline with a sense of humor and smile, and skillfully completed a dozen other important tasks. This catalog would not be without Bridget's work.

A multiyear project of this scope would not be possible without institutional support, including the New York State Board of Regents, Chancellor Betty Rosa, and Commissioner of Education MaryEllen Elia. Mark Schaming, director of the NYSM and deputy commissioner for Cultural Education, supported this project since the beginning. He gave us a wide berth and let us create the exhibition we envisioned. Most importantly, Mark made the suffrage centennial a priority for the museum years before 2017.

We are indebted to our families for their support. Our husbands, mothers, and in-laws cared for our children while we were on research trips across the state, read and commented on the manuscript, and listened to our rants on the injustices bestowed upon women over the past 150 years. Lastly, we thank our children. They serve as reminders of why the history of the suffrage and women's rights movement are important.

JENNIFER A. LEMAK AND ASHLEY HOPKINS-BENTON
New York State Museum

CONTRIBUTORS

Votes for Women features collections from the New York State Museum, New York State Library, and the New York State Archives, as well as artifacts and images from historical institutions and private collections across the state:

Albany Institute of History & Art

Bellevue Alumnae Center for Nursing History Archive, Center for Nursing at the Foundation of New York State Nurses

Binghamton University

Bryn Mawr College

Buffalo History Museum

Chautauqua County Historical Society, McClurg Museum

Clinton Historical Society

Coline Jenkins, Elizabeth Cady Stanton Family

Coreen Hallenbeck

Cornell University—PJ Mode Collection of Persuasive Cartography

Cortland County Historical Society

Department of Rare Books and Special Collections, University of Rochester Libraries

Diana Mara Henry Photography

Eleanor Roosevelt National Historic Site, Val-Kill

Elizabeth Cady Stanton Trust

Elizabeth Meaders

Fenimore Art Museum Research Library

FDR Presidential Library and Museum

Geneva Historical Society

Howland Stone Store Museum

Keene Valley Library

Kheel Center, Cornell University

Laura Bierman

League of Women Voters of New York State

Library of Congress

Marguerite Kearns

Matilda Joslyn Gage Foundation

Ms. magazine

Museum of the City of New York

National Museum of American History, Smithsonian

National Susan B. Anthony Museum & House

New York Public Library

New York State Department of Labor

New York State Office of Parks, Recreation, and Historic Preservation,
    Lorenzo State Historic Site

Onondaga Historical Association

Pam Elam Collection

Rochester City Historian

Rochester Historical Society

Ronnie Lapinsky Sax Collection

Seneca Falls Historical Society

Sophia Smith Collection, Smith College

University of Rochester Libraries, Department of Rare Books
    and Special Collections

Women's Rights National Historic Park

Contributors to the catalog:

Robert Chiles
Lecturer, Department of History
University of Maryland, College Park
Essay—"'An Infusion of Hope': New York Women in the Post-Suffrage Era"

Jessica Derleth
Binghamton University
Essay—"'These Model Families': Romance, Marriage, and Family in the New York Woman Suffrage Movement"

Susan Goodier
Book Review Editor, New York History Journal
Department of History, Women's and Gender Studies Affiliate
State University of New York at Oneonta
Essay—"'Bound Together by the Ties of Humanity': Sarah Jane Thompson Garnet"

Traci Langworthy
Associate Professor of History
Jamestown Community College
Essay—"'Just Cause to Feel Proud': Chautauqua County's Leading Role in Grassroots Suffrage Activism"

Karen Pastorello
Professor of History/Chairperson Women and Gender Studies
Tompkins Cortland Community College (SUNY)
Essay—"Recognizing Rights: Men in the Woman Suffrage Campaign"

Shannon M. Risk
Associate Professor of History
Director, Public History and Women's Studies Minors
Niagara University
Essay—"'Give Her of the Fruit of Her Hands': Women's Suffrage Activity on the Buffalo-Niagara Frontier"

Lauren C. Santangelo
Writing Program
Princeton University
Essay—"A 'Monstrous Absurdity': The 1886 Suffrage Protest of the Statue of Liberty"

Sally Roesch Wagner
Founding Director, Matilda Joslyn Gage Center
Adjunct Faculty, The Renée Crown University Honors Program, Syracuse University
Essay—"Breaking the Law for Freedom: The Campaign of Non-Violent Civil Disobedience for the Vote"

Judith Wellman
Director, Historical New York Research Associates
Professor Emerita, State University of New York at Oswego
Essay—"'All Men and Women Are Created Equal': The Legacy of Seneca Falls"

In New York State, we hold dear a simple truth: we are one community. We share each other's benefits and burdens. When all of us do not have the same rights and privileges, we must stand up for one another, because it means that each one of us is lowered. Many movements for equal rights and justice have been born in New York because it is who we are and what we live, and it sends a clear message to the world that this is what America is supposed to be. The women's suffrage movement that began in Seneca Falls embodies this unyielding pursuit of fairness, and set a precedent that continues to this day: New Yorkers simply do not settle for less.

In the 100 years since women gained the right to vote in New York State – three years before the ratification of the 19th Amendment – we have come a long way. However, there is still work to do, and New York will continue to lead the way. We will not turn the clock back on reproductive rights, and we will not allow the important progress of the women's movement to be stopped. As Governor, I have worked to expand rights and protections for women, including measures to end gender discrimination in workplaces, protect young women against sexual assault on college campuses, and provide paid family leave for working families. In New York, we know that women's rights are human rights. Each one of us has benefitted from the milestones achieved by generations of women who actively crusaded against injustice.

As the father of three daughters, I am grateful to the women and men from New York and across the nation who worked tirelessly for suffrage and women's rights. As a human being, I am humbled by their sacrifices and their conviction that we are all equal. As a New Yorker, I am proud of their legacy, and the important lessons we can learn from them still today: none of us are bystanders to history. We can and must take charge. We must address injustices, we must persist, and we must protect these hard-won rights.

The spirit of the women who dedicated their lives to earning the right to vote, many of whom did not live to see their triumph over discrimination, lives on in New Yorkers to this day. We will continue to hold the torch high for people of every gender, religion, background, and sexual orientation, reaching ever upward in the fight for equality and justice for all.

Sincerely,

Governor Andrew M. Cuomo

MESSAGE FROM SENATOR KIRSTEN GILLIBRAND

On Election Day in 1872, a woman from Rochester named Susan B. Anthony went to the polls like any engaged citizen would and cast her ballot. About a week later, she was arrested. Her crime? Voting. For more than half of our country's history, it was illegal for a woman to vote in the United States of America.

It is hard to imagine an arrest like that happening today—an American woman being hauled into the police station simply because she cast a ballot. Most Americans aren't old enough to remember a time when women weren't allowed to vote, and many New York women today serve in elected office, from city council to mayor to lieutenant governor—and even as a candidate for president of the United States.

But when the idea was proposed in Seneca Falls, in 1848, that women should be allowed to vote, to many people it was blasphemy. It was dangerous. It was shocking. It took many decades for the country's mood to shift, and by the time the Nineteenth Amendment passed through Congress in 1919, and then was ratified in 1920, the idea that women and men should have the same political rights wasn't so shocking anymore.

This was a monumental change. In just a few generations, our country had gone from arresting women for voting to amending our Constitution and guaranteeing a woman's right to vote. How did this happen? Because brave and brilliant New York women, from Elizabeth Cady Stanton to Susan B. Anthony, Matilda Joslyn Gage to Eleanor Roosevelt, along with the men who supported them, were willing to raise their voices about extraordinary injustices. Without their willingness to speak out, to march, to protest, and even to risk arrest, would American women today be allowed to vote?

We should all feel proud to be New Yorkers. The women's suffrage movement was born in New York State, it was planned here, it was developed here, and now, nearly a century after the Nineteenth Amendment was passed, New York continues to be at the forefront of fighting for women's rights. The long and difficult battle to give women the right to vote is over—we won with the Nineteenth Amendment—but there are many issues today that affect women, that people may not have been thinking about in 1919, and that we still have to work hard to solve.

We are the only industrialized country that doesn't guarantee its workers some form of paid leave, which means many new mothers and other women who need to take care of sick family members can't without giving up a paycheck or being fired. Women make up two-thirds of minimum wage earners, but our minimum wage is well below the poverty line. Quality daycare is unaffordable for many families, especially the large and growing number of families in which the woman is the primary breadwinner. And the final injustice sounds like a relic from 1919, but it still exists today: the average American woman is still paid just eighty cents for every dollar a man makes. We still don't have equal pay for equal work.

Who will be the next Susan B. Anthony and Elizabeth Cady Stanton? Who will fight these twenty-first-century battles for women's rights? The New York State Museum has put on an extraordinary exhibit to commemorate the women's suffrage movement and the Nineteenth Amendment, and I hope it inspires a new generation of women and men to raise their voices about all the injustices in their lives.

KIRSTEN GILLIBRAND
United States Senator for New York State

MESSAGE FROM LIEUTENANT GOVERNOR
ᛕATHY HOCHUL

Here in New York State, we have a long-standing reputation to uphold. It's an enduring legacy of empowerment and equal rights that began nearly 170 years ago. And the voices of its champions echo today in the corridors of power around the globe. Voices of bold women who stood against the tides of their time.

This year marks the one hundredth anniversary of women's suffrage in New York State, which led the fight to get women the right to vote, setting the stage for future battles against workplace discrimination, to achieve pay equity and to preserve a woman's right to make decisions about her health care.

The first-ever women's rights convention, held in Seneca Falls, was organized by Lucretia Mott and Elizabeth Cady Stanton. Sixty-nine years later, women in New York State won the right to vote. Three years after that, the Nineteenth Amendment was ratified, granting all women the right to vote as protected by the United States Constitution.

As chair of the New York State Women's Suffrage 100th Anniversary Commemoration Commission, I am proud to lead an effort to promote this anniversary through a series of statewide programs and events large and small and through this exhibit at the New York State Museum. We are celebrating the accomplishments of women and their contributions to our history and taking the message of women's equality across the state.

At the same time, as the state's highest-ranking elected woman, I hope we can inspire the next generation of young women who want to arise and achieve great things themselves.

In Congress, only 19 percent of our representatives are women. In the New York State Legislature, women are very proud to have moved up to 26 percent. But across the nation in local government, where many elected leaders get their start, only 13 percent of women are chief administrative officers like mayors, supervisors, or county executives. And that number hasn't moved since 1970.

We still have a long way to go, yes, but let's seize the opportunity we have in the coming years and join to lift and inspire the next generation of women leaders. One hundred years from now, when women in the future look back to 2017–2020, what are they going to say about us? What will they be celebrating about the men and women in New York State from our era, and what are we doing to further the legacy of the courageous women on whose shoulders we now stand?

I hope you will join me and the other commission members at events in every corner of the state in the years ahead. Bring your friends and, most importantly, share these occasions with younger generations. Together, we can continue our progress forward and make our foremothers proud.

KATHY HOCHUL
Lieutenant Governor of the State of New York

MESSAGE FROM
BOARD OF REGENTS CHANCELLOR BETTY A. ROSA
AND COMMISSIONER OF EDUCATION MARYELLEN ELIA

New York State plays a central role in American history. Many New Yorkers—the nation's greatest thought leaders, innovators, artists, and everyday people—have changed the world. In fact, it was here in the Empire State that the women's rights movement was born.

In 2017 we celebrate the centennial of New York State granting women the right to vote. The struggle of gaining the vote was long sought and long fought. Thousands of New Yorkers—both women and men—advocated for women's suffrage for decades.

When New York granted women the right to vote in 1917, it was one of the first states east of the Mississippi River to do so. A few years later, in 1920, the Nineteenth Amendment was ratified and added to the US Constitution, stating "the right of citizens of the United States to vote shall not be denied or abridged by the United States or by any state on account of sex."

A century later, we reflect on New York's women's suffrage centennial with an exhibition at the New York State Museum: Votes for Women. As an educational institution under the State Education Department and the Board of Regents, the State Museum is charged with serving the lifelong educational needs of New Yorkers.

To accomplish this mission, the State Museum worked with its sister institutions—the New York State Library and New York State Archives—to feature objects from their world-class collections in the exhibition. In addition, Votes for Women includes artifacts from historical institutions and private collections throughout the state—from the Susan B. Anthony House to the Elizabeth Cady Stanton Trust. The State Education Department is grateful to all lending institutions for helping to truly make this exhibition representative of the fight for women's suffrage across the state.

The story of how women in New York fought and won the right to vote records not only a pivotal moment in history; it's also an educational opportunity. From lesson plans to professional development workshops for teachers, the museum has resources to support educators. Teachers can show students how the fight for women's rights began in New York with powerful women like Elizabeth Cady Stanton, Sojourner Truth, and Inez Milholland. Students can learn how New York women used multiple strategies, all peaceful, to make their voices heard, even though they did not yet have the vote.

We cannot understand where we are today or where we are going in the future without learning about our past. The women's suffrage movement in New York not only teaches us about the struggle for women's rights, but it also teaches us about our cultural heritage, activism, democracy, and the struggle for equal rights.

The fight for women's rights and equality continues across the world. To close with the words of Susan B. Anthony, women's rights activist and staunch leader of the women's suffrage movement in New York: "Failure is impossible."

BETTY A. ROSA
New York State Board of Regents Chancellor

MARYELLEN ELIA
New York State Education Commissioner

ƎNTRODUCTION

In 1923, Alice Paul, leader of the National Woman's Party, used the power of history when she proposed the Equal Rights Amendment in Seneca Falls on the seventy-fifth anniversary of the Woman's Rights Convention. Paul stated, "We tie this amendment to the 1848 movement. It is easier to get support for something with tradition behind it . . ."[1] Seventy-five years earlier, Elizabeth Cady Stanton and Lucretia Mott also summoned the past when they based the Declaration of Sentiments on the language of the Declaration of Independence, stating, "We hold these truths to be self-evident: That all men *and women* are created equal." These women understood the power of the past and used it to gain freedoms that were not awarded to them by the Founding Fathers.

On November 6, 1917, New York State passed the referendum for women's suffrage. This victory was an important event for New York State and the nation for several reasons. Passage of women's suffrage in New York State was the national suffrage movement's first electoral triumph east of the Mississippi River. The Empire State carried forty-seven electoral votes and assured forty-five seats in the US House of Representatives. Suffrage in New York State signaled that the national passage of suffrage would soon follow, and in August 1920, "Votes for Women" were constitutionally guaranteed.

Women began asserting their independence long before 1848. However, the coordinated work for women's suffrage began in earnest in 1848. The Seneca Falls convention served as a catalyst for debates and action on both the national and state levels. Women like Susan B. Anthony and Matilda Joslyn Gage organized and rallied for support of women's suffrage throughout upstate New York at women's rights conventions that culminated with the third national meeting held in Syracuse in 1852 (the first two meetings were held in Worcester, Massachusetts). Reforms during this time were not strictly focused on voting rights. Women wanted equal access to education; better jobs; changes in marriage, divorce, and property laws; and dress reform.

Prior to the Civil War, advocates for the rights of women were first involved with abolitionist activities, but after the war debates over the Fourteenth and Fifteenth Amendments split the women's movement. Some women's rights advocates (including Elizabeth Cady Stanton and Susan B. Anthony) refused to support any suffrage amendment that did not include women, while others (Frederick Douglass and Lucy Stone) felt that supporting African American males would be a pathway toward women's suffrage. In response to this split, in 1869, Stanton and Anthony organized the National Woman Suffrage Association (NWSA) in New York City to work toward woman suffrage. This group advocated for a federal amendment to ensure women the vote until it merged with the American Woman Suffrage Association (AWSA) in 1890, thus creating the National American Woman Suffrage Association (NAWSA). Elizabeth Cady Stanton was elected as its first president.

By the dawn of the twentieth century, the political and social landscape was much different in New York State than fifty years before. The state had experienced dramatic advances in industrialization and urban growth, and several large waves of immigrants settled there. Many women worked outside the home and, as a result, the reformers' priorities shifted to labor issues, health care, and temperance, in addition to women's suffrage. At this time, a new group of reformers from across the state began, again, working toward suffrage with new tactics. Harriot Stanton Blatch formed the Women's Political Union, Carrie Chapman Catt organized the state's suffrage workers under the Empire State Campaign Committee, and thousands of other women organized, marched in parades, attended meetings, and signed petitions. During this time, anti-suffrage sentiment was strong and the New York State suffrage amendment was voted down in 1915. Nonetheless, two years later, on November 6, 1917, New Yorkers finally approved women's suffrage with 53 percent voting yes. Immediately following this victory, the state's reformers used New York's momentum to help propel the passage of the Nineteenth Amendment in 1920.

After New York's women won the vote, its leaders continued reform efforts throughout the twentieth century. African American women made progress for civil rights through club activities—the Empire State Federation of Women's Clubs worked with the National Association for the Advancement of Colored People (NAACP) and the National Urban League. First Lady Eleanor Roosevelt and Secretary of the Department of Labor Frances Perkins made history on the state and national levels. Betty Friedan wrote the *Feminine Mystique* in 1963 and three years later helped to found the National Organization for Women (NOW), a feminist organization whose leaders worked toward equal job opportunities and pay for women. In the 1970s, Gloria Steinem and others founded *Ms.* magazine, which served as a voice for the new feminist movement. In 1972, pathbreaker Shirley Chisholm of Brooklyn became the first African American woman to run for the office of president for the Democratic Party, and in more recent decades, New York women, including Bella Abzug, Geraldine Ferraro, Hillary Rodham Clinton, and Kirsten Gillibrand, sought and were elected to positions in public office, continuing the work that began in Seneca Falls in 1848.

The *Votes for Women* catalog presents research about and artifacts from the exhibition at the New York State Museum between November 4, 2017 and May 13, 2018. Focused essays from historians on various aspects of the suffrage and equal rights movements around New York State provide greater detail about local stories with statewide significance. Judith Wellman writes about the powerful mix of diversity in Seneca Falls and the zeitgeist of its geographic location that helped to start the women's rights movement. Sally Roesch Wagner's essay discusses how a small group of New York women used civil disobedience to sway the opinions set by passage of the Fourteenth and Fifteenth Amendments. Shannon Risk and Traci Langworthy write about the movement in western New York; Risk focuses on Buffalo and the numerous women's rights workers and organizations at the local level, while Langworthy focuses on Chautauqua County and area grassroots organizations there that supported suffrage such as the Grange and the Woman's Christian Temperance Union. Karen Pastorello's essay discusses the role of men and their collaborations with women in the fight for suffrage in New York State, while Susan Goodier's essay focuses on Sarah Jane Thompson Garnet, an African American woman who worked to combat both racism and sexism and led the Colored Women's Suffrage League in Brooklyn in the late nineteenth century.

Anita Pollitzer and Alice Paul at Susan B. Anthony gravesite, July 1923, Rochester, New York, photograph.

Jessica Derleth writes about the role of marriage and motherhood in the suffrage movement. Lauren Santangelo recounts the protest organized in 1886 by Lillie Devereux Blake at the dedication ceremony of the Statue of Liberty in New York Harbor. The irony of a giant female statue dedicated to women was not lost on the New York City suffragists. Lastly, Robert Chiles writes about women's voting patterns and how New York politicians dealt with their new constituency.

The centennial of women's suffrage in New York State provides an opportunity to reexamine the efforts of the state's women and men who worked for the vote and the efforts toward equality since the vote. In June 2016, on the evening when Hillary Rodham Clinton was the first female to be declared the presumptive presidential nominee from a major political party, she evoked the power of the past: "Tonight's victory is not about one person, it belongs to generations of women and men who struggled and sacrificed and made this moment possible. In our country, it started right here in New York, a place called Seneca Falls."[2]

It is with the idea that there is power in the past that we celebrate the centennial of the passage of women's suffrage in New York State in 2017.

SECTION 1

Agitate! Agitate!
1776–1890

"Abigail Adams, Mrs. Washington, Mrs. Hamilton, Mrs. Madison, Louisa C. Adams," engraving, R. Soper, in *Godey's Lady's Book*, date unknown.

This illustration, depicts the wives of some of the founding fathers, including Abigail Adams. Despite living in an era where they were generally seen as an accompaniment to their respective husbands, this group of women boasts a lengthy list of achievements. Courtesy of the New York State Museum, H–1940.17.1420.

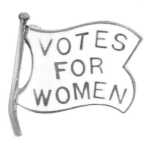

The 1848 women's rights convention, held in Seneca Falls, New York, is often referenced as a starting point of the women's rights movement in the United States. Certainly, this event propelled the cause to a much more prominent place in the reform discussions of the nineteenth century. However, women and men had been talking, writing, and working for equality for a long time.

IN WRITING AND IN SPEECH

During the Revolutionary War, many American women closely followed the discussions of patriots, hoping for better rights for both women and men. Abigail Adams expressed this hope, to her husband, John Adams, as he served in the Continental Congress. Abigail made frequent entreaties that as the representatives worked to set up a new government, they should "remember the ladies and be more generous and favorable to them than your ancestors."[1] She also declared the need for greater education for women, writing to John,

> If you complain of neglect of Education in sons, What shall I say with regard to daughters, who every day experience the want of it. With regard to the Education of my own children, I find myself soon out of my depth, and destitute and deficient in every part of Education. I most sincerely wish that some more liberal plan might be laid and executed for the Benefit of the rising Generation, and that our new constitution may be distinguished for Learning and Virtue. If we mean to have Heroes, Statesmen and Philosophers, we should have learned women.[2]

Abigail complained, "whilst you are proclaiming peace and goodwill to Men, Emancipating all Nations, you insist upon retaining an absolute power over Wives."[3]

Following the war, there were new expectations for the education of men, for them to become self-reliant and productive citizens. While women were still barred from participating in government through voting, their role as the mothers who prepared future citizens was recognized. Through this concept of "republican motherhood," women experienced some expansion of their educational opportunities, just as Adams had called for.

"Frances Wright," engraving, ca. 1881.

Elizabeth Cady Stanton, Susan B. Anthony, and Matilda Joslyn Gage honored Frances Wright's contributions to the women's rights movement by featuring her portrait on the frontispiece of the first volume of the *History of Woman Suffrage*. They focused on Wright's attacks on the lack of separation of church and state, the impact the relationship had on women, as well as the persecution Wright received for speaking out on these views. In *History of Woman Suffrage*, Vol. 1, frontispiece. Courtesy of the New York State Library, Manuscripts and Special Collections, 324.3 S79 V.1.

British author and educator Mary Wollstone-craft (1759–1797) published the treatise *A Vindication of the Rights of Woman* in 1792. In it, she pointed to the lack of educational opportunities for middle-class women as the root of their oppression. Wollstonecraft's essay was certainly on the minds of women reformers in America, since she was frequently cited in their writings through the mid-nineteenth century.

Born in Scotland, Frances "Fanny" Wright (1795–1852) traveled extensively in the United States in the early nineteenth century. Her observations about American life during her first visit to the states (1818–1820), especially concerning slavery and women, made their way back to Europe in her letters, and she later published her experiences in *Views of Society and Manners in America*.[4] During her second visit, she began speaking on "theology, slavery, and the social degradation of woman," gaining the opposition of the clergy and the moniker of "infidel." She was the "first woman who gave lectures on political subjects in America."[5]

In 1839, Margaret Fuller (1810–1850) began her first series of guided discussions in Boston, which she called "conversations." Initially open only to women, the gatherings were intended as an intellectual outlet, since women could not attend Harvard like their male peers. Discussion often centered on women's rights, through the lens of ancient philosophy.[6] Elizabeth Cady Stanton wrote later in life about attending a series during her time in Boston (likely the 1842–1843 season), and she later held her own weekly meetings "in imitation of Margaret Fuller's Conversationals."[7]

Fuller recorded some of her thoughts on women's rights in an essay, "The Great Lawsuit," published in *The Dial* in 1843. It was later reprinted as the book *Woman in the Nineteenth Century* in 1845. Fuller encouraged women to embrace self-fulfillment as individuals, rather than as men's subordinates, and argued for equality for women in marriage and opportunities for women in education and employment.

Judge Elisha P. Hurlbut (1807–1889) published his *Essay on Human Rights* in 1845.[8] Hurlbut, of Albany, was elected to the New York State Supreme Court the same year as Elizabeth Cady Stanton's father, Daniel Cady. He argued that government existed to protect the rights of citizens, not take them away, and that all humans were entitled to a set of rights, determined by an individual's ability to contribute to society, not by sex or race. Hurlbut's book was cited in women's rights circles, and as late as 1876, Stanton contacted him to obtain extra copies to give away.[9]

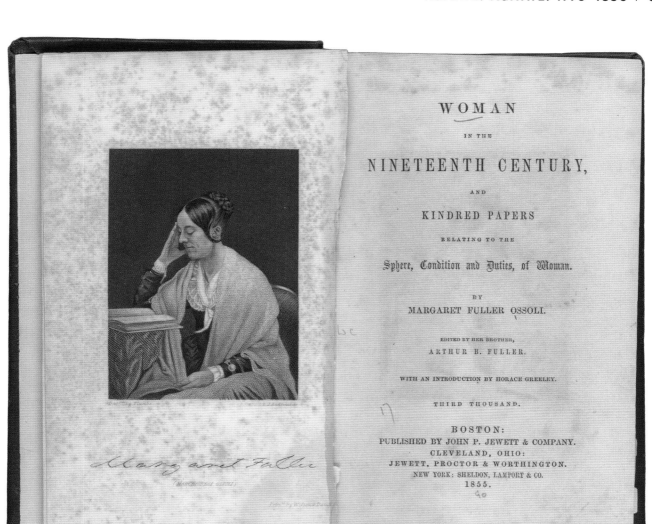

PETITIONING THE NEW YORK STATE GOVERNMENT

Petitions to various government bodies were an important tool used by reform movements in the nineteenth century. Several petitions relating to women's rights issues were sent to the New York State legislature prior to 1848, and they became even more frequent following the Seneca Falls Convention. The first of such petitions asking for married women's property rights was compiled by Ernestine Rose in 1836.

In 1846, six women from Jefferson County wrote a petition that was sent to the New York State constitutional convention. Signed by Eleanor Vincent, Susan Ormsby, Lydia A. Williams, Amy Ormsby, Lydia Osborn, and Anna Bishop, the petition was presented to the convention by delegate Alpheus S. Greene. Its sentiments were in keeping with Hurlbut's view that government existed to protect rights, not limit them. The

Woman in the Nineteenth Century, book, Margaret Fuller Ossoli (1810–1850), 1855.

This 1855 edition of *Woman in the Nineteenth Century* was published with the help of Fuller's friends, after her untimely death in a shipwreck off Fire Island. It includes writings from Fuller's papers, recovered after the shipwreck, which were not included in the 1845 edition. Courtesy of the General Research Division, the New York Public Library, Astor, Lenox and Tilden Foundations.

"Ernestine L. Rose," engraving, ca. 1881.

petitioners declared that New York State had "widely departed from the true democratic principles upon which all just governments must be based by denying to the female portion of community the right of suffrage and any participation in forming the government and laws under which they live," including imposing upon them taxation without representation. They requested that the government modify "the present Constitution of this State, so as to extend to women equal, and civil political rights with men."[10] Three other similar petitions were sent to the New York State Legislature in 1846 alone.[11]

Central to the discussions during the 1846 New York State constitutional convention was the idea of married women's property rights. Modeled after English common law, New York State law stated that a woman's property went to her husband at marriage. This was a concern to even wealthy conservatives, who could watch assets left to their daughters be squandered away by their daughters' husbands. In fact, the law had not always worked this way in New York State: under Dutch rule, women could and did own and inherit property. A law to protect women's property upon marriage was first proposed by Thomas Herttell in 1836, and again in 1837. The law finally passed in 1848, after twelve years of bills, petitions, and much debate, making New York the first state to secure equal property rights.[12]

ERNESTINE L. ROSE

Ernestine L. Rose (1810–1892) was born in the ghetto of Piotrków, Poland, the daughter of a rabbi. Following the death of her mother, a falling out with her father over a marriage he had arranged for her, and her successful defense in court of her own inheritance from the spurned suitor, Ernestine left home to travel Europe. In England, she met Robert Owen and became active in the Owenite movement. Owen believed that man is a product of his environment: "Surround him with evil circumstances or conditions and his thoughts and conduct must become evil; while when surrounded through life with good conditions only, his thoughts and conduct must be good."[13]

Ernestine met and married fellow Owenite William Ella Rose, and the two set sail for New York. Upon her arrival in 1836, Ernestine immediately set out on a petition campaign in support of married women's property rights. After passage of the law following twelve years of petitioning, she spoke on reform, and changes in public opinion: "Agitate! Agitate! ought to be the motto of every reformer. Agitation is the opposite of stagnation—the one is life, the other death."[14] She did not, however, feel that the work was done, reporting to the 1851 women's rights convention in Worcester, Massachusetts:

> According to a late act, the wife has a right to property she brings at marriage, or receives in any way after marriage. Here is some provision for the favored few; but for the laboring many, there is none. The mass of people commence life with no other capital than the union of head, hearts and hands. To the benefit of this best of capital the wife has no right. If they are unsuccessful in married life, who suffers more the bitter consequences of poverty than the wife? But if successful, she has not a dollar to call her own . . .[15]

Rose was active on the lecture circuit, and was well known as an orator. She traveled extensively and addressed new immigrants in several languages (which she had taught herself during her travels in Europe). Rose attended every National Women's Rights Convention between 1850 and 1869.

In 1869, Rose and her husband retired to England, and Elizabeth Cady Stanton and Susan B. Anthony were unsuccessful in persuading them to return.[16] Anthony counted Rose as a major influence in the early movement, referring to her as "that noble worker for the cause of women's rights."[17]

REFORM BREEDS REFORM

Discussions about women's rights were also happening within other reform movements, and the changes sought by reformers often prompted thinking about women's rights as well. While working within the abolition movement, for example, women gained political experience, which enlightened their views about their abilities, but they also suffered attacks for their public participation.[18]

By the 1830s, discussions had begun within the anti-slavery movement about the propriety of including women and the extent to which they should be involved. William Lloyd Garrison argued that women had an important role in the movement, asking, "When woman's heart is bleeding, shall woman's voice be hushed?"[19] Female anti-slavery societies began appearing in the United States in the 1830s, including one in New York City in 1835. In 1837, several of the female anti-slavery societies coordinated to hold a joint national meeting in New York City. Called the Anti-Slavery Convention of American Women, this was the first national women's convention held in the United States. The convention met the following year in Philadelphia.[20]

Women like Abby Kelley, Sarah Grimké, and Angelina Grimké made the rounds lecturing for the cause, at first exclusively to females, and eventually to mixed audiences, referred to derisively as "promiscuous assmeblies."[21] Responding to such criticisms, Sarah wrote, "Men and women were CREATED EQUAL, they are both moral and accountable beings and whatever is *right* for man to do, is *right* for woman."[22]

A rift developed in the American Antislavery Society during their 1840 convention in New York. Abby Kelley was elected to the business committee, just a year after the decision to admit both female and male delegates equally. The split resulted in the formation of a rival group, the American and Foreign Anti-Slavery Society.[23] Shortly after, in London, female delegates were barred from the 1840 World Anti-Slavery Convention (they were ultimately allowed to attend, but not speak). A large portion of discussion at the convention turned to the role of women within the movement. Elizabeth Cady Stanton later cited her attendance there, where she also met Lucretia Mott for the first time, as an impetus for the women's rights convention in 1848: "The action of this convention, was the topic of discussion, in public and private, for a long time, and stung many women into new thought and action and gave rise to the movement for women's political equality both in England and the United States."[24]

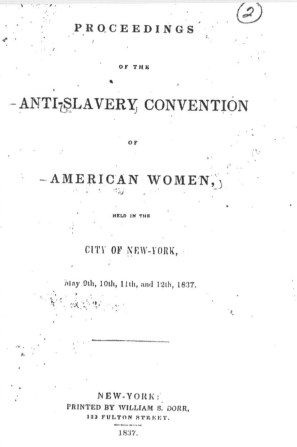

PROCEEDINGS

OF THE

ANTI-SLAVERY CONVENTION

OF

AMERICAN WOMEN,

HELD IN THE

CITY OF NEW-YORK,

May 9th, 10th, 11th, and 12th, 1837.

NEW-YORK:
PRINTED BY WILLIAM S. DORR,
123 FULTON STREET.
1837.

APPEAL

TO THE WOMEN

OF THE

NOMINALLY FREE STATES.

"The trembling earth, the low murmuring thunders, already admonish us of our danger; and if females can exert any saving influence in this emergency, it is time for them to awake."—Catharine E. Beecher.

BELOVED SISTERS,

The wrongs of outraged millions, and the foreshadows of coming judgments, constrain us, under a solemn sense of responsibility, to press upon your consideration the subject of American Slavery. The women of the North have high and holy duties to perform in the work of emancipation—duties to themselves, to the suffering slave, to the slaveholder, to the church, to their country, and to the world at large, and, above all to their God. Duties, which if not performed now, may never be performed at all.

Multitudes will doubtless deem such an address ill-timed and ill-directed. Many regard the excitement produced by the agitation of this subject as an evidence of the impolicy of free discussion, and a sufficient excuse for their own inactivity. Others, so undervalue the rights and responsibilities of woman, as to scoff and gainsay whenever she goes forth to duties beyond the parlor and the nursery. The cry of such is, that the agitation of this subject has rolled back the cause of emancipation 50, or 100, or it may be 200 years, and that this is a *political* subject with which women have nothing to do. To the first, we would reply, that the people of the South are the *best judges* of the effects of Anti-Slavery discussions upon their favorite "domestic institution;" and the universal alarm which has spread through the Slave States, is conclusive evidence of *their* conviction that *Slavery*

"An Appeal to the Women of the Nominally Free States, Issued by an Anti-Slavery Convention of American Women," speech, Angelina Grimké (1805–1879), in *Proceedings of the Anti-Slavery Convention of American Women held in the City of New-York, May 9th, 10th, 11th, and 12th, 1837.*

In this pamphlet published following the 1837 Anti-Slavery Convention of American Women, Angelina Grimké addressed some of the objections to women's involvement in abolitionist reform work, including the idea that women should not be involved in political concerns. She argued that the issue of slavery was not only political but also moral and religious and that "All moral beings have essentially the same rights and the same duties, whether male or female." Courtesy of the New York State Library, Manuscripts and Special Collections, 324.3 S79 V.2.

Throughout its history, the women's rights movement was also intertwined with the temperance movement. Temperance supporters argued for abstinence from "strong drink," often citing the injurious effects drunkards had on their wives and children. Many early supporters of women's rights also made rounds on the temperance circuit, including Susan B. Anthony and Amelia Bloomer.

With discussions circulating about women's rights, and with an air of change driven by other reform movements, including anti-slavery and temperance, the time was ripe for a women's rights convention. It was in this climate that five women in the Finger Lakes region began to plan for a meeting in Seneca Falls.

WHAT WAS IT LIKE FOR A WOMAN IN THE EARLY NINETEENTH CENTURY?

- Very few professions were open to women. If a woman did work, she was expected to hand over all her earnings to her husband—even if he squandered all the money and did not provide for her and her children.

- Women had few opportunities for education. Oberlin College in Ohio was the first to admit women, including African American women, in 1833. The first bachelor's degree was granted to a woman in 1840, from Wesleyan College in Macon, Georgia. Elizabeth Blackwell was

FEMALE  ADVOCATE.

Published at the Office of the Genius of Temperance.

Vol. 1.   NEW-YORK, FRIDAY, AUGUST 10, 1832.   No. 16.

the first woman to graduate from medical school in the United States, earning a degree from Geneva Medical School in 1849. It took many years for women to be widely accepted to institutions of higher learning, and to be allowed to take the same rigorous courses as men once they were accepted.

- Upon marriage, a woman became invisible to the law and a charge of her husband. This concept, called "coverture," made its way into American law from English common law. An unmarried woman ("feme sole") retained right to her own property and the ability to make contracts, but a married woman's ("feme covert") legal rights were taken over by her husband.

- Women could not sue, be sued, or make legal contracts.

- A woman had no rights to her own children. In rare cases of divorce, the husband was legally entitled to sole guardianship of the children. If she became a widow, her husband could make arrangements to give the children away upon his death.

- Widows were treated as dependents and were only given a portion of the estate, even if they had brought money or land in through work or inheritance.

The Female Advocate, newspaper, August 10, 1832.

The Female Advocate was published biweekly in New York City, in 1832 and 1833, and marketed to women in the temperance movement. Courtesy of the New York State Library, Manuscripts and Special Collections. 305.4 fF329 215-113 1832 AUG–1833 AUG.

- Women were not allowed to vote. Their sole means of expressing their political opinion was through petitions. Petitions were used successfully in the temperance movement, but they often represented a very slow means of change.

ELIZABETH CADY STANTON

Elizabeth Cady Stanton (1815–1902) was born in Johnstown, New York, to Daniel and Margaret Livingston Cady. She recalled being made aware of the different opportunities for boys and girls when her father remarked, "Oh, my daughter, I wish you were a boy," while grieving the death of her brother Eleazar. Daniel Cady had a law office in Johnstown and served in the New York State Assembly. Stanton spent hours in her father's office studying his books, talking with his law clerks, and hearing the plight of widows who faced losing all their property, even that which they had brought into their marriages. She felt such treatment of widows unfair and threatened to physically cut the relevant laws out of her father's law books.

Stanton's eyes were open to the world of reform, and specifically to anti-slavery, through her time at her cousin Gerrit Smith's house. In Smith's household, she relished the dinner table discussion on anti-slavery, and she developed a close friendship with Smith's daughter, Elizabeth Smith Miller, who also became involved in women's rights.

Elizabeth Cady met Henry Stanton at the Smith household in 1839. They married in 1840, with Elizabeth leaving "obey" out of their vows. Henry was deeply involved in the anti-slavery movement, and for their honeymoon, they traveled to London for the World Anti-Slavery Convention. There, Elizabeth was exposed to the conflict over women's place in the abolition movement, and her frustration grew. Ultimately, she turned her anger into her lifelong work for the cause of women's rights.

Elizabeth Cady Stanton's rocking chair, ca. 1840.

Courtesy of the Seneca Falls Historical Society.

Elizabeth Cady Stanton with Baby, daguerreotype, ca. 1842.

The first image many people conjure of Elizabeth Cady Stanton is that of an older woman, with white curly hair, after many years of devotion to women's rights. Her work for the cause actually began much earlier, when she was a young woman, grappling with the difficulties of running a household with small children in the remote location of Seneca Falls, often alone while her husband, Henry, traveled for work. Motherhood was a very important role to Elizabeth, and she and Henry ultimately had seven children. The difficulties of her life with young children and little help opened Elizabeth's eyes to many women's rights concerns. Courtesy of the Seneca Falls Historical Society.

Declaration of Sentiments Table, ca. 1825.

After the M'Clintocks' mahogany table was used by the women who drafted the Declaration of Sentiments, the M'Clintocks gifted it to Elizabeth Cady Stanton. Stanton, in turn, presented it to Susan B. Anthony as an eightieth birthday present. Upon Anthony's death, the table was owned by the National American Woman Suffrage Association (NAWSA), who pasted a copy of the Declaration of Sentiments to the underside. In 1920, following passage of the Nineteenth Amendment, NAWSA was invited to exhibit the table at the Smithsonian, and it was donated to the National Museum of American History. Courtesy of the Division of Political History, National Museum of American History, Smithsonian Institution.

SENECA FALLS, 1848

Planning for the Seneca Falls women's rights convention officially began on July 9, 1848, in the home of Quakers Jane and Richard Hunt, in Waterloo, New York. That afternoon, the Hunts hosted a tea for several fellow Quakers, including Lucretia Mott, who was visiting from Philadelphia. Elizabeth Cady Stanton, a friend of Mott, was invited as well. According to Stanton, she and Mott had discussed the idea of a women's rights meeting during their time at the World Anti-Slavery Convention in 1840. When the topic of women's rights came up at tea, it was decided that it was time for such a convention. Joining them in planning for the meeting in Seneca Falls were Martha Coffin Wright (Mott's sister), Mary Ann M'Clintock, and Jane Hunt.

Dates for the convention were set for July 19–20, just ten days later, so that it could take place while Mott was still in town. A notice was placed in local papers:

> WOMAN'S RIGHTS CONVENTION.—A Convention to discuss the social, civil, and religious condition and rights of woman, will be held in the Wesleyan Chapel, at Seneca Falls, N.Y., on Wednesday and Thursday, the 19th and 20th of July, current; commencing at 10 o'clock A.M. During the first day the meeting will be exclusively for women, who are earnestly invited to attend. The public generally are invited to be present on the second day, when Lucretia Mott, of Philadelphia, and other ladies and gentlemen, will address the convention.[25]

On Sunday, July 16, Stanton returned to the M'Clintock home for help revising her draft of a declaration she was writing for the convention. Discussion ultimately led to adoption of the Declaration

Letter, Elizabeth Cady Stanton to Lucretia Coffin Mott, October 22, 1852.

"I am at length the happy mother of a daughter. Rejoice with me all Womankind, for lo! a champion of thy cause is born. I have dedicated her to this work from the beginning. I never felt such sacredness in carrying a child as I have this one, feeling all the time strongly impressed with the belief that I was cherishing the embryo of a mighty female martyr—Glorious hope! may she wear the crown of martyrdom bravely & patiently, and leave her impress on the world for goodness & truth." Elizabeth wrote this letter upon the birth of her fifth child, and first girl, Margaret Livingston Stanton. While not as actively involved in the suffrage movement as her sister, Harriot Eaton Stanton Blatch, Margaret worked later in life, with her brother Theodore Weld Stanton, to collect and publish materials about their mother's career and keep Elizabeth Cady Stanton's legacy alive. (Gordon, *The Selected Papers of Elizabeth Cady Stanton and Susan B. Anthony*, 1:212.) Courtesy of Coline Jenkins, Elizabeth Cady Stanton Family.

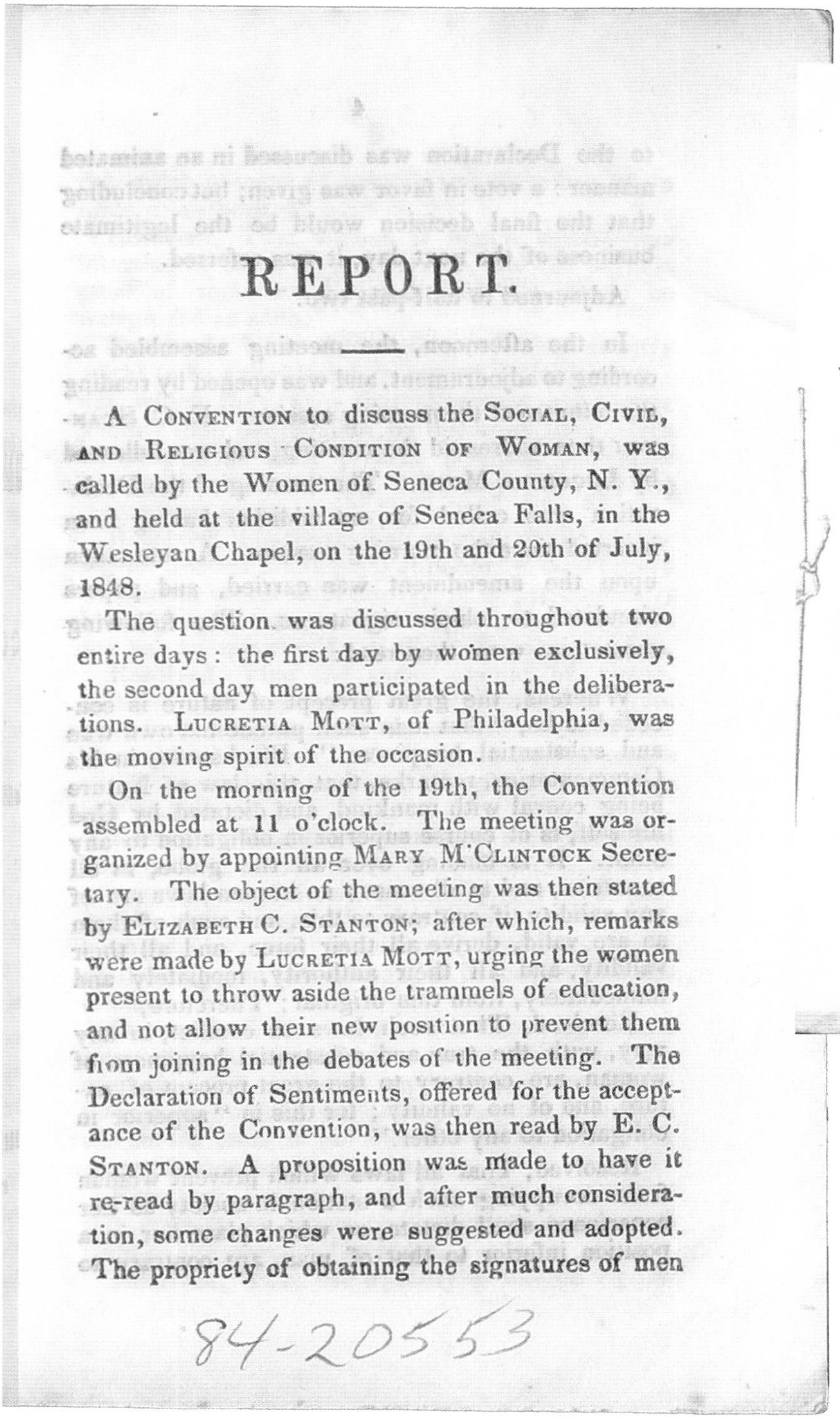

REPORT.

A CONVENTION to discuss the SOCIAL, CIVIL, AND RELIGIOUS CONDITION OF WOMAN, was called by the Women of Seneca County, N. Y., and held at the village of Seneca Falls, in the Wesleyan Chapel, on the 19th and 20th of July, 1848.

The question was discussed throughout two entire days: the first day by women exclusively, the second day men participated in the deliberations. LUCRETIA MOTT, of Philadelphia, was the moving spirit of the occasion.

On the morning of the 19th, the Convention assembled at 11 o'clock. The meeting was organized by appointing MARY M'CLINTOCK Secretary. The object of the meeting was then stated by ELIZABETH C. STANTON; after which, remarks were made by LUCRETIA MOTT, urging the women present to throw aside the trammels of education, and not allow their new position to prevent them from joining in the debates of the meeting. The Declaration of Sentiments, offered for the acceptance of the Convention, was then read by E. C. STANTON. A proposition was made to have it re-read by paragraph, and after much consideration, some changes were suggested and adopted. The propriety of obtaining the signatures of men

REPORT

OF THE

WOMAN'S RIGHTS

CONVENTION,

Held at SENECA FALLS, N. Y., July 19th and 20th, 1848.

ROCHESTER:
PRINTED BY JOHN DICK,
AT THE NORTH STAR OFFICE.
—
1848.

Report on the Woman's Rights Convention, Held at Seneca Falls, N.Y., July 19th and 20th, 1848, pamphlet, printed by John Dick, North Star Office, Rochester, 1848.

The report of the women's rights convention in Seneca Falls was published in Frederick Douglass's printing office for the newspaper the *North Star*, located in Rochester. After the Civil War, the report was reprinted, as leaders of the early movement sought to interest new recruits in the foundations of the women's rights movement. Courtesy of the New York State Library, Manuscripts and Special Collections, 323.42 W872 84-20553.

of Independence as the model for the document.[26] The new declaration, called the "Declaration of Sentiments," began with the addition of two words to the original, familiar text (emphasis added):

> We hold these truths to be self-evident; that all men *and women* are created equal; that they are endowed by their Creator with certain inalienable rights; that among these are life, liberty, and the pursuit of happiness; that to secure these rights governments are instituted, deriving their just powers from the consent of the governed.[27]

It then went on to replace the colonists' grievances against the king with a list of the ways in which women were repressed in government, in the home, in the professions, in education, and in the church. While the women's rights movement at times focused its attention singularly on getting the vote, the Seneca Falls convention took a holistic approach. The addition of the right to elective franchise, which Stanton later took credit for adding, was not supported by all the planners. Lucretia Mott worried that including voting rights might "make the convention ridiculous," as it was a more revolutionary and less agreed-upon statement than their other sentiments.[28] Stanton, however, felt that enfranchisement was the key to women securing their other rights.

The first day of the meeting, to which only women were invited, was well attended. Stanton read the Declaration of Sentiments, and it was requested that the gathering review the document paragraph by paragraph. Changes were proposed and made, and the group discussed eleven resolutions to accompany it. There was a great deal of conversation on the matter of whether to allow men to sign in support of the declaration on the second day of the meeting, a matter which was not completely resolved. Elizabeth M'Clintock also gave a speech; a satirical article by Martha Coffin Wright, "Hints for Wives," was read; and Lucretia Mott closed out the day as the evening speaker, putting women's rights into context in the other reform movements.

The second day of the meeting was open to men and women, and attendees packed the church. James Mott, Lucretia's husband, was asked to serve as chair. The Declaration of Sentiments was read, and then extensively discussed, before being adopted unanimously. Ultimately, sixty-eight women signed in approval, and thirty-two men signed separately, "in favor of the movement." The resolutions set out on the first day were also adopted, with the most discussion centered on the urge to secure elective franchise for women, found in the ninth resolution.[29] Frederick Douglass spoke in support of the ninth resolution, and ultimately, it passed.

ROCHESTER, 1848

Two weeks after the convention at Seneca Falls, a second women's rights convention was held in Rochester, planned by Amy Post, Sarah D. Fish, Sarah C. Owen, and Mary H. Hallowell. Abigail Bush was elected as president of the convention, despite initial reservations of some attendees who thought it was a "most hazardous experiment to have a woman President."[30]

Speeches and discussion at the Rochester convention focused on the rights of women in the workplace and equal pay, as well as the role of women in marriage with regard to the governing of the household and the taking of a husband's name.[31] There was also discussion on the topic of women's right to suffrage. On this matter, Frederick Douglass lent his support, as he had in Seneca Falls, and made an appeal "for the complete equality of woman in all the rights that belong to any human soul."[32] The Declaration of Sentiments was again read and discussed, and it was ultimately adopted and signed by many supporters.[33]

Conventions like those at Seneca Falls and Rochester were central to the organization of the early women's rights movement. National conventions were held annually between 1850 and 1860, and numerous smaller conventions were held in New York and other states.[34]

"ALL MEN AND WOMEN ARE CREATED EQUAL"

The Legacy of Seneca Falls

Judith Wellman

Professor Emerita, State University of New York at Oswego

On July 19, 1848, thirty-two-year-old Elizabeth Cady Stanton stood at the front of the Wesleyan Chapel in Seneca Falls. As she looked out at the audience, she found herself so nervous that she considered "suddenly abandoning all of her principles and running away." But she did not. The result was the Seneca Falls women's rights convention and the beginning of the organized women's rights movement in the United States. Stanton would call the women's movement "the greatest movement for human liberty recorded on the pages of history—a demand for freedom to one-half the entire race."[i] Stanton had a point. Those voices at Seneca Falls captured the attention of the nation and the world and echoed far into the future. They raised questions that citizens of the world continue to debate in the twenty-first century.

For two hot summer days in the Wesleyan Chapel at Seneca Falls, about three hundred people considered equal rights for women. In a culture that denied women political, legal, economic, social, and religious equality, the convention took a step that crystallized American commitment to equality. One hundred people—sixty-eight women and thirty-two men, all European Americans except Frederick Douglass—signed a Declaration of Sentiments. In a brilliant move, organizers patterned the Declaration of Sentiments after the Declaration of Independence. They proclaimed, "We hold these truths to be self-evident, that all men and women are created equal." Just as the Declaration of Independence included colonial accusations against King George III, so the Declaration of Sentiments listed women's claims of oppression by a male-dominated world. Beginning with the statement that man "has never permitted her to exercise her inalienable right to the elective franchise," the declaration dealt with inequalities in the law, property, family, morality, employment, education, and religion.[ii]

Without compromise, these women's rights advocates asserted the right of every woman to follow her own vision, to define for herself what she wanted to do and what she wanted to become. One statement summed it all up: "He [man] has usurped the prerogative of Jehovah himself, claiming it as his right to assign for her a sphere of action, when that belongs to her conscience and to her God." And they demanded "immediate admission to all the rights and privileges which belong to them [women] as citizens of the United States."

Signers of the declaration did not intend that the Seneca Falls convention would be a one-time event. It was to be the beginning of a movement. "We shall use every instrumentality within our power to effect our object," they announced. "We shall employ agents, circulate tracts, petition the State and national Legislatures, and endeavor to enlist the pulpit and the press in our behalf. We hope this Convention will be followed by a series of Conventions, embracing every part of the country."

And, indeed, it was. Newspapers across the country picked up the story of Seneca Falls and the Declaration of Sentiments. For many Americans, women's rights made common sense. It was rooted in the ideal of equality upon which this country had been founded. If women were indeed citizens (and no one denied that free women, although not enslaved women, were citizens), then they should be entitled to all the "rights and privileges" of citizenship. Period.

The Seneca Falls women's rights convention immediately inspired similar meetings. Two weeks after Seneca Falls, women's rights advocates held a second convention in Rochester, New York. In 1850, they held the first women's rights convention to attract a national audience in Worcester, Massachusetts. In the 1850s, women organized a women's rights convention every year except one, 1857 (when Susan B. Anthony complained that all her fellow workers were having babies).

After the Civil War, partly because so many young men (more than six hundred thousand of them, North and South, of all ethnic backgrounds) had been killed in the conflict, opportunities for women expanded in education, jobs, family, property rights, and religion. Political rights took longer. Not until 1917 did New York State recognize women's right to vote. In 1920, seventy-two years after the Seneca Falls convention, the Nineteenth Amendment finally guaranteed voting rights to all women across the country.

For all its national importance, the Seneca Falls convention began as a local movement. Who came to this convention and why? Why did three hundred local people, with less than a week's notice, pack the Wesleyan Chapel in Seneca Falls on July 19–20, 1848?

East view of Seneca Falls village.

"East View of Seneca Falls Village," engraving, 1841.

This view shows the bustling village of Seneca Falls, full of industry after the arrival of the canals. Where the artist was standing would have been near the Stanton house. In *Historical Collections of the State of New York; containing a general collection of the most interesting facts, traditions, biographical sketches, anecdotes, &c., relating to its history and antiquities, with geographical descriptions of every township in the state,* 1841, John Warner Barber, p. 526. Courtesy of the New York State Library, Manuscripts and Special Collections, 974.7 B23a3.

The geographic position of Seneca Falls and its sister community of Waterloo offers part of the answer. Both villages were located the middle of rich agricultural land, once controlled by Haudenosaunee people, with major potential for industrial development, too. Straddling the Seneca River, the "falls" of Seneca Falls had one of the highest drops of water—forty-three feet—east of the Mississippi River. After the American Revolution, European Americans and some African Americans flooded into these two villages. Seneca Falls had nine gristmills, a textile factory, and a pump factory. Waterloo had a nationally significant textile factory. Both villages offered transportation to New York City and the west by canal and railroad. Lawyers found a good business locally, filing patents for new inventions.

Seneca Falls and Waterloo had another geographic feature important for our story: they were located where the major migration route from the east intersected with a route from the southeast. From the east came Yankees from New England, Dutch and English heritage families from the Hudson River and lower Mohawk River valleys, and Irish and English who came directly from western Europe through New York City. From the southeast came a strong infusion of Quaker families and a few African Americans from Philadelphia and the Chesapeake Bay.

The combination of economic opportunity and cultural diversity created a lively and often volatile environment. Social bonds stretched and sometimes snapped. Institutions that normally kept communities in good order—family, church, and political institutions—faced challenges and change. People from different regions, religions, classes, and cultures had to find common ground.

In the face of all their differences, Seneca Falls residents, like local people all over the country, shared an identity as citizens of the United States. They all recognized the Declaration of Independence as the founding document of their country. They did not, however, agree about the meaning of "all men are created equal." Even if they ignored Native Americans (who were often outside their own experience), even if they discounted distinctions of wealth (possible, in any case, to change), they still faced daily inequalities—encased in laws, institutions, and personal relationships—based on race and sex. As people worked against slavery and for the rights of African Americans, they created a model for and emerging movement for women's rights.

We know the names of the one hundred people who signed the Declaration of Sentiments. With the exception of Lucretia Mott, Frederick Douglass, perhaps Martha Wright and Amy Post, and Elizabeth Cady Stanton herself, few of them achieved national recognition.

These signers were not linked by class or economic status. Some of the signers were among the richest people in the area. Richard P. Hunt, for example, was worth $50,000 according to the 1850 census, more than any other person in Seneca County. Others were among the poorest. Margaret Pryor was on the list of poor women to whom Gerrit Smith gave money around 1850.

Instead of wealth, the signers were linked by a shared commitment to equal rights, based on religious and political values. They were influenced by one major event in April 1848 and two more events in June 1848. Elizabeth Cady Stanton acted as a catalyst. With personal ties to each event, she brought people together to form the first women's rights convention.

In April 1848, New York State passed its first Married Women's Property Act. Married women's property had generated debates about women's rights in families and neighborhoods across the state for a dozen years. Stanton was intimately connected to these legal issues through her lawyer father Daniel Cady.

In June 1848, two major groups, one spiritual and one political, both associated with national abolitionist movements, emerged with particular intensity in Seneca Falls and Waterloo. Elizabeth Cady Stanton had personal ties to both.

The first group was composed of Quakers affiliated with the American Anti-Slavery Society. Without these Quakers, there would have been no women's rights convention in Seneca Falls. Historically committed to equal rights for all people, they worked with Stanton as the convention's main organizers. Stanton was connected to Quakers through her friendship with Lucretia Mott, perhaps the best-known woman preacher in America. On her honeymoon, Stanton had attended the World Anti-Slavery Convention in London, where Mott powerfully impressed her with her commitment to equal rights.

Many of these Quakers had moved to central New York from Pennsylvania, New Jersey, or Long Island. Locally, they were part of Junius Monthly Meeting in Waterloo. Through Genesee Yearly Meeting, meeting annually in the 1816 Quaker Meetinghouse in Farmington, New York, they were connected to an extended network across central and western New York, upper Canada, and Michigan. In 1838, ten years before the Seneca Falls convention, Genesee Yearly Meeting formally recognized the equality of decisions made by women in Quaker meetings with those made by men.

In June 1848, Quakers in Genesee Yearly Meeting at Farmington split over issues relating to equality, both within Quaker meetings and in the larger world. A month later, the Seneca Falls women's rights convention offered an opportunity to meet and figure out the boundaries of Quaker commitment to equal rights.

These reform Quakers became the single largest religious group at the Seneca Falls convention. On Friday, July 15, 1848, the M'Clintock family (including Thomas, clerk of Genesee Yearly Meeting from 1838 to 1843, Mary Ann, and their children Elizabeth, Mary Ann, Julia, and Charles) welcomed Elizabeth Cady Stanton to their home to finish writing the Declaration of Sentiments. Stanton credited "one of the company" with suggesting the Declaration of Independence as a model. The M'Clintocks were connected to an extended family network that included at least eleven people in the Hunt, Mount, and Vail families. This was the largest family group to sign the Declaration of Sentiments. Elizabeth M'Clintock acted as one of the convention's main organizers, writing letters of invitation and recruiting attendees. Her sister Mary Ann acted as the convention's secretary.

The second major group who came to the Seneca Falls convention was also defined by a commitment to equal rights, not as a new religious group but as a new political party. In May 1848, the United States and Mexico ended a two-year war, leaving the United States with ownership of much of the northern part of Mexico. Abolitionists organized a new Free Soil Party to keep slavery out of this territory.

Seneca Falls was a hotbed of Free Soil enthusiasm. More than four hundred adult male voters committed themselves to Free Soil in the *Seneca County Courier* in the summer of 1848. Among them were Stanton's husband, Henry B. Stanton, a major Free Soil organizer, and many of her neighbors, including her nearest neighbor, Jacob Chamberlain, president of the local Free Soil meeting in June 1848.

A month after Quaker reformers walked out of Genesee Yearly Meeting of Friends and Free Soilers left their traditional political parties, the women's rights convention offered an opportunity for both groups to meet with like-minded people and to discuss the boundaries of their commitment to women's rights.

But what about the idea of women's right to vote? That was another thing entirely. Neither Quakers nor Free Soil advocates had ever discussed this. Stanton alone took credit for introducing voting rights at the Seneca Falls convention. She faced intense opposition from her closest allies. Her husband was "thunderstruck" and "amazed at her daring." He was so disgusted that he refused to attend the convention, telling Elizabeth, "You will turn the proceedings into a farce."

Even Lucretia Mott, who rarely backed down from any radical idea, responded, "Lizzie, thou wilt make the convention ridiculous." To put Mott's comment into context, Quakers generally did not vote at all. Stanton persevered: "I must declare the truth as I believe it to be," she asserted.[iii]

What Stanton did not tell us was that her cousin Gerrit Smith also supported women's right to vote. Smith had been nominated as a candidate for president of the United States on June 2, 1848, by the newly formed Liberty League, an alternative to Henry Stanton and the Free Soil Party. Smith undoubtedly stayed with the Stantons in Seneca Falls on his way to the National Liberty Convention in Buffalo. Whether he was influenced by Elizabeth Cady Stanton or she found strength from Smith's own views, both introduced the idea of women's right to vote in major public speeches that summer. Smith went first. On June 14–15, he gave a speech at the Buffalo convention, advocating "universal suffrage in its broadest sense, females as well as males being entitled to vote."[iv] Stanton felt she could do no less. So she introduced women's right to vote at the women's rights convention in Seneca Falls a month later.

Today, Seneca Falls is a small village bisected by the Seneca River and the Seneca and Cayuga Canal. Much of its historic fabric remains intact. Women's Rights National Historical Park interprets the Wesleyan Chapel, the Stanton house, and the M'Clintock home in Waterloo. Voices of Elizabeth Cady Stanton, Lucretia Mott, Frederick Douglass, and the M'Clintock family still echo the phrase "all men and women are created equal." They continue to offer a challenge to Americans and citizens of the world today.

Notes

i. *Report of the International Council of Women* (Washington, DC: National Woman Suffrage Association, 1888), 32.

ii. Laura Curtis Bullard, "Elizabeth Cady Stanton," in *Our Famous Women*, ed. Elizabeth Stuart Phelps (Hartford: A. D. Worthington, 1884).

iii. Bullard, "Elizabeth Cady Stanton," 613–614.

iv. *Proceedings of the National Liberty Convention, Held at Buffalo, N.Y., June 14th and 15th, 1848* (Utica: S. W. Green, 1848), 14.

AT THE POLLS.

"The Election—At the Polls," engraving, W.J.H., 1857.

On top of the questions that were raised about whether women were intellectually fit to vote, many opponents to woman suffrage questioned the propriety of women actually going to cast votes. Nineteenth-century polling places were known as boisterous spaces prone to violence, and reserved for men. Published in *Harper's Weekly*, vol. 1, 7 November 1857, p. 712. Courtesy of the Library of Congress.

DEFINING CITIZENSHIP

Throughout the nineteenth century, Americans grappled with how exactly to define what it meant to be a citizen and, in turn, who could vote. Early laws defined citizenship through land ownership, but as the dynamics of wealth tied to the land changed, this definition was no longer appropriate. Lawmakers discussed requirements of service and limitations based on race and gender.

The matter of what defined a citizen voter was of great interest regarding both women's suffrage and African American suffrage. The debate would rage for many years.

LUCRETIA MOTT AND MARTHA COFFIN WRIGHT

Sisters born in Massachusetts and raised in Philadelphia, Lucretia Mott (1793–1880) and Martha Coffin Wright (1806–1875) were both active at the Seneca Falls convention in 1848 and were central to the nineteenth-century women's rights movement in New York State and nationally. Raised as Quakers, the Coffin family fell on the "Hicksite" side of a schism that occurred among Quakers in 1827–1828. Unlike the Orthodox Quakers who stressed the importance of the scriptures, Hicksites, named for Elias Hicks, emphasized the importance of one's "inner light" to guide faith and conscience.[35] Mott remained a devout

Lucretia Mott, carte de visite, 1879.

This carte de visite of Lucretia Mott is from the family collection and is inscribed on the back, "Truth for authority not authority for truth. 1879—86 yrs. Old." Courtesy of the Sophia Smith Collection, Garrison Family Papers, Smith College.

Hicksite Quaker and was inaugurated into the ministry of the Society of Friends. Wright, disassociated with the Society of Friends upon her first marriage to a non-Quaker, became skeptical of religion.

Both sisters and their families were deeply involved in the anti-slavery movement. The Wrights regularly hosted anti-slavery speakers and hid runaways in their home in Auburn, New York. Mott spoke passionately for abolition and the fact that slavery was sinful, and she served as a head of the American Equal Rights Association.

LUCRETIA MOTT

Lucretia Mott was already a respected reformer and speaker at the time of the 1848 Seneca Falls convention. As such, the dates for the meeting were chosen to correspond with her visit to central New York, her presence lending weight to the gathering and bringing a following. The refusal of women delegates at the 1840 World Anti-Slavery Convention in London, which included Mott, marked a turning point for her, and she focused on both anti-slavery and women's rights work for the rest of her life.[36]

Mott laid out her theories on women's rights in her "Discourse on Woman," delivered at the assembly buildings in Philadelphia, on December 17, 1849. She began, "There is nothing of greater importance to the well-being of society at large—of man as well as woman—than the true and proper position of woman."[37] Mott then addressed the biblical foundations for women's inferior place in society and asked, "Why should not woman seek to be a reformer?"

> We would admit all the difference, that our great and beneficent Creator has made, in the relation of man and woman, nor would we seek to disturb this relation; but we deny that the present position of woman, is her true sphere of usefulness: nor will she attain to this sphere, until the disabilities and disadvantages, religious, civil, and social, which impede her progress, are removed out of her way. These restrictions have enervated her mind and paralyzed her powers.[38]

Although Mott lived in Philadelphia, she remained deeply involved in the movement in New York through her correspondence with her sister, as well as friends including Stanton. Mott was chosen to preside over numerous conventions, both local and national.

MARTHA COFFIN WRIGHT

Wright was present for both the planning meetings and the convention at Seneca Falls, although she admitted to being less active than she would have liked since she was six months pregnant with her seventh child. As part of the proceedings, Stanton read "Hints for Wives," a satirical article written by Wright and first published in 1846. In response to a serious article that called for wives to have "unremitting kindness"

Lucretia Mott's bonnet, ca. 1843–1847.

Newspapers frequently reported on Mott's stately appearance on convention stages, as well as her reserved Quaker dress. Courtesy of the Albany Institute of History & Art.

Martha Coffin Wright, daguerreotype, ca. 1845.

Courtesy of the Sophia Smith Collection, Garrison Family Papers, Smith College.

and "a cheerful smile" for their husbands, Wright asked, "Why is it not oftener insisted upon, that the husband should always return to his fireside with a smile, and endeavor to soothe the perturbed spirit, that has for hours been subjected to the thousand annoyances of the nursery and the kitchen?"[39] Wright was a fixture at many women's rights meetings, both before and after the Civil War, serving frequently as secretary, and occasionally as president.

Wright carried the idea of equality of the sexes into her child rearing and frequently defied gender norms with her children. Her boys began their education at the Auburn Female Academy, and they learned to knit, as Wright felt that it was an important skill for filling idle time, regardless of gender. While she showed great love for her children and interest in their lives, she also expressed a desire for more family planning, writing to her sister, "No one is fonder of 'children in the abstract' than I am, but when it comes to the *concrete* it becomes suggestive of the remark of the psalmist relative to 'too much of a good thing.'"[40] In her letters to family, she recorded household discussions on equality, including an incident in which she was upset that their seamstress was paid less than half of what they paid the hired hand, arguing with her husband, David, that sewing was also injurious to one's health, and that she should make enough to put aside money for "the age of rheumatism and poor sight."[41]

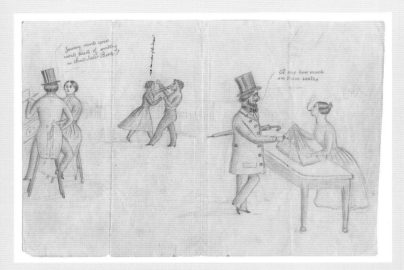

"Female Store Clerks," drawing, attributed to Elizabeth M'Clintock and Maria Mott Davis, pen and ink, ca. 1849.

A series of drawings survive from both sides of M'Clintock and Southwick's unsuccessful applications. This drawing depicts women successfully working in traditional men's roles. All the women involved in the incident wielded the pen, in their letters, drawings, and "drama." Courtesy of the Sophia Smith Collection, Garrison Family Papers, Smith College.

Paulina Kellogg Wright Davis, engraving, J. C. Buttre based on a photograph by Manchester Bros., ca. 1850–1881.

Paulina Kellogg Wright Davis, planner of the first National Women's Rights Convention in Worcester, Massachusetts, was active in the suffrage, abolition, and temperance movements. Following the death of her first husband in 1845, she was independent and wealthy, and she turned to the study of medicine. Her lectures on anatomy inspired other women to follow in her footsteps to become physicians. After remarrying in 1849 to Rhode Island congressmen Thomas Davis, she moved to Washington, DC, where she remained a leader in the national suffrage movement. From there she published the newspaper *The Una*, which focused on women's rights and was in print from 1853 to 1855. Following the Civil War, she helped found the New England Woman Suffrage Association. Courtesy of the Library of Congress.

LADIES AS MERCHANTS?

Perhaps emboldened by the publicly made sentiments in support of women's rights in 1848, Elizabeth M'Clintock and Anna Southwick applied for positions in the historically male workplace of a Philadelphia textile wholesaler in 1849. The business was owned by Edward M. Davis, son-in-law of Lucretia Mott, and Elizabeth Cady Stanton sent along a letter in support of their application. Not only were their applications refused, but a series of caricatures, drawn by male clerks, depicting how women would fail in business, were sent back. The women responded in kind, with a series of drawings of their own, as well as a written "drama." Martha Coffin Wright wrote with sympathy to M'Clintock: "In the stagnation that occurs periodically in those wholesale establishments it is not surprising that your application should have raised a 'tempest in a teapot' and set Market Street in a ferment."[42]

1850: FIRST NATIONAL WOMEN'S RIGHTS CONVENTION, WORCESTER, MASSACHUSETTS

Following local suffrage conventions in Seneca Falls, Rochester, and Salem, Ohio, the first National Women's Rights Convention was planned by Paulina Kellogg Wright Davis (1813–1876) in Worcester, Massachusetts. National conventions were then held annually (except for 1857) in the years leading up to the Civil War. Statewide conventions were also held in numerous states, including New York, during these years. While some accused the women of doing nothing for their cause but talking, these meetings were an important way to refine their list of grievances, as well as

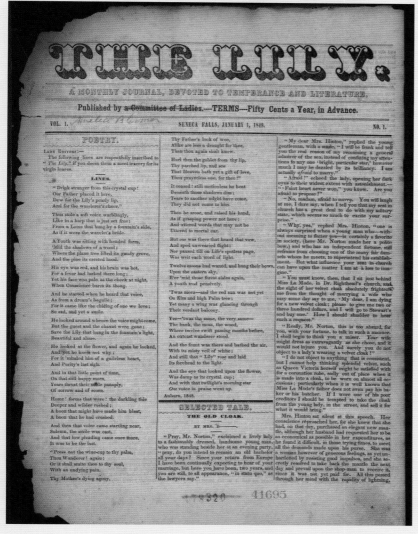

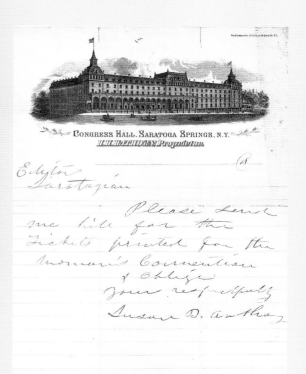

The Lily, newspaper, January 1, 1849.

This copy of *The Lily* in the collection of the New York State Library belonged to Amelia Bloomer. It bears a correction to the masthead in her hand. Prior to coming to the library, it was exhibited at the 1893 World Columbian Exposition in Chicago. Courtesy of the New York State Library, Manuscripts and Special Collections, 051 xL731 206-882 1849-1853.

Letter, Susan B. Anthony to the editor of *The Saratogian*, ca. 1870.

This letter from Susan B. Anthony addresses some of the planning that went into conventions. Statewide conventions for women's rights were held in Saratoga Springs on several occasions, both before and after the Civil War. Courtesy of the New York State Library, Manuscripts and Special Collections, V23251.

their methods for resolving them, and advance their thoughts on women's rights. They were also a successful means to recruit new members.

AMELIA BLOOMER AND *THE LILY*

Born in Homer, New York, Amelia Bloomer (1818-1894) served as the publisher of *The Lily*, the first newspaper for women. The publication began with a focus on temperance, as the journal of the Seneca Falls Ladies Temperance Society. Originally, the masthead read "published by a committee of ladies," but after 1850, it listed Bloomer's name.

Stanton, a friend of Bloomer, was a major contributor to the journal, publishing under the penname "Sunflower." Stanton's articles discussed temperance, raising children, education, unjust laws, and women's rights, leading *The Lily* to a wider focus than its original temperance roots.

In 1854, Bloomer sold the publication to Mary Birdsall, but she remained a contributing editor. The final issue of the paper was December 15, 1856.

"The New Costume," engraving from *The Lily*, July 1851.

An engraving of "the new costume" appeared in *The Lily* in July 1851. Following publication of the image, readership of the paper grew. Courtesy of the New York State Library. Manuscripts and Special Collections, 051 xL731 206-882 1849-1853.

"Amelia Bloomer," engraving from *The Lily*, September 1851.

Following the demands of readers, Bloomer published an engraving of herself in what became known as the "Bloomer costume." Courtesy of the New York State Library. Manuscripts and Special Collections, 051 xL731 206-882 1849-1853.

Amelia Bloomer, daguerreotype, ca. 1851.

Courtesy of the Seneca Falls Historical Society.

Elizabeth Smith Miller, daguerreotype, ca. 1851.

Credit for introducing the bloomer costume to the women's rights movement was widely given to Elizabeth Smith Miller, daughter of abolitionist Gerrit Smith and cousin of Elizabeth Cady Stanton. Courtesy of the Seneca Falls Historical Society.

DRESS REFORM

Popular dress for women in the nineteenth century was often listed by reformers as one of the many things holding women back.[43] In the 1840s and '50s, standard attire for a woman included floor-length skirts over layers of petticoats and a boned corset, a heavy and cumbersome arrangement. John Humphrey Noyes, leader of the Oneida Community in central New York, declared, "Woman's dress is a standing lie. It proclaims that she is not a two-legged animal, but something like a churn standing on castors!" Soon after, women in the community adopted a shorter dress over loose pants. A similar costume was

"The Bloomer Schottisch, dedicated to Mrs. Bloomer and the ladies in favor of the Bloomer costume," sheet music, 1851.

Composer William Dressler, publisher William Hall & Son, New York. Courtesy of the New York State Library, Manuscripts and Special Collections, SCO344.

Bloomer costume, ca. 1851.

This Bloomer costume is one of the few known surviving examples from the nineteenth century. It was found in a trunk, deep in a bank vault in Cortland, New York. The waistband of the bloomers is signed, in ink, "M.M. Carpenter," a reference to Meriva Carpenter, of Homer, New York. (Laura J. Ping, "Clothes as Historical Sources: What Bloomers Reveal about the Women Who Wore Them," *AHA Today* (blog), American Historical Association, February 13, 2017, http://blog.historians.org/2017/02/clothes-historical-sources-bloomers-reveal-women-wore/). Courtesy of the Cortland County Historical Society.

"Bloomer, or New Costume Polka," sheet music, 1851.

Composer Edward LeRoy, publisher Firth Pond & Co., New York. Courtesy of the New York State Library, Manuscripts and Special Collections, SCO BC12861 V3-2.

After its adoption by the women's rights movement, the Bloomer costume initially received mixed and even some favorable reviews. The costume made appearances in popular culture, including in multiple sheet music publications.

supported by reformers in the hydropathy (water-cure) movement, where it was felt that standard dress caused "our ladies to totter and hobble along like a cripple or a fettered criminal." Water-cure reformers called the dress the "short dress," "the shorts," "Turkish dress," "the American costume," and "the reform dress." By 1852, however, opinion turned to ridicule, and many reformers gave up on wearing it. On her choice to abandon the new costume, Susan B. Anthony wrote, "The attention of my audience was fixed upon my clothes instead of my words."

Susan B. Anthony, carte de visite, 1856.

Courtesy of the Department of Rare Books and
Special Collections, University of Rochester
Libraries.

SUSAN B. ANTHONY

Susan B. Anthony (1820–1906) was born in Adams, Massachusetts, to a
Hicksite Quaker family that eventually included six children who survived to adulthood. The family resettled twice, first to Battenville, New
York, and then to Rochester, the city Susan called home for most of her
life. The family was involved in anti-slavery reform, hosting meetings at
their farmhouse and attending conventions. Susan also became involved
in the temperance movement, giving speeches on the temperance circuit before she became involved in women's rights.

Susan B. Anthony's dress, ca. 1870.

Courtesy of the Rochester Historical Society.

Susan B. Anthony, photograph, ca. 1870.

Courtesy of the Seneca Falls Historical Society.

Susan B. Anthony's dress, in the collection of the Rochester Historical Society, appears to be the same one she is wearing in the photograph from the collection of the Seneca Falls Historical Society.

Through Susan's work as a teacher, she quickly became aware of the wage gap between men and women in the profession. Susan's mother, Lucy Anthony, and sister, Mary Anthony, attended the Rochester women's right's convention in 1848, but Susan did not attend. Susan became involved in women's rights soon after meeting Elizabeth Cady Stanton in 1851, and she eventually put her other reform work to the side to devote her life to the fight for women's suffrage.

Alligator purse and Shawl, dates unknown.

Susan B. Anthony was known for wearing a red shawl to speaking engagements and for carrying this alligator skin satchel. In the purse, she carried her speaking notes, as well as pamphlets and a copy of the transcript of her 1873 trial for voting. The bag especially was so ubiquitous that it was mentioned in a children's schoolyard rhyme, recorded by the press in California while Anthony campaigned for suffrage there:

> Miss Lulu had a baby, she called him tiny Tim.
> She put him in the bathtub, to see if he could swim.
> He drank up all the water! He ate up all the soap!
> He tried to swallow the bathtub, but it wouldn't go down his throat!!
> Call for the doctor!
> Call for the nurse!
> Call for the lady with the alligator purse!
> "Mumps!" said the doctor. "Measles!" said the nurse.
> "Vote!!" said the lady with the alligator purse!!

(National Susan B. Anthony Museum & House, exhibition label text, "So Much More Than a Purse.")

Alligator purse, Courtesy of the National Susan B. Anthony Museum & House.

Shawl, Courtesy of the Division of Political History, National Museum of American History, Smithsonian Institution.

LIFELONG PARTNERS:
ELIZABETH CADY STANTON AND SUSAN B. ANTHONY

In *History of Woman Suffrage*, Stanton wrote, "We were at once fast friends, in thought and sympathy we were one, and in the division of labor we exactly complemented each other. In writing we did better work together than either could alone. While she is slow and analytical

in composition, I am rapid and synthetic. I am the better writer, she the better critic. She supplied the facts and statistics, I the philosophy and rhetoric, and together we have made arguments that have stood unshaken by the storms of thirty long years: arguments that no man has answered. Our speeches may be considered the united product of our two brains."[44]

Susan B. Anthony and Elizabeth Cady Stanton, photograph, ca. 1888–1891.

Courtesy of the Seneca Falls Historical Society.

Anthony-Stanton-Bloomer, sculpture, Ted Aub, bronze, 1999.

This sculpture depicts Amelia Bloomer introducing Elizabeth Cady Stanton and Susan B. Anthony in 1851, on the street in Seneca Falls. Anthony was visiting the village to attend an anti-slavery meeting, and the two quickly became friends and partners in the fight for women's rights.

    Their respective skills and personalities complemented each other well. Anthony was an organizer and had the freedom to travel to conventions and lectures. Stanton was more tied to home and family in the earlier years but was a prolific and talented writer. Anthony often took charge of Stanton's children while visiting, giving Stanton the opportunity to write.

    That is not to say that Stanton and Anthony did not have disagreements and fallings out from time to time. Stanton's ideals occasionally led her down paths that Anthony felt diluted their primary message (suffrage), or even hurt the image of the women's rights movement. In these cases, however, they provided balance to each other, Stanton pushing them to think more broadly about issues that were important to women's rights, and Anthony considering the big picture of the fight for suffrage and reining them in. Courtesy of the Seneca Falls Historical Society; original full-scale sculpture in Seneca Falls, New York.

Trunk, ca. 1870–1900.

Susan B. Anthony traveled tirelessly on the lecture circuit, speaking on suffrage, abolition, women's property rights, and temperance. In the early years, she was responsible not only for her travel arrangements but for setting up a place to speak, promotion, and production of handouts in each town she visited. (Flexner and Fitzpatrick, *Century of Struggle*: The Woman's Rights Movement in the United States, Cambridge: The Belknap Press of Harvard University Press, 1996, 81–82.)

Anthony's status as an unmarried woman, without children, allowed greater freedom of time to promote these causes in large and small communities around New York State, and across the country. Even to modern viewers accustomed to travel by modern transportation methods, her lecture schedule seems daunting. Her diary entries record endless travel, unfamiliar rooms, and often small audiences. Anthony's biographer, Ida Husted Harper, wrote of one particularly hard winter of travel: "Many towns were off the railroad and could be reached only by sleigh. After a long ride she would be put up for the night into a room without a fire, and in the morning would have to break the ice in the pitcher to take that sponge bath from head to foot which she never omitted. All that she hoped from a financial standpoint was to pay the expenses of the trip, and had she desired fame or honor, she would not have sought it in these remote villages." (Ida Husted Harper, *The Life and Work of Susan B. Anthony*, Vol. 1, Indianapolis: Brown-Merrill Company, 1899, 107.) Courtesy of the National Susan B. Anthony Museum & House.

ADDRESSING THE NEW YORK STATE LEGISLATURE, 1854

Susan B. Anthony's work as an organizer of the women's rights movement began in 1854, as she took on a petition campaign directed at the New York State legislature. Anthony worked with sixty women, one designated as a captain in each county. In ten weeks, they collected six thousand signatures on the petition that called for women's control over their own earnings, women's guardianship of children in cases of adoption, and the right to vote.[45]

In February of 1854, Elizabeth Cady Stanton delivered an address to the women's rights convention in Albany, regarding women's position in the laws of New York State. William Channing made a motion to

Elizabeth Cady Stanton's writing desk, ca. 1855.

"I love Mrs. Stanton for the ardor and energy she shows in advocating our cause, and envy her ability to clothe her thoughts in words that burn!" (Martha Coffin Wright to Elizabeth M'Clintock, 8 January 1850, Garrison Family Papers, Sophia Smith Collection, Smith College.)

In the early years of the women's rights movement, Stanton was in the midst of birthing and raising seven children. Her travel was limited by her family obligations, which were exacerbated by the fact that her husband was frequently away for work. She could not be out on the road speaking the way others in the movement could. Her writing, then, became a powerful tool, and she used it to communicate her ideas through newspaper articles, in addresses to conventions she could not attend in person, and in speeches delivered by Susan B. Anthony.

Stanton was not alone—many women in the movement had to balance travel for the cause and work from home in the form of writing articles and locally distributing petitions. Courtesy of Coline Jenkins, Elizabeth Cady Stanton Family.

Address to the Legislature of New-York Adopted by the State Woman's Rights Convention, Held at Albany, pamphlet, Elizabeth Cady Stanton, 1854.

Courtesy of the New York State Library, Manuscripts and Special Collections, 324.623 S792 200-4134.

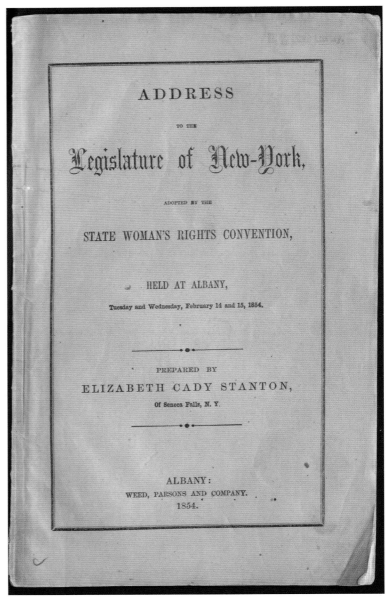

ADDRESS

TO THE

Legislature of New-York,

ADOPTED BY THE

STATE WOMAN'S RIGHTS CONVENTION,

HELD AT ALBANY,

Tuesday and Wednesday, February 14 and 15, 1854.

PREPARED BY

ELIZABETH CADY STANTON,

Of Seneca Falls, N. Y.

ALBANY:
WEED, PARSONS AND COMPANY.
1854.

adopt the speech as the convention's address to the state legislature, and the motion carried, with printed copies soon being made available to legislators. Many years later, Stanton erroneously remarked that she had spoken directly to the legislature, a detail which has been oft repeated as fact.[46]

Neither Anthony's petition nor Stanton's speech was successful in gaining legislation for the rights they demanded.

MATILDA JOSLYN GAGE

Like many in the women's rights movement, Matilda Joslyn Gage (1826–1898) was raised in an abolitionist home. A native of Syracuse, Gage leapt into the women's rights movement when she presented a speech at the 1852 National Women's Rights Convention, held in her city. Though not anticipated on the program, hers was the only speech of the convention to be reprinted in the paper, and she made a call to

The *National Citizen and Ballot Box*, newspaper, May 1878.

Gage served as the owner, editor, and contributor to the monthly journal the *National Citizen and Ballot Box*. The paper began as *The Ballot Box*, published by an Ohio suffrage association, and was purchased and renamed by Gage in 1878. In its prospectus, Gage declared that "women of every class, condition, rank and name will find this paper their friend." (Accessible Archives, "National Citizen and Ballot Box," Accessible Archives, Inc., http://www.accessible-archives.com/collections/national-citizen-and-ballot-box accessed May 28, 2016.) Courtesy of the Matilda Joslyn Gage Foundation.

The National Citizen

AND BALLOT BOX.

SELF-GOVERNMENT IS A NATURAL RIGHT AND THE BALLOT IS THE METHOD OF EXERCISING THAT RIGHT.

SYRACUSE, N. Y., FEBRUARY, 1880.

Matilda Joslyn Gage's writing desk, ca. 1890.

Stanton recalled that Gage "was always a student, an omnivorous reader and liberal thinker, and her pen was ever at work answering the attacks on the woman movement in the county and state journals." (Stanton, Anthony, and Gage, *History of Woman Suffrage*, 1:465.) Courtesy of the Matilda Joslyn Gage Foundation.

"Let Syracuse sustain her name for radicalism."[47] Gage, along with Anthony and Stanton, founded the National Woman Suffrage Association, and she served in many leadership roles within the organization.

Gage developed deep friendships with her Native American neighbors and was adopted by the Haudenosaunee into the Wolf Clan, writing, "I received the name of Ka-ron-ien-ha-wi, or 'Sky Carrier,' or *She who holds the sky*."[48] In her work with the Haudenosaunee, she discovered a culture that had a vastly different view toward women than her own. Gage and Stanton both wrote, publicly and privately, of a more equal division of power and labor in Haudenosaunee society, of women's role in choosing clan leaders, and of the matrilineal organization of Haudenosaunee families.[49]

SOJOURNER TRUTH

Sojourner Truth (ca. 1797–1893) was born into slavery as Isabella Baumfree in Ulster County, New York. In 1827, when her master failed to uphold a promise to free her, she escaped, or as she later declared, "I did not run away, I walked away by daylight."[50] After experiencing a religious conversion, Truth became a preacher and chose the name by which she is known today.

Truth became active in the abolition movement and then, in the 1850s, in the women's rights movement as well. She is perhaps best known for a speech she delivered to the Ohio Women's Rights Convention of 1851, which carried the plea "Ain't I a Woman?" Truth's first language was Dutch, so the dialect added to the speech when it was printed is not likely accurate, but her message that African American women's rights should not be ignored is clear:

That man over there says that women need to be helped into carriages, and lifted over ditches, and to have the best place everywhere. Nobody ever helps me into carriages, or over mud-puddles, or gives me any best place! And ain't I a woman? Look at me! Look at my arm! I have ploughed and planted, and gathered into barns, and no man could head me! And ain't I a woman? I could work as much and eat as much as a man—when I could get it—and bear the lash as well! And ain't I a woman? I have borne thirteen children, and seen most all sold off to slavery, and when I cried out with my mother's grief, none but Jesus heard me! And ain't I a woman?[51]

Following the Civil War, African American women held a precarious place within both the women's rights movement and among anti-slavery reformers. With arguments over whether the African American vote or women's votes should come first, African American women were left out. Several black women, including Truth and Frances Ellen Watkins Harper, became involved in the American Equal Rights Association, which was formed in 1866 "to secure Equal Rights to all American citizens, especially the right of suffrage, irrespective of race, color or sex." Harper stated that the two causes were "all bound up together."[52]

1860 CONVENTION, NEW YORK CITY

What a pretty kettle of hot water you tumbled into at New York!

—Parker Pillsbury to
Elizabeth Cady Stanton, 1860[53]

The Tenth National Women's Rights Convention, the last to be held before the suspension of conventions during the Civil War, was held on May 10–11, 1860, at the Cooper Union in New York City. The convention is most notable for a series of resolutions presented by Stanton on the second day, addressing marriage and divorce. The idea of divorce reform, in cases of cruelty, abandonment, and drunkenness, were not new—beginning in 1850, they were introduced into the New York State Legislature annually.[54] Nevertheless, the topic brought on fierce debate, with Wendell Phillips leading the opposition. Ultimately, the measure was defeated after a vote.

AFTER THE CIVIL WAR

Women's rights conventions were suspended during the Civil War, and many women in the movement worked to support the Union cause. After the war, suffragists felt that their patriotic contributions would help their cause as well, and the second volume of the *History of Woman Suffrage* starts with a chapter on "Woman's Patriotism in the War."

With the passage of the Thirteenth Amendment, which emancipated the slaves, women found new promise in the discussions over the Constitution and what it meant to be a United States citizen. As reformers and politicians discussed African American suffrage, many hoped that woman suffrage could be passed at the same time.

THE AMERICAN EQUAL RIGHTS ASSOCIATION

At the close of the Civil War, reformers founded the American Equal Rights Association (AERA), which was designed to promote the cause of both women's and African American rights, through universal suffrage.

Sojourner Truth, framed carte de visite, 1864.

To support her family, Sojourner Truth sold photographs of herself like this one, at events such as the thirtieth anniversary women's rights convention held in Rochester in 1878. Courtesy of Coline Jenkins, Elizabeth Cady Stanton Family.

At an 1866 convention in Albany, Charles L. Remond summarized the organization's goal, saying, "The time is soon to come when we shall go to the ballot box with our wives and sisters, as the late slaveholders shall with their emancipated blacks."[55] State referenda on both woman and "negro" suffrage in Kansas in 1867, as well as discussions at the New York State constitutional convention the same year, brought expanding the franchise to the forefront.[56]

"Universal Suffrage Convention!", broadside, 1866.

In 1866, the American Equal Rights Association called a universal suffrage convention in Albany's Tweddle Hall, which had approximately 250 attendees. The convention was to address goals for achieving support of universal suffrage at the 1867 New York State constitutional convention, and a call was made for female representatives to be included. Qualifications for suffrage were also discussed, including "intelligent suffrage," which called for an educational test. Stanton opposed the measure, saying, "The ballot is itself an education," and Douglass concurred, as he "found great difficulty in applying any qualification to the right of suffrage beyond that of a common humanity—manhood, womanhood." It was resolved that "Equal Rights" clubs be organized throughout the state.

The beginnings of the fracture of the AERA were also apparent in the proceedings. When Frederick Douglass spoke of a victory in African American suffrage, "giving suffrage to everybody," Elizabeth Cady Stanton reminded him, "Except women, Mr. Douglass, except women." Later, Douglass worried, "I am afraid, from the preponderance of women on this platform, that this will be a Woman's Rights Convention nearly, and that the Negro will only be lugged in incidentally. But I cannot give up the Negro. I can see the importance of enfranchising woman. But with the Negro, I see that enfranchisement is a matter of life and death." ("Equal Rights Convention," The Argus (Albany, NY), 21 November 1866; "Albany: Equal Rights Convention," New York Times, 22 November 1866). Courtesy of the New York State Library, Manuscripts and Special Collections, BRO0119+.

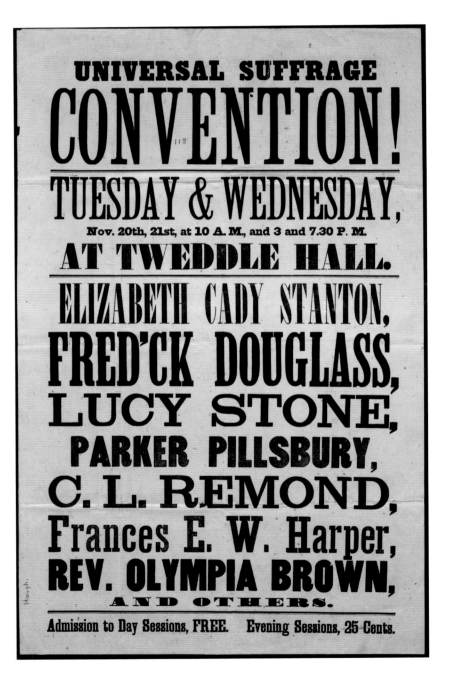

Tweddle Hall, Albany, New York, photograph, 1876.

Interior of Tweddle Hall, Albany, New York, photograph, ca. 1860–1880.

Tweddle Hall was built in 1859 and featured a performance hall that could seat one thousand people. Spaces like this in cities across the state frequently hosted suffrage and other reform conventions, as well as individual speakers. Tweddle Hall burned down in 1883. Courtesy of the Albany Institute of History & Art.

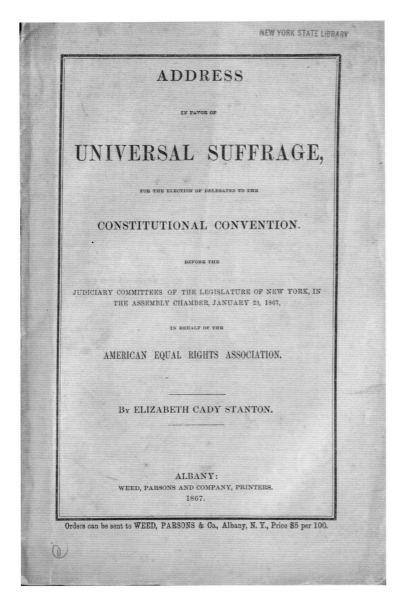

NEW YORK STATE LIBRARY

ADDRESS

IN FAVOR OF

UNIVERSAL SUFFRAGE,

FOR THE ELECTION OF DELEGATES TO THE

CONSTITUTIONAL CONVENTION.

BEFORE THE

JUDICIARY COMMITTEES OF THE LEGISLATURE OF NEW YORK, IN
THE ASSEMBLY CHAMBER, JANUARY 23, 1867,

IN BEHALF OF THE

AMERICAN EQUAL RIGHTS ASSOCIATION.

By ELIZABETH CADY STANTON.

ALBANY:
WEED, PARSONS AND COMPANY, PRINTERS.
1867.

Orders can be sent to WEED, PARSONS & Co., Albany, N. Y., Price $5 per 100.

Address in Favor of Universal Suffrage, for the Election of Delegates to the Constitutional Convention, before the Judiciary Committees of the Legislature of New York in the Assembly Chamber, January 23, 1867, in Behalf of the American Equal Rights Association, pamphlet, Elizabeth Cady Stanton, 1867.

Courtesy of the New York State Library, Manuscripts and Special Collections, 324.623 S792 92-5737.

THE FOURTEENTH AMENDMENT

Discussion of the Fourteenth Amendment, the first to add the word "male" to the United States Constitution in defining citizenship, presented a strain on the membership of the American Equal Rights Association. Despite the foundations of the organization, many members felt that, politically, it was not possible to achieve African American and woman suffrage at the same time. Wendell Phillips, president of AERA, declared that it was the "Negro's hour."[57]

Stanton and Anthony broke ranks from the organization, with Stanton arguing for "educated suffrage," or suffrage based on an educational test.[58] Stanton adopted an anti-immigrant and racist stance, arguing white women's superiority over the other groups that would gain voting rights under the amendment.[59]

With the passage of the Fourteenth Amendment, suffragists were left to wonder whether women were even considered citizens.

THE 1867 NEW YORK STATE CONSTITUTIONAL CONVENTION

In 1867, New York State held a constitutional convention, the first since the Seneca Falls convention (the previous New York State constitutional convention was held in 1846). Like the discussions surrounding the Fourteenth Amendment, the focus of many New Yorkers was on striking the word "white" from the state constitution, not removing the qualifier "male." Horace Greeley, editor of the *New York Tribune*, a paper that had been sympathetic to the women's rights cause, reminded Stanton and Anthony that the immediate post-war period had been declared "the negro's hour," to which they responded:

> No, no, this is the hour to press woman's claims; we have stood with the black man in the Constitution over half a century, and it is fitting now that the constitutional door is open that we should enter with him into the political kingdom of equality. Through all these years he has been the only decent compeer we have had. Enfranchise him, and we are left outside with lunatics, idiots and criminals for another twenty years.[60]

Stanton appeared before the New York State Legislature on January 23, 1867, demanding that "male" be stricken from Section 1, Article II, and that women be allowed to vote for representatives at the convention. Her speech was rich with citations of legal precedent and was reprinted in papers across the state.[61]

The convention assembled in June. Ezra Graves proposed a committee to authorize a vote for women only to determine if they were interested in suffrage, but his proposition was tabled.[62] On June 19, William A. Wheeler, president of the convention, appointed a committee to review the "right of suffrage, and the qualifications for holding office," with Horace Greeley as chair. The committee heard petitions related both to woman and African American suffrage and granted hearings to Stanton, Anthony, Lucy Stone, and George Francis Train.[63] Stanton and Anthony spoke on June 27, after the report of the committee had

Prospectus for *The Revolution*, ca. 1868.

Train offered the suffragists a voice in the press through his newspaper, *The Revolution*. In it, Stanton and Anthony, feeling left behind by the Republican Party, took on the racist arguments for women suffrage that were supported by the Democrats. Courtesy of the Department of Rare Books and Special Collections, University of Rochester Libraries.

"Geo. Francis Train, Mrs. E. Cady Stanton, Susan B. Anthony, Corinthian Hall," ticket, 1867.

George Francis Train was an outspoken and eccentric lecturer who used racist views to support woman suffrage, including the idea that white women should gain suffrage to counteract the black vote. Anthony and Stanton first joined forces with Train in Kansas, where he had been invited to speak in favor of suffrage during the 1866 campaign, to the chagrin of many of their radical friends. Courtesy of the Department of Rare Books and Special Collections, University of Rochester Libraries.

already been completed. During questioning, they were asked about the other strides women had made in legislation, specifically pertaining to property rights. Regarding their support of women and men being "indiscriminately drawn upon juries," they were asked if they felt the same about the draft, which they agreed, despite opposing war.[64] In the *History of Woman Suffrage*, this exchange was reported with more drama and sarcasm:

> Greeley: "Ladies, you will please remember that the bullet and ballot go together. If you vote, are you ready to fight?"

> Stanton and Anthony: "Certainly. We are ready to fight sir, just as you fought in the late war, by sending your substitutes."[65]

Ultimately, an amendment proposed by George William Curtis suggesting the removal of the word "man" from the constitution was voted down.[66]

THE FIFTEENTH AMENDMENT

Only six months after the passage of the Fourteenth Amendment, the Fifteenth Amendment was introduced to build on it, declaring, "The right of citizens of the United States to vote shall not be denied or abridged by the United States or any State, on account of race, color, or previous condition of servitude."

Arguments over the Fifteenth Amendment further deepened the divide in the American Equal Rights Association. In May 1869, Stanton warned the organization, "'Manhood suffrage' is national suicide and women's destruction," and she again put down male immigrants and African American men who would be protected by the amendment.[67] Frederick Douglass argued back that the violence faced by African Americans and their families gave them "an urgency to obtain the ballot."[68] Ultimately, the AERA voted in favor of supporting the Fifteenth Amendment. Stanton and Anthony left, however, to form the National Woman Suffrage Association.[69]

"Celebration in Honor of the Ratification of the 15th Amendment," ticket, Washington, DC, 1870.

Courtesy of the New York State Museum, H-2014.26.10.

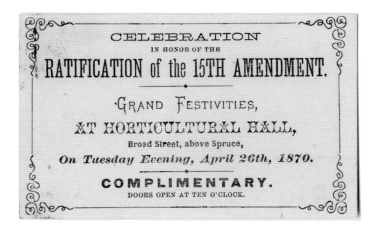

BREAKING THE LAW FOR FREEDOM

The Campaign of Non-Violent Civil Disobedience for the Vote

Sally Roesch Wagner

Matilda Joslyn Gage Center and Syracuse University

After the Civil War and the passage of the Fourteenth and Fifteenth Amendments, the government became an oligarchy of sex, a dictatorship of gender. The Fourteenth defined citizens as "male" for the first time in the Constitution, and the Fifteenth gave African American men—but not women—the right to vote. All men now had the vote; all women didn't. The exception was the men of Native nations, who were citizens of their own sovereign nations and didn't want forced citizenship in the United States.

The hypocrisy worsened when male traitors—former Confederate officials—were given back the vote to rule over loyal women of the North who had wrapped the bandages, supplied the hospitals, and raised over $92 million through the Sanitary Commission, essentially providing medical care for the Union Army.[i]

The suffragists didn't ask for the right to vote. They had it by virtue of being citizens of a government based on the consent of the governed. They were demanding that the federal government protect that right against the states that had passed laws denying women suffrage. How to do that? Direct action was their answer. The charge was led by New York women of the National Woman Suffrage Association (NWSA) most notably the leadership triumvirate of Susan B. Anthony (Rochester), Matilda Joslyn Gage (Fayetteville), and Elizabeth Cady Stanton, organizer of the first local woman suffrage convention in Seneca Falls.[ii]

Taxation without representation is tyranny, whether in 1776 or 1876, the suffragists contended, launching their campaign of non-violent civil disobedience with a national tax protest announced as the government celebrated the centennial of the Boston Tea Party in 1873. "*Oh, wise men,*" questioned Matilda Joslyn Gage, "*can you tell why he means she, when taxes are to be assessed, and does not mean she, when taxes are to be voted upon?*"[iii] The Anti-Tax League refused to financially support the government until it gave them representation. The tax resistance was more than a token gesture; one petition alone of many sent to the New York legislature represented $9,000,000 of women's money among its few signers.[iv]

It was against the law for women to vote. Women by the hundreds, across the country, broke the law and voted, to push their point. Susan B. Anthony was arrested; hers was the test case. Matilda Joslyn Gage (who had tried to vote a year before) joined Anthony in a campaign to educate potential jurors on the issue in a whirlwind tour of sixteen townships in Ontario County, New York, where the trial was to be held, in the twenty-two days before the trial began.

"The United States is on trial," Matilda Joslyn Gage announced in her speech, "not Susan B. Anthony." Anthony had the right to vote. But New York State law made it a crime for women to vote. The trial of Susan B. Anthony for voting was really a trial about whether the federal government had a responsibility to protect its citizens against anyone that denied them their rights, even if that denial came from a state.[v]

The judge did not allow the jury to decide the case, nor did he consult them. Judge Hunt ordered the jury to find Susan B. Anthony guilty of voting, an act expressly forbidden to women under New York law, and fined her one hundred dollars, plus the costs of the prosecution. She refused to pay.[vi]

An indignant Gage told the National Woman Suffrage Association annual convention that year:

> What better is it today for Susan B. Anthony, for any woman, to be a citizen of the United States, than it was for our fathers to be subjects of Great Britain? They were taxed without being represented, so are all women. . . . We have rulers set over us whom we are forbidden to help elect. . . . Can the nation play fast and loose at will with things so sacred? Is the very key of personal and national liberty a ball to be tossed from nation to state, and state to nation, to suit the whims of shallow states-men, and unprincipled politicians?[vii]

When the nation prepared to celebrate the centennial, the National Woman Suffrage Association declared, "The women of the United States, denied for one hundred years the only means of self-government, the ballot," are "political slaves," and "have greater cause for discontent, rebellion and revolution, than the men of 1776." "As Abigail Adams predicted," they continued, "we are determined to foment a rebellion, and will not hold ourselves bound by laws in which we have no voice or representation."[viii]

Renting headquarters in Philadelphia where they held nightly meetings, these radical suffragists decided to "demand justice for the women of this land" by presenting a Woman's Declaration of Rights at the official ceremonies on July 4. Matilda Joslyn Gage and Elizabeth Cady Stanton penned the document, and then were denied permission to present it on the grounds that, "if granted, it would be the event of the day—the topic of discussion to the exclusion of all others." The women decided to go ahead with their plan, risking the possibility of arrest, to "place on record for the daughters of 1976, the fact that their mothers of 1876 had thus asserted their equality of rights, and thus impeached the government of today for its injustice towards women."[ix]

On July 4, 1876, five women: Matilda Joslyn Gage, Susan B. Anthony, Sara Andrews Spencer, Phoebe Couzins, and Lillie Devereux Blake, took their seats in the press section facing a crowd of 150,000 in Independence Square. They had only a few seconds to make their presentation after the reading of the Declaration of Independence, knowing there was a good chance they would be stopped before they reached the speaker's platform by the guards surrounding it. Anthony went first, followed by Gage, who held concealed the three-foot scroll containing the declaration. They moved rapidly and as they approached the stand, the foreign guests, military officers, and guards—taken by surprise—all made way. Gage passed their document to Anthony, who placed it in the hand of a startled Vice President Ferry saying, "We present this Declaration of Rights of the women citizens of the United States." With his silent acceptance, the declaration became an official part of the day's proceedings.

The final words of the Woman's Declaration read: "We ask justice, we ask equality, we ask that all the civil and political rights that belong to citizens of the United States, be guaranteed to us and our daughters forever."[x]

The protests continued. Charging that the existing political parties had "raised no great moral or political issue" but rather "presented to people the same old platitudes," the feminists formed an Equal Rights Party and ran a well-known woman lawyer for president in 1884. Belva Lockwood, from Lockport, New York, became the first woman to carry out a campaign for the presidency. Her party's commitment was to "equal and exact justice" for all citizens, regardless of "color, sex or nationality." An international peace pact (because "war is a relic of barbarism belonging to the past") joined an end to monopolies ("the tendency of which is to make the rich richer, and the poor poorer") as top priorities in the platform. Belva Lockwood and Marietta Stow received 4,149 popular votes and the entire electoral vote of Indiana in the election.[xi]

When the Statue of Liberty was unveiled in 1886, women's rights advocates called it "the greatest hypocrisy of the 19th century" to depict liberty as a woman "while not one single woman throughout the length and breadth of the Land is as yet in possession of political Liberty." The New York Woman Suffrage Association decorated a rented steamer with suffrage banners and joined the three-mile-long aquatic parade that sailed past a crowd of thousands on the Battery and then circled Bedloe's Island during the official unveiling ceremonies in New York Harbor on October 18.[xii]

It was inevitable that the ceremonies that "fittingly brought to a conclusion" the "noble series of celebrations in commemoration of the birth of a mighty nation" would find the radical suffragists staging their final protest. At the anniversary celebration of the Constitution on September 17, 1887, New York City suffragist Lillie Devereux Blake made the presentation of the suffragists' protest. "Precisely at nine o'clock the cheering outside announced the coming of the Chief Magistrate," Blake reminisced.

> A moment later he entered the room, and was presented to the city officials. Then there was a pause, and this was my opportunity. I at once advanced, holding a copy of the protest with the autograph signatures. As Mr. Cleveland saw me, he smiled pleasantly, shook hands, and greeted me cordially. "I have the honor, Mr. President," I said, "to present to you this protest, on behalf of the National Woman Suffrage Association."[xiii]

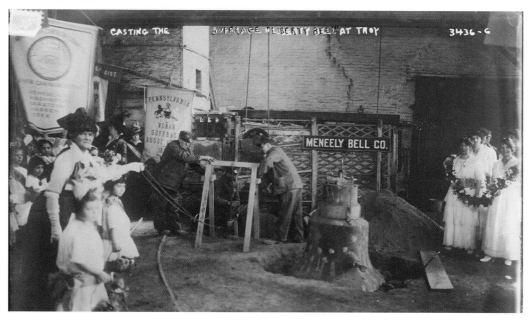

Casting the Suffrage "Liberty Bell" at Troy, photograph, ca. 1915.

The suffrage movement frequently called on the theme of liberty and alluded to the struggles of the American Revolution, especially the call for "no taxation without representation." In 1915, Katharine Wentworth Ruschenberger commissioned a replica of the Liberty Bell to be used in parades and events in Pennsylvania. The bell was cast by the Meneely Bell Company, in Troy, New York, where a ceremony was held following the casting. Sometimes referred to as the "Justice Bell," the bell crisscrossed Pennsylvania in silence, since its clapper was chained down until the Nineteenth Amendment was passed. Courtesy of the Library of Congress.

But justice was not being granted, and the position of women needed transformation on all fronts, not just politically. Gage and Stanton came increasingly to believe that the vote was not an end itself but simply a tool by which to remove the "*four-fold bondage of women*" at the hands of "*the State, the Church, the capitalist, and the home.*"[xiv]

Gage left words to encourage the women who would come after to move in the dramatic ways of their foremother suffragists: "Let all government cease from off the face of the earth, if we cannot build up a government of equality. A rebel! How glorious the name sounds when applied to woman. Oh, rebellious woman, to you the world looks in hope. Upon you has fallen the glorious task of bringing liberty to the earth and all the inhabitants thereof."[xv]

Notes

i. *New Northwest*, 4 August 1876; Belle Squire, *The Woman Movement in America* (Chicago: A. C. McClurg, 1911), 107–108; "Volunteer Relief," *Syracuse Journal*, 22 November 1861.

ii. Matilda Joslyn Gage, "Woman's Rights Catechism" (Fayetteville, NY), *Weekly Recorder*, 27 July 1871.

iii. *Syracuse Journal*, 7 May 1871.

iv. "Women Tax Payers" (Fayetteville, NY), *Weekly Recorder* [1873], Scrapbook of Writings, Matilda Joslyn Gage Collection, Schlesinger Library; "Tea and Taxes," *Chicago Tribune* [1873] and Call for December 16, 1873, Mass Meeting, Matilda Joslyn Gage scrapbook, Library of Congress.

v. *An Account of the Proceedings of the Trial of Susan B. Anthony, on the Charge of Illegal Voting, at the Presidential Election in November, 1872* (Rochester: Daily Democrat and Chronicle Book Print, 1874; reprint ed., New York: Arno Press, 1974), 178.

vi. *An Account of the Proceedings of the Trial of Susan B. Anthony*, 205.

vii. Elizabeth Cady Stanton, Susan B. Anthony, and Matilda Joslyn Gage, *History of Woman Suffrage* 6 vols. (Reprint ed., Salem NH: Ayer Company, 1985), 2:689.

viii. (Boston) *New Age*, 1 July 1876, 1.

ix. *History of Woman Suffrage*, 3:29–30.

x. *History of Woman Suffrage*, 3:34. Chapter 27, "The Centennial Year" (1–56) has a complete and vivid description of events during the year.

xi. (Oakland, CA) *Woman's Herald of Industry*, November 1884. This paper, edited by Marietta Stow, is the major source of information on the 1884 campaign of the Equal Rights Party. In December of 1884, the paper became the *Equal Rights Party*.

xii. Katherine Devereux Blake and Margaret Louise Wallace, *Champion of Women: The Life of Lillie Devereux Blake* (New York: Fleming H. Revell, 1943), 165; *The Woman's Journal*, 16 and 23 October 1886.

xiii. Blake's report was carried in her regular column, "Our New York Letter," in *The Woman's Journal*, 24 September 1887; Susan B. Anthony, Matilda Joslyn Gage, Rachel G. Foster, Mary Wright Sewall, and Lillie Devereux Blake, "Protest Against the Unjust Interpretation of the Constitution Presented on Behalf of the Women of the United States by Officers of the National Woman Suffrage Association," 17 September 1887, Blake collection, Missouri Historical Society.

xiv. Lois W. Banner, *Elizabeth Cady Stanton* (Boston: Little, Brown, 1980), 145.

xv. "Our New York Letter," in *The Woman's Journal*, 24 September 1887.

THE SUFFRAGE MOVEMENT SPLITS: NWSA AND AWSA

THE NATIONAL WOMAN SUFFRAGE ASSOCIATION

With their discontent over the American Equal Rights Association's support of the Fifteenth Amendment, Stanton and Anthony departed to form the National Woman Suffrage Association (NWSA) in May of 1869. Despite their opposition to the Fifteenth Amendment, they recognized that it set a new precedent: federal regulation of voting. NWSA set its goal on pressing Congress for a federal amendment allowing woman suffrage, and it promoted efforts for a Sixteenth Amendment to do so. This amendment was first introduced to Congress by George Julian, of Indiana, in 1869.[70]

THE AMERICAN WOMAN SUFFRAGE ASSOCIATION (AWSA)

A second suffrage oriented group also emerged from the AERA, in November 1869: the American Woman Suffrage Association (AWSA). Many of its members, including its leader, Lucy Stone, came from the ranks of the New England Woman Suffrage Association. The organization supported a state-focused strategy, promoting state referenda and state constitutional conventions, rather than a federal constitutional amendment.[71]

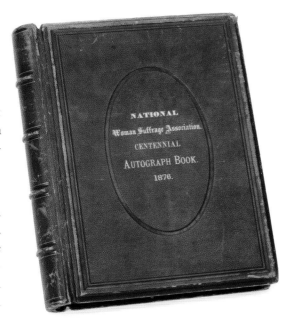

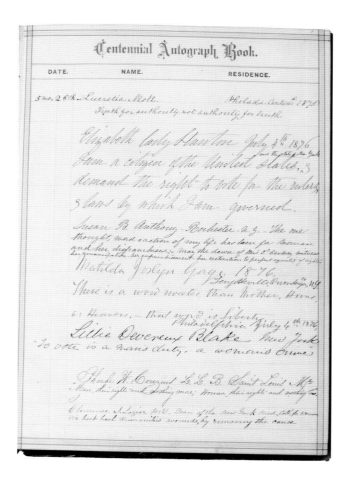

National Woman Suffrage Association Centennial Autograph Book, 1876.

Suffragists saw the 1876 centennial celebrations as an opportunity to highlight their cause, as the country looked back on the American Revolution and the fight for "no taxation without representation." The National Woman Suffrage Association rented rooms in Philadelphia as a summer headquarters, convenient to the Centennial Exposition grounds. Matilda Joslyn Gage developed a "Declaration of Rights of the Women of the United States," which began: "While the Nation is buoyant with patriotism, and all hearts are attuned to praise, it is with sorrow we come to strike the one discordant note, on this hundredth anniversary of our country's birth." (Tetrault, *The Myth of Seneca Falls*, 99–101.) The suffragists applied for an opportunity to present the declaration at the official ceremonies of the exposition—and were denied. Susan B. Anthony and others attended the ceremonies anyway and marched on stage to present the declaration to the acting vice president, while Gage distributed printed copies to the crowd. Courtesy of the Onondaga Historical Association.

Lucy Stone, photograph, ca. 1850.

Lucy Stone, of Massachusetts, was a leading organizer of the New England Woman Suffrage Association, and of the American Woman Suffrage Association. Stone was also an abolitionist, and she was active as an orator for both causes. Courtesy of the Library of Congress.

THE 1872 ELECTION AND SIXTEEN ROCHESTER WOMEN

Following passage of the Fourteenth and Fifteenth Amendments, many in the suffrage movement saw hope in a new theory and plan of attack, called "the New Departure." Supporters felt that under the US Constitution and existing amendments, women already had the right to vote. The philosophy was laid out by Francis Minor in a set of resolutions he wrote for the Missouri Woman Suffrage Association, which were reprinted by the National Woman Suffrage Association in October 1869.[72]

The New Departure was adopted as a strategy of the NWSA, and the plan gained further national attention when it was espoused by Victoria Woodhull in her January 1871 speech to the House Judiciary Committee. Woodhull was later asked to repeat her speech to the Union Association convention, where the strategy was also adopted.

In November of 1872, sixteen women in Rochester took to the polls. Among them were Susan B. Anthony and Rhoda Degarmo, a suffragist who was active at the 1848 Rochester women's rights convention. Anthony was arrested and made a test case for a number of women who had voted, across the country. Prior to the trial, Anthony made the rounds speaking in each of the postal districts of Monroe County, where the trial was to take place. When the trial was moved to Ontario County, she worked with Matilda Joslyn Gage to speak in all postal districts there as well, drumming up support among potential jurors.[73]

Anthony's defense was that she considered herself legally able to vote and did so in good faith. Anthony was not permitted as a witness, and upon completion of the testimony, Justice Ward Hunt directed the jury to find a guilty verdict and read a prepared statement declaring her guilty. Anthony was fined one hundred dollars plus the costs of the prosecution, which she did not pay.[74]

"'Susannah, Don't You Cry,'
Miss Susan B. Anthony Fined $100 for Voting," the *New York Herald*, June 29 ,1873.

This article recounts the close of Anthony's trial for voting, Judge Ward Hunt's guilty determination, and the resulting $100 fine. Courtesy of Laura Bierman.

Maurice Leyden's journal, 1872.

Maurice and Maggie Leyden were active in the suffrage movement in Rochester, New York. In Maurice's daily journal, he records some of their suffrage activities and work with Susan B. Anthony and Matilda Joslyn Gage. In November of 1872, Maggie registered and voted in Rochester, along with sixteen other women, and Maurice wrote, "The ladies of the 8th ward are confident that they are right & determined to offer their votes. I think they are right & as citizens can vote beyond a doubt." Maurice went on to record the arrest and trials of the elections officers related to the incident. Courtesy of the Maurice Leyden Collection, Binghamton University Libraries' Special Collections and University Archives, Binghamton University, State University of New York.

"BOUND TOGETHER BY THE TIES OF HUMANITY"

SARAH JANE SMITH THOMPSON GARNET

Susan Goodier
State University of New York at Oneonta

MRS. SARAH J. S. GARNET

Sarah Jane Smith Thompson Garnet, illustration, ca. 1910.

Courtesy of the New York Public Library.

Most African American women strongly supported the right of women to vote. They usually had to do so in conjunction with their other activist work, rarely able to devote their time exclusively to woman suffrage. Unfortunately, most white women's suffrage clubs and organizations remained reluctant to include black women in the mainstream movement. Complicating our understanding of black women's suffrage activism, very little evidence of activist work on the part of black suffragists exists in the archives. To appreciate black women's activism for suffrage, we have to understand that it does not always parallel—or integrate neatly with—white women's suffrage activism. Rather, black women did not separate political rights for women from other rights they considered necessary. Black women saw the potential of the vote "as a cure from many of their ills"—as a way to promote education, alleviate "sexual exploitation," end prostitution and other "moral evils," challenge black men's disenfranchisement, and support workers' rights—supporting women's enfranchisement for reasons similar to those of white women.[i] Having to confront racism at virtually every level complicated, but did not suppress, the suffrage movement for African American women.

As the suffrage movement dragged on to the dawn of the twentieth century, many white suffragists began to endorse an "expediency" theory that encouraged the exclusion of black women from voting rights. This theory promoted states' rights, whereby individual states could determine the limits of suffrage. Under these ideas, many white suffragists could "practice racist principles without censure from other suffragists."[ii] So, to promote the cause of woman suffrage, black women had to confront the societal racism they had long faced, as well as the racism more boldly justified by the movement they found essential for the uplift of their race. Among the many black women in New York State who confronted these challenges, Sarah Jane Smith Thompson Garnet stands out as a dynamic advocate of the cause of woman suffrage.

Born on July 30, 1831, the first of eleven children of Sylvanus and Annie Springstead Smith, both of whom claimed Long Island Native American ancestry, Sarah Jane joined a prosperous Queens County family. The family earned a good living from farming and Sylvanus' work as a pork merchant.[iii] Her maternal grandmother gave Sarah an elementary-level education, and then

Sarah attended school in the New York public school system. She must have stood out as a capable and intelligent young woman, for by the age of fourteen, she worked as a monitor under the supervision of John Peterson.[iv] Like many other educated black women of her time, Sarah Smith decided on a career in teaching.

She began teaching in the nearby Brooklyn neighborhood of Williamsburg in 1854. Around the same time, she married the Episcopal reverend James Thompson and bore two children, neither of whom survived to adulthood.[v] Her personal life did not seem to interfere with her career, as she became the first black principal of an integrated New York public school, the Manhattan Grammar School No. 4, on April 30, 1863. Eventually, she moved on to Public School No. 80 as a principal, a position she kept until her retirement in 1900; she worked in education for a remarkable fifty-six years.[vi] In addition to her full-time work as a school administrator, she operated a seamstress shop in her home from 1883 to 1911.

James Thompson died in the late 1860s, and in 1879 Sarah Smith Thompson married the well-known abolitionist and minister Henry Highland Garnet. Henry Garnet served at the time as minister of the Shiloh Presbyterian Church in Brooklyn. The marriage does not seem to have been a particularly successful one; according to one source, the couple separated after only a year.[vii] Subsequently, Henry Garnet left the United States by himself to serve as ambassador to Liberia, dying in Monrovia in 1882. Sarah Garnet, again widowed, focused her energies on her activism for suffrage and other feminist causes.

Garnet believed that women had the "same human intellectual and spiritual capabilities as men," and that no democracy should deny women the right to vote.[viii] Her activism manifested itself at both the local and national levels. On the local level, Garnet, with her younger sister Susan Maria Smith McKinney Steward, the first black female physician to practice in New York State, and others, founded the Colored Women's Equal Suffrage League of Brooklyn in the late 1880s, holding meetings in her seamstress shop in the back of her home. The group met to discuss voting and citizenship rights for women. When the league became too popular to continue meeting in Garnet's home, they adjourned to the local church or YMCA on Carlton Avenue.[ix] Most meetings opened with a musical performance, followed by speeches presented by members or special guests, and closed with a report relating the group's accomplishments since the previous meeting. Although ostensibly a women's club, men attended many of the meetings.

The league held a memorial service for Susan B. Anthony in April 1906 where both black and white women spoke in memory of the suffrage leader.[x] They honored author Harriet Beecher Stowe at another meeting a few years later.[xi] Sometimes the league hosted white suffragists, such as when Mary E. Craigie spoke at a league meeting. Arguing that "we are all bound together by the ties of humanity," she contended that women wanted the right to vote because "we want to be human individuals."[xii] On another occasion the league enjoyed the speech of Anne Cobden-Sanderson of London, who also "listened with deep interest to Mrs. S. J. S. Garnet, who told of the efforts of the black women to organize and assist with the women's suffrage work."[xiii]

The league also participated in political playacting. For example, in July 1908, members held a mock national Republican convention, and Garnet, appointed as the "one woman delegate," voted for the controversial Joseph B. Foraker, who disagreed with Theodore Roosevelt over the Brownsville Affair two years before, whereby Roosevelt had dismissed an entire black battalion for allegedly terrorizing a town in Texas.[xiv] League members assisted with preparations for helping to host a meeting of the National Association of Colored Women, held the same summer.[xv] Although Sarah Garnet gave up her role as president of the Equal Suffrage League to another prominent African American suffragist and activist, Dr. Verina Morton-Jones, she consistently attended its meetings. The newspapers often referred to Garnet as the league's "leading spirit."[xvi]

Garnet also worked for woman suffrage and racial uplift at the national level. As a member of the National Association of Colored Women, Garnet served as head of the special suffrage division. In this capacity, she helped educate members of the association about woman suffrage, distributing literature and giving speeches. Garnet gave "an excellent talk" on woman suffrage at the fourth convention of the association in St. Louis, Missouri, in July 1904. The association represented about forty thousand women and worked to overcome some of the racist and sexist challenges black women faced. She also served as superintendent of the National Federation of Colored Women's Clubs.[xvii] At every opportunity, Garnet promoted the woman suffrage cause.

Like most black women suffragists, Garnet also worked for social justice in other fields. She sought to end race-based discrimination against African American teachers and advocated for equal pay for women and better retention for educators. According to the biography written by prominent educator Maritcha Remond Lyons, Garnet, accompanied by Bishop W. B. Derrick and the lawyer T. McCants Stewart, traveled to Albany to "confront the legislature with indisputable facts" regarding the discrimination black teachers faced.[xviii] Garnet maintained an active schedule to improve the education of black children. She also worked for this goal nationally as a member of the National Teachers' Association, one of very few African American women who belonged to the organization. In addition, she served as a manager for the Howard Orphan Asylum.[xix]

Garnet attended the anti-lynching event with Ida B. Wells Barnett and other activists, held in October 1892 at Lyric Hall in New York City. The event, organized by Sarah Garnet, her sister, Dr. Susan McKinney, Victoria Earle Matthews of the White Rose Working Girls Home, and Maritcha Lyons, drew 250 supporters. The women contributed $500 so that Wells could write her anti-lynching pamphlet, *Southern Horrors: Lynch Law in All Its Phases.* Following the meeting, Garnet, McKinney, Lyons, Matthews, Elizabeth Frazer, and others organized the Women's Loyal Union of New York and Brooklyn to continue Wells' anti-lynching work, with Matthews serving as president. Its focus included education for African Americans and the "desire to increase their happiness in every way consistent with law and reason."[xx] Woman suffrage would help to achieve all the goals of the Loyal Union.

In 1911 Garnet and her sister, Susan McKinney Steward, traveled to the University of London to attend the first meeting of the Universal Races Congress, held July 26 to 29, so that Steward could present a paper, "Colored American Women." While in London, she listened to other activists who discussed the status of people of color outside of the United States and gathered information on various topics, including woman suffrage. Upon their return to Brooklyn, the Colored Women's Suffrage League held a welcome home reception for Garnet in her home on September 7. In addition to the usual playing of music and reading of poetry, several attendees read papers. Susan Steward read the paper she had presented at the London Congress. Garnet distributed the suffrage material she had collected. People in attendance included Atlanta professor John Hope and his wife, Lugenia Burns Hope, W. E. B. Du Bois, Verina Morton-Jones, and other members of the Equal Suffrage League.[xxi]

Just ten days after the reception, on September 17, 1911, Sarah J. Smith Thompson Garnet died quietly in her Hancock Street, Brooklyn, home. Suffragist and national lecturer for the YWCA, Addie Waites Hunton and W. E. B. Du Bois spoke at her memorial service, held at the Bridge Street African Methodist Episcopal Church on October 29, 1911, while Fannie Garrison Villard, Ida B. Wells Barnett, and others sent letters to be read at the service.

While many black women worked for the woman suffrage cause, most found white women generally excluded them from attending their suffrage meetings. Nevertheless, black activists refused to back away from the goal of political enfranchisement, rarely separating their goals related to political equality from their other goals for economic and social equity. By promoting political education, as well as the full engagement and support of black men in the political process, black women's suffrage activism aided the mainstream suffrage cause.

Notes

i. Paula Giddings, *When and Where I Enter: The Impact of Black Women on Race and Sex in America* (New York: Bantam Books, 1984), 121; Karen Garner, "Equal Suffrage League," in *Organizing Black America: An Encyclopedia of African American Associations*, ed. Nina Mjagkij (New York: Garland, 2001), 224; Mrs. Sarah J. S. Garnet, Seventh Report, file #358, New York City Municipal Archives, New York, NY.

ii. Giddings, *When and Where I Enter*, 127.

iii. Hallie Q. Brown, *Homespun Heroines and Other Women of Distinction* (New York: Oxford University Press, 1988), 111.

iv. Carla L. Peterson, *Black Gotham: A Family History of African Americans in Nineteenth-Century New York City* (New Haven: Yale University Press, 2011), 355–356.

v. Maritcha Lyons, Garnet's biographer, seems to have misremembered the reverend's name, stating it as "Tompkins." Some historians have repeated this error. Brown, *Homespun Heroines*, 114.

vi. Brown, *Homespun Heroines*, 112; Mrs. Sarah J. S. Garnet, Seventh Report, file #358, New York City Municipal Archives, New York, NY.

vii. Peterson, *Black Gotham*, 356.

viii. Garner, "Organizing Black America," 224; Peterson, *Black Gotham*, 355–356.

ix. The Brooklyn and Queens YMCA Carlton Avenue Branch, the first branch in Brooklyn for African Americans, opened in 1902 and closed in 1955. http://special.lib.umn.edu/findaid/html/ymca/ygny0025.phtml (accessed 2 April 2015).

x. "Susan B. Anthony Memorial," *Brooklyn Daily Eagle*, 1 April 1906, 22.

xi. "Honor Harriet B. Stowe," *Brooklyn Daily Eagle*, 16 June 1910, 6.

xii. "Mrs. Craigie Wants to Vote," *Brooklyn Daily Eagle*, 29 April 1907, 5.

xiii. "Afro-American Notes," *Brooklyn Daily Eagle*, 5 January 1908, 22.

xiv. "Afro-American Notes," *Brooklyn Daily Eagle*, 1 July 1908, 8.

xv. "Afro-American Notes," *Brooklyn Daily Eagle*, 29 May 1908, 13.

xvi. "Afro-American Notes," *Brooklyn Daily Eagle*, 5 January 1908, 22.

xvii. Report of the "Fourth Convention of the National Association of Colored Women," 29, Microfilm, Burke Library, Hamilton College, Clinton, NY; "Civilization in Africa," *Brooklyn Daily Eagle*, 9 February 1906, 10.

xviii. Brown, *Homespun Heroines*, 115.

xix. "For Colored Orphans," *Brooklyn Daily Eagle*, 16 December 1892, 9; "Howard Orphan Asylum," *Brooklyn Daily Eagle*, 16 October 1900, 13.

xx. "Colored Women Organize," *Brooklyn Daily Eagle*, 21 February 1893, 4.

xxi. "News of Greater New York," *New York Age*, 14 September 1911, 7; Brown, *Homespun Heroines*, 116.

PRE-SUFFRAGE WOMEN WHO RAN FOR PRESIDENT

VICTORIA CLAFLIN WOODHULL

Victoria Claflin Woodhull (1838–1927), and her sister, Tennessee (Tennie) Claflin (1844–1923), were born into a family that embraced spiritualism, and as young teens, the sisters were put on the road as child mediums and healers. Woodhull's first marriage, to Dr. Canning Woodhull at age 14, ended in divorce due to his alcoholism. Victoria was left destitute with two children, one of whom was mentally handicapped. These experiences informed Victoria's views on women's rights and free love.

In 1868, Victoria and Tennie set out for New York City to pursue new opportunities. They quickly sought out Cornelius Vanderbilt and, winning his favor, used his assistance to set up their own stock brokerage. They were the first women to run such a firm, and the press gave them a great deal of attention, calling them "Queens of Finance" and "Bewitching Brokers."[75]

In *The Revolution*, Susan B. Anthony remarked, "These two ladies (for they are ladies) are determined to use their brains, energy, and their knowledge of business to earn them a livelihood. . . . The advent of this woman's firm in Wall Street marks a new era."[76] In 1870, the sisters also began their own newspaper, *Woodhull and Claflin's Weekly*, which focused on broad social reform.

After becoming involved in the suffrage movement as an observer in 1869, Victoria announced her candidacy for president in April of 1870. In a letter to the *New York Herald*, she wrote, "I therefore claim the right to speak for the unfranchised women of the country, and believing as I do that the prejudices which still exist in the popular mind against women in public life will soon disappear, I now announce myself as a candidate for the Presidency."[77]

In the fall of 1870, Woodhull took up residence in the Willard Hotel in Washington, DC, with the goal of lobbying for a Sixteenth Amendment for woman suffrage. Her mission soon changed, and through collaboration with Benjamin Butler, she promoted the idea that the Fifteenth Amendment already gave women the right to vote. Victoria petitioned Congress to confirm her interpretation and ultimately presented before the House Judiciary Committee (the first woman to address a congressional committee), as well as the national suffrage convention.[78]

Woodhull was a supporter of "free love," promoting women's right to their own bodies and supporting their right to say no to loveless marriages. She actively spoke out against the sexual double standard, which judged women more harshly than men for supposed transgressions,

Victoria C. Woodhull, carte de visite, ca. 1870.

Victoria Woodhull and Tennessee Claflin garnered a great deal of publicity when they became the first female brokers on Wall Street, and carte de visites like this one were available for sale. It is noteworthy that Woodhull is labeled "broker." Courtesy of the Collection of Ronnie Lapinsky Sax.

AGITATE! AGITATE! 1776–1890 / 55

CONVENTION IN APOLLO HALL, NEW YORK CITY. VICTORIA CLAFLIN WOODHULL NOMINATED FOR PRESIDENT OF THE UNITED STATES, 1872.

"Victoria Woodhull Being Nominated for the Presidency by the Equal Rights Party in New York City, May 10, 1872," engraving in *One Moral Standard for All: Extracts from the Lives of Victoria Claflin Woodhull, Now Mrs. John Biddulph Martin, and Tennessee Claflin, Now Lady Cook*, M. F. Darwin, ca. 1915.

By the spring of 1872, Woodhull had taken over the meeting of the Union Association to create a new "People's Party," which was soon renamed the Equal Rights Party. This matched her expanding presidential platform, which took on a broader reform agenda, and embraced the Labor movement. Woodhull was nominated as the party's presidential candidate, and Frederick Douglass, unbeknownst to him, was chosen as her running mate. Courtesy of the New York State Library, Manuscripts and Special Collections, 323.34092 D228 91-26981.

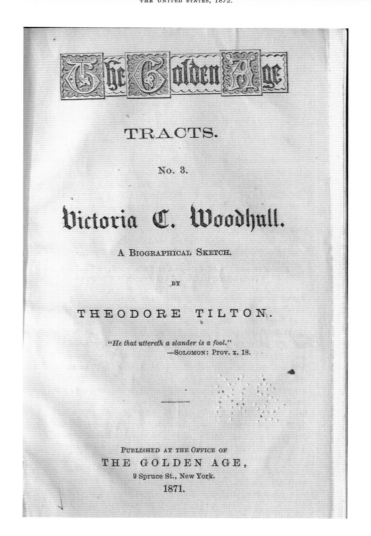

The Golden Age

TRACTS.

No. 3.

Victoria C. Woodhull.

A BIOGRAPHICAL SKETCH.

BY

THEODORE TILTON.

"He that uttereth a slander is a fool."
—SOLOMON: Prov. x. 18.

PUBLISHED AT THE OFFICE OF
THE GOLDEN AGE,
9 Spruce St., New York.
1871.

Victoria C. Woodhull, A Biographical Sketch, book, Theodore Tilton, 1871.

As Woodhull came under growing scrutiny in the press for her private life, she decided that having an author publish her biography would be a means to provide clarity on her background. She hoped, in turn, that her personal history would illicit sympathy in the press. Victoria developed a close friendship with editor and abolitionist Theodore Tilton, and his reputation lent status to the publication. Courtesy of the New York State Library, Manuscripts and Special Collections, 396.09 M38t.

while men carried on behind the scenes. In October 1872, she put these beliefs into practice when she exposed the affair of the prominent minister Henry Ward Beecher with his parishioner and friend's wife, Elizabeth Tilton. Woodhull was jailed for obscenity, and the negative publicity from the highly publicized trial destroyed her candidacy and hurt the suffrage movement.

BELVA ANN LOCKWOOD

Born near Royalton, New York, Belva Ann Lockwood (1830–1917) began a teaching career immediately after finishing school herself. Like Anthony, she quickly realized that she was making less than half of what male teachers were being paid. After the early death of her first husband, Lockwood concluded that the key to bettering her situation was education. She made the difficult decision to leave her young daughter with family and pursued studies at Genesee Wesleyan Seminary, which had just begun accepting women. Even after graduation, as a school principal, her wages were far lower than those of her male peers.[79]

Inspired by taking a law class in Lockport, New York, Lockwood and her daughter moved to Washington, DC, where Lockwood became a devoted political observer and founded her own school. She remarried and decided to pursue her goal of becoming a lawyer. After many rejections, she was finally admitted to the National University School of Law, with eighteen other women. When Lockwood and one other woman completed their coursework, they were both denied degrees, until Lockwood petitioned President Grant, Chancellor ex-officio of the university. She faced similar battles in her application to the bar, finally being admitted to practice before the Supreme Court in March of 1879, the first woman to do so.

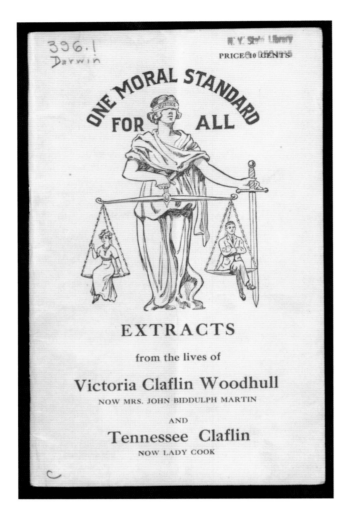

One Moral Standard for All: Extracts from the Lives of Victoria Claflin Woodhull, Now Mrs. John Biddulph Martin, and Tennessee Claflin, Now Lady Cook, book, M. F. Darwin, ca. 1915.

At the end of their lives, Victoria and Tennie returned to the idea of biography as a way to cast their history in a positive light. Both had moved to England and married respectable Englishmen. The title, *One Moral Standard for All*, alludes to Woodhull's fight against the sexual double standard. Courtesy of the New York State Library, Manuscripts and Special Collections, 323.34092 D228 91-26981.

"Belva A. Lockwood, Attorney and Solicitor," advertisement in the *National Citizen and Ballot Box*, May 1878.

Courtesy of the Matilda Joslyn Gage Foundation.

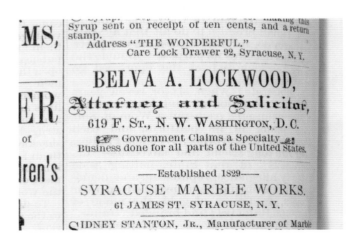

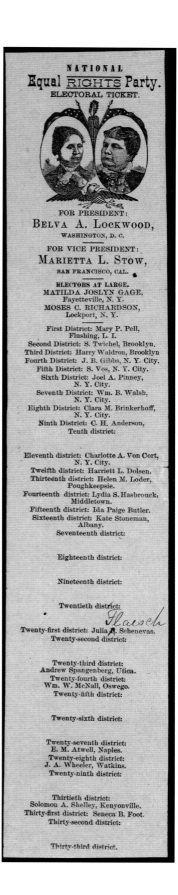

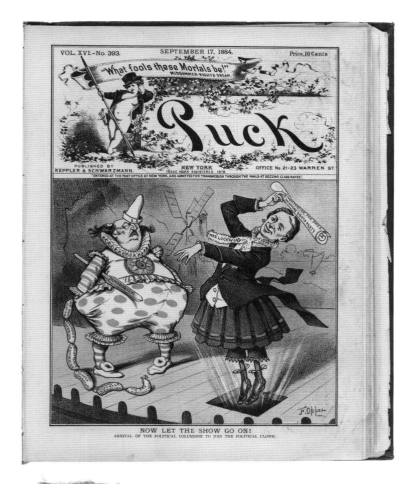

National Equal Rights Party Electoral Ticket, Belva A. Lockwood and Marietta L. Stow, 1884.

Courtesy of the New York State Library, Manuscripts and Special Collections, BRO5765.

Puck, September 17, 1884, Vol. 16, No. 393.

Courtesy of the Library of Congress.

Bell-V-Lock-Wood pictogram ribbon, 1888.

In both her 1884 and 1888 campaigns, Lockwood encountered an intense barrage of satirical images, faux campaign materials, mock "Belva Lockwood Clubs," and "Mother Hubbard" protest parades (where men in dresses carried torches and rag babies). This ribbon is believed to be a satirical piece from her adversaries. Courtesy of the Collection of Ronnie Lapinsky Sax.

The New Woman.

*The masculine spirit now groans,
With a grief that's enough to move stones.
Lest he on his visiting Case,
Shall be forced to conditions so hard,
As writing Mrs. Metilabel
Jones!
Although Mr. Jones
has been told for the 99th
time that there is nothing
new under the Sun,—much
less a new woman, he
still bars and it haunts
him.* *He a p*

Manuscript draft of speech titled "The New Woman," Belva Ann Lockwood, ca. 1879–1904.

Following her runs for office, Belva Lockwood took on a busy public speaking career. Her topics included women's rights and marriage, including her speech "Is Marriage a Failure? No Sir!" In her speech "The New Woman," Lockwood questions men's fears about women who have grown out of traditional gender roles and discusses the ways in which women can benefit from involvement in professions and government, and in an active lifestyle. In addition, she appeared before Congress twice, promoting the passage of a constitutional amendment guaranteeing women the right to vote. Courtesy of the Farmers' Museum, Gift of Mrs. Julia H. Winner, Belva Ann Lockwood Papers: The Ormes-Winner Collection, Coll. No. 213.1/3.

Having won the right to practice in various courts, Lockwood turned her attention to women's rights. In an 1884 letter to Marietta L. Stowe, editor of *The Woman's Herald* of Indiana, Lockwood suggested that although women could not legally vote, there was nothing in the law that said they could not be voted for. Stowe printed the letter, and it got the attention of the National Equal Rights Party, who promptly nominated Lockwood as their candidate for president. Lockwood accepted and ran an earnest campaign, with a platform of women's rights, universal peace, improved education, citizenship for Native Americans and allotment of tribal lands, improved trade with South America, and improvement of the civil service system, specifically, fair allotment of positions to both men and women.[80] Lockwood lost to Grover Cleveland but earned an impressive 4,149 votes, amid reports of votes being dumped. The Equal Rights Party nominated her again in 1888.[81]

HISTORY OF WOMAN SUFFRAGE

History writing was a popular and political act in the decades following the Civil War. As men wrote volume after volume documenting their history of the war, and leaving out the contributions of women to the war effort, many in the suffrage movement felt the need for a written history of their own. They recognized that not only would a published history give legitimacy to their work, but it could help gain the support of young women ready to learn more and join the fight. Additionally, the work had the potential to unify the movement that was critically fractured in the years following the war.

Stanton, Anthony, and Gage finally sat down to begin the work of writing and compiling in 1880 and published volume 1 in 1881. Ultimately, six volumes were produced, with volume 4 being edited by Susan B. Anthony and Ida Husted Harper, and volumes 5 and 6 by Harper alone. Each volume contains primary sources collected from colleagues in the movement, including the text of speeches, convention reports, and excerpts of newspaper articles. There are also personal narratives and essays on the movement in each state.

Publication of the *History of Woman Suffrage* was not without controversy within the women's rights movement. Complaints were made about the heavy-handiness of the editing and the addition or deletion of material. The American Woman Suffrage Association is almost absent from the books, and many leaders from New England, including Lucy Stone, felt it inappropriate that their history be written by leaders of the National Woman Suffrage Association (with which Stanton, Anthony, and Gage were affiliated).[82]

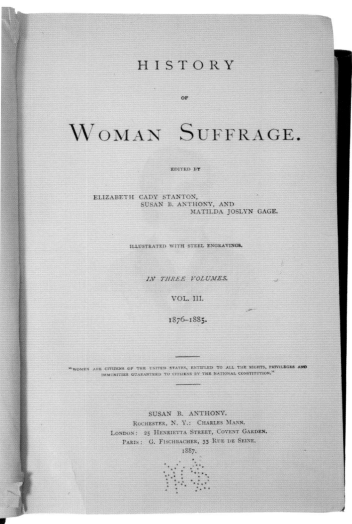

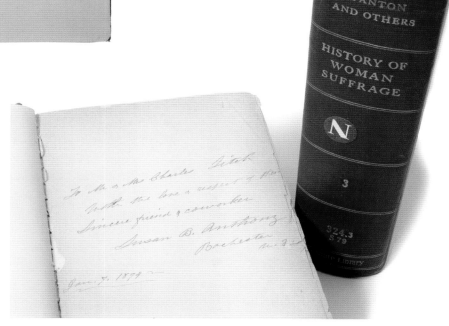

"The History of Woman Suffrage, from 1848 to 1877, with its preceding causes," advertisement, in *National Citizen and Ballot Box*, August 1878.

Parts of *History of Woman Suffrage* were serialized in Matilda Joslyn Gage's newspaper, *The National Citizen and Ballot Box*. Courtesy of the Matilda Joslyn Gage Foundation.

History of Woman Suffrage, books, Vol. 1: 1848–1861 and Vol. 3: 1876-1885, Elizabeth Cady Stanton, Susan B. Anthony, and Matilda Joslyn Gage.

After the completion of the third volume, Anthony sent complimentary sets to public libraries and universities across the country, as well as to politicians and activists. Some institutions, including Harvard and Vassar, rejected the donation. This set was inscribed by Anthony to Mr. and Mrs. Charles Fitch, 1894. It is possible that these copies replaced others lost in the 1911 Capitol fire. New York State Library, Manuscripts and Special Collections, 324.3 S79 V.1.

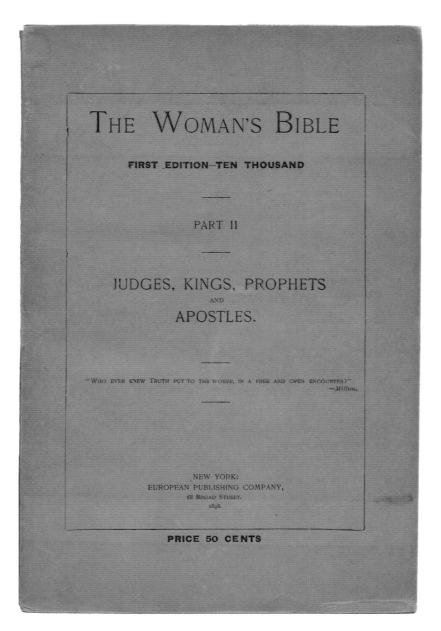

The Woman's Bible, book, Elizabeth Cady Stanton, 1895.

Courtesy of Coline Jenkins, the Elizabeth Cady Stanton Family.

THE WOMAN'S BIBLE

At the end of her life, Stanton returned in earnest to the broader view of women's rights that she had promoted in the beginning. At Seneca Falls, she was the one to insist on woman suffrage being added to the list of demands, but she did not believe that suffrage was the only way in which women's lives could be improved. In 1892, she declared, "I have said all I have to say on the subject of suffrage."[83]

Stanton turned her energy and pen to the church, which she had long believed played a major role in women's oppression. Opponents of women's rights regularly quoted the Bible, which Stanton believed was "a book that curses woman in her maternity, degrades her in marriage, makes her the author of sin, and a mere afterthought in creation and baptizes all this as the word of God cannot be said to be a great blessing to the sex."[84] Instead, she began a new interpretation of biblical texts, *The Woman's Bible*, which was published in 1895. To complete the task, she consulted with a "revising committee" of twenty-five women, which included Matilda Joslyn Gage, Reverend Olympia Brown, and Reverend Phebe Hanaford, and consulted with women from around the world.

Reaction to the book within the suffrage movement was not positive. The growing ranks of temperance women in the suffrage movement, who were deeply Christian, found it offensive. Others worried about the impact the book would have on opinions of the movement in general, as ministers declared it proof that the suffragists were heretics. The National Woman Suffrage Association moved to censure Stanton and have "no official connection with the so-called 'Woman's Bible,' or any theological publication."[85] Ultimately, the official censure and surrounding drama helped book sales.

ESSAY

A "MONSTROUS ABSURDITY"

THE 1886 SUFFRAGE PROTEST OF THE STATUE OF LIBERTY

Lauren C. Santangelo
Princeton University

"The New Freedom," lithograph after the drawing
by Ray O. Evans, in *Puck,* October 30, 1915.

The Statue of Liberty continued to serve as a rallying
point for suffragists into the twentieth century, and
it was used in both demonstrations and in political
cartoons. Courtesy of the Library of Congress.

The suffrage parades up and down Fifth Avenue in the 1910s captured journalists' attention, drew thousands of onlookers, and dominate our memory of the movement. They brought midtown Manhattan—perhaps the nation's busiest district—to a standstill.[1] Women proudly marched on the boulevard, brandishing banners, riding horses, and pushing strollers. As historians have argued, organizers were mobilizing city streets to create a spectacle.[2] But long before suffragists curated such stunts, they used the urban landscape as a site for protest. The most remarkable instance of this was in 1886 when activists first politicized the Statue of Liberty.

Frenchmen, led by Édouard de Laboulaye and Auguste Bartholdi, dreamt up the Statue of Liberty in the 1870s. They envisioned a gift from France that would celebrate America's centennial. Newspapers detailed the monument's progress, tracking the fundraising campaign in both France and the United States. When the budget for the project ran dry in 1876, Bartholdi brought over the statue's arm with torch in hand. It sat in Madison Square Park—a scheme to raise more funds and a disembodied reminder of the incomplete present. The drama and publicity surrounding construction only served to amplify excitement over the finished product. And October 28, 1886, marked the unveiling of the impressive, 305-foot landmark.[3]

For suffragists, unveiling day—a public holiday in Gotham—presented a prime opportunity to broadcast their cause. Formed in 1869, the New York State Woman Suffrage Association remained a struggling organization throughout the Gilded Age. What it lacked in finances and constituents, Lillie Devereux Blake, its president, made up for in sheer willpower. Even before the Statue of Liberty stood atop her pedestal, Blake eyed the debut ceremony. "Looking as we do upon this huge Pharos as an omen of the future day when women will be free," she penned in spring 1886, "it is quite right that women should aid in uplifting it [by fundraising]. The question arises whether, when the day of unveiling comes, women will be permitted to take any part in the ceremonies."[4] She received an answer a few weeks prior to the celebration: planners would not invite suffragists to Bedloe's Island.[5]

The gendered iconography of the statue made this doubly insulting for activists. "Yes, the men of the nation, presidents, governors, and potentates, propose in solemn state to unveil this Statue of Liberty," Blake seethed in the suffrage newspaper, "What a monstrous absurdity that men should unite to do honor to Liberty, represented by a woman, while refusing liberty to woman [*sic*]!" With that, the state leader discursively transformed the Statue of Liberty's celebration of American independence into a painful reminder of women's disfranchised status. And then she promised a protest.[6]

That Blake was willing to spend the last of the association's budget on this rally indicates how seriously she took the affront. With only four dollars left in the treasury, she chartered a boat for one hundred dollars—selling tickets to make up the difference.[7] Blake and her peers planned to steer the vessel close to Bedloe's Island to protest their ballot-less state, politicizing the patriotic festival in the process. The cheapest one they could secure was a cattle barge, which the owner promised to "scour" to eliminate any animal odor.[8] Those celebrating on Bedloe's Island might not see the suffrage remonstration amid the fanfare, but those involved felt committed to demonstrating anyway—even if doing so was uncomfortable.

It is unlikely that those aboard the *John Lenox* heard President Grover Cleveland's promise as he officially accepted the gift. "We will not forget," he pledged, "that Liberty has here made her home."[9] But, the comment's gendered shortsightedness would have only exacerbated the anger those onboard already felt. After the veil fell from Lady Liberty's face, Blake held an "indignation meeting" on the vessel's lower deck. "[I]n erecting a statue of Liberty embodied as a woman in a land where no woman has political liberty," she mocked, "men have shown a delightful inconsistency, which excites the wonder and admiration of the opposite sex."[10]

While suffragists never exited the cattle barge, clinging to the safe space of the boat, their protest was largely without precedent.[11] Previously, they generally isolated themselves in rented halls or individual supporters' homes. Now, they were taking public action to protest women's disfranchised state and doing so by reappropriating one of the metropolis' landmarks.[12] It was enough for newspapers to take notice; the *New York Times* detailed the day's events under the jarring subtitle: "Woman Suffragists Think the Ceremonies an Empty Farce."[13]

The event itself only involved two hundred people. But, the Statue of Liberty protest in 1886 became a folkloric memory in the New York City movement—even if we have largely forgotten it since then. The *History of Woman Suffrage*, the official account of the movement, described it. Suffragists spoke about it into the twentieth century. And Blake's daughter recounted it in the biography of her mother that she coauthored.[14]

Discussion of the protest came up again in 1915 when a new generation of supporters used the landmark once more as a backdrop to demand political equality. But, unlike the earlier display, the 1915 one reflected twentieth-century activists' stunt-driven mind-set. This time leaders disembarked their vessel to listen to the "Appeal for Liberty," read by a woman "dressed as a Goddess of Liberty." When a speaker inquired whether Lady Liberty endorsed the ballot, a supporter who had climbed atop the monument ventriloquized, "Votes for women." They then took to the city streets, traveling to Riverside Drive and later to Columbus Circle with a "Liberty Chariot" in a "torchlight" procession.[15]

A nighttime parade, open-air meetings, and large-scale publicity stunts would have been difficult for those in 1886 to fathom. Brimming with panache and bravado, these later spectacles have shaped our understanding of the suffrage movement. The earlier protests, however, established the precedents. The Statue of Liberty demonstration in 1886 might have been one of the first times organizers mobilized an urban landmark for their cause. But, it would not be the last.

Notes

i. For a detailed description of the parades, see Pamela Cobrin, *From Winning the Vote to Directing on Broadway: The Emergence of Women on the New York Stage, 1880–1927* (Newark: University of Delaware Press, 2009), chap. 1.

ii. See, for instance, Susan Glenn, *Female Spectacle: The Theatrical Roots of Modern Feminism* (Cambridge: Harvard University Press, 2009), chap. 5.

iii. For a history of the Statue of Liberty, see Edward Berenson, *Statue of Liberty: A Transatlantic Story* (New Haven: Yale University Press, 2012).

iv. Lillie Devereux Blake, "Our New York Letter," *The Woman's Journal*, 17 April 1886.

v. "They Enter a Protest," *New York Times*, 29 October 1886.

vi. Lillie Devereux Blake, "Our New York Letter," *The Woman's Journal*, 16 October 1886.

vii. Katherine Devereux Blake and Margaret Louise Wallace, *Champion of Women: The Life of Lillie Devereux Blake* (New York: Fleming H. Revell Company, 1943), 165.

viii. Transcript of Lillie Devereux Blake Diary with Katherine Devereux Blake's note, 10 October 1886, Box 2, Folder 21, Lillie Devereux Blake Papers, Missouri Historical Society.

ix. "The Statue Unveiled," *New York Times*, 29 October 1886; "Unveiling the Goddess," *New-York Tribune*, 29 October 1886.

x. "They Enter a Protest," *New York Times*, 29 October 1886.

xi. "Current News," *Albany Times*, 20 October 1886.

xii. One exception is the demonstration for Home Rule for Ireland in Union Square, in which suffragists participated. See Lillie Devereux Blake, "Our New York Letter," *The Woman's Journal*, 10 July 1886.

xiii. "They Enter a Protest," *New York Times*, 29 October 1886.

xiv. Blake and Wallace, *Champion of Women*, 165.

xv. "Women Ask Votes at Liberty's Feet," *New York Times*, 6 July 1915; " 'Votes for Women,' First Words of Miss Liberty by the Sea," *New York Tribune*, 6 July 1915.

SECTION 2

Winning the Vote, 1890–1920

Group of State Presidents and Officers of the N.A.W.S.A. at Nat. Convention, 1892.

1. Mrs. Jean Greenleaf, Pres. N.Y. Assn.   4. Isabella Beecher Hooker, Pres. Conn. Assn.   7. Anna Howard Shaw, Nat. V. Pres.   28 Clara B. Colby, Ed. Woman's Tribune.

2 Lillie Devereau Blake, N.Y.C. Assn. Pres.   5. Susan B. Anthony, Pres. National Assn.   9. Mary B. Clay, Pres. Kentucky Assn.   32, Emmily Howland,   32, Emmiline Wells, Pres. Utah.

3 Rev. Olympia Brown, Pres. Wisconsin Assn.   6 Mrs. Jane Spoffard, Treas   "   "   15. Lucy Anthony.   16 Rachel F. Aver.   35. Harriet T. Upton. 34. Mrs. Osborn.

State presidents and officers of the National American Woman Suffrage Association, photograph, 1892.

Anna Howard Shaw (*seated in the front row, third from the right*) was instrumental in the merging of NWSA and AWSA. She also served as president of NAWSA between 1904 and 1915, always pushing for a national constitutional amendment for women's suffrage. NAWSA grew under her tenure as president from an organization with seventeen thousand to two hundred thousand suffrage workers, as well as the passage of full suffrage in Arizona, Kansas, and Oregon in 1912. "Dr. Anna H. Shaw, Suffragist, Dies," *New York Times*, 3 July 1919. Courtesy of the Bryn Mawr College Special Collections.

By the dawn of the twentieth century, the political and social landscape was much different in New York State than fifty years prior in Seneca Falls. The state had experienced dramatic advances in industrialization and urban growth, and several large waves of immigrants made New York their new home. Many women worked outside the home and, thus, reformers' priorities shifted to labor issues, health care, and temperance, in addition to women's suffrage.

A new group of reformers from across the state began working toward suffrage. Harriot Stanton Blatch formed the Women's Political Union; Carrie Chapman Catt made New York City and the immigrant working class an integral part to her plan for winning suffrage; millionaire Alva Belmont donated large sums of money to keep the cause going; Ella Hawley Crossett of Warsaw, New York, was elected president of the New York State Woman Suffrage Association (NYSWSA) in 1902; and thousands of other women organized, marched in parades, attended meetings, and signed petitions. During this time, anti-suffrage sentiment was strong. Supported by many upstate voters, liquor advocates, and political conservatives, the New York State suffrage amendment was voted down in 1915. Nonetheless, two years later, on November 6, 1917, New Yorkers finally approved women's suffrage with 53 percent voting yes.

CREATION OF THE NATIONAL AMERICAN WOMAN SUFFRAGE ASSOCIATION

In the last decades of the nineteenth century, the women's rights movement in New York State was in transition. By 1896, women could vote in four western states—Wyoming, Utah, Colorado, and Idaho. Susan B. Anthony and Elizabeth Cady Stanton were still leading the charge for reform in both the state and nation, but change was on the horizon. As the new century began, so too did a modern women's rights movement.

The disagreements that split the suffrage movement during Reconstruction, such as the addition of the word "male" into the Constitution and universal black male suffrage, diminished in importance as the nineteenth century wore on. In 1890, the National Woman Suffrage Association (Elizabeth Cady Stanton and Susan B. Anthony) and the American Woman Suffrage Association (Lucy Stone, Henry Blackwell, and Julia Ward Howe) merged to form the National American

NAWSA Convention in Buffalo, ribbon, 1908.

In 1893 the NAWSA voted to hold annual conventions in Washington, DC, every other year and then at various spots around the country to increase visibility. Susan B. Anthony was vehemently against this decision because she felt leaving Washington, DC, would take the pressure off Congress. The NAWSA met in Buffalo in 1908 to celebrate the sixtieth anniversary of the Seneca Falls convention. This was the first time the organization met in New York State. Courtesy of the Collection of Ronnie Lapinsky Sax.

Women's ballot box, ca. 1870s.

Women's suffrage across the country came slowly and conditionally. When women were allowed to vote, they were restricted to only those issues men felt women had a vested interest in such as the education of their children. Oftentimes, they were made to use separate ballots and ballot boxes. This example was made by George D. Barnard & Co., a manufacturer of office fixtures and equipment, in St. Louis, Missouri. Courtesy of the Collection of Ronnie Lapinsky Sax.

Woman Suffrage Association (NAWSA). NAWSA served as the umbrella organization for hundreds of smaller state and local suffrage groups. Its main goal was to push for suffrage on the state level, theorizing that if enough states passed women's suffrage into law, a federal amendment would be inevitable. Elizabeth Cady Stanton was elected as the first president and Susan B. Anthony as vice president. Anthony took over as president in 1892 when Stanton resigned, serving until 1900.[1]

Even though the two largest groups devoted to woman's suffrage merged, it appeared that not much was accomplished by NAWSA until 1913 when there was a concerted effort to try new tactics and push for a national amendment. However, new groups of women, including college women, and immigrant and working women joined the movement during this time. On the state level, New York had a dedicated group of women with new ideas and new supporters working toward the goal of suffrage.

THE NEW YORK STATE WOMAN SUFFRAGE ASSOCIATION

The New York State Woman Suffrage Association was organized in 1869, serving as the umbrella organization for the political equality and suffrage clubs across the state. The annual convention of the NYSWSA was held in a different city each year. NYSWSA had the largest membership of any state-level suffrage organization and consistently gave the national association the largest amount of money each year. The single plank in the platform of the NYSWSA was: "The object of this organization shall be to secure to the Women of the State of New York and of the United States their right to vote, by appropriate state and national legislation." Martha Coffin Wright (1869–1875), Matilda Joslyn Gage (1875–1876, 1878), Susan B. Anthony (1876–1877), Lillie Devereux Blake (1879–1890), Jean Brooks Greenleaf (1890–1896), Mariana W. Chapman (1896–1902), Ella Hawley Crossett (1902–1910), Harriet May Mills (1910–1913), Gertrude Foster Brown (1913–1915), and Vira Boarman Whitehouse (1915–1917) all served as president.

NYSWSA Convention, Buffalo, photograph, 1902.

Anna Howard Shaw, the president of the National American Woman Suffrage Association, is pictured here in the front row, fourth from the left. Standing to her left is Ella Hawley Crossett of Warsaw, New York, who was elected president of the New York Woman Suffrage Association at this convention. Courtesy of Susan B. Anthony Memorial, Inc. papers. Courtesy of the Department of Rare Books and Special Collections, University of Rochester Libraries.

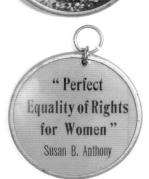

New York State Woman Suffrage Association convention ribbons, 1903, 1904, 1906, and 1907.

The photographs on these ribbons represent leaders in the New York State and national suffrage movements: Carrie Chapman Catt (1903), Anna Howard Shaw (1904), Susan B. Anthony (1906), and Elizabeth Smith Miller (1907). Despite Shaw never living in New York, she had a constant presence in the state. She was often a speaker at the NYSWSA annual conventions and at events throughout the state. In 1903 alone, Shaw spoke in thirty of New York State's counties. Courtesy of the Collection of Ronnie Lapinsky Sax.

NYSWSA thirty-seventh annual convention in Rochester, October 24–27, 1905, ribbon and pendant with photograph of Susan B. Anthony.

The 1905 annual convention of the New York State Woman Suffrage Association in Rochester honored the work of Susan B. Anthony, who was eighty-five years old at the time. Courtesy of the National Susan B. Anthony Museum & House.

Reverse side of the 1905 NYSWSA pendant.

Collection of Ronnie Lapinsky Sax.

CLUBWOMEN LEAD THE CHARGE, 1890–1910

This wave of the suffrage movement, both nationally and in New York State, took shape through an organized network of women's clubs.[2] By the end of the nineteenth century, technology and innovation gave women more leisure time than ever before. As a result, women began to organize into clubs to discuss literature, celebrate the arts, work toward domestic reforms, and eventually, some clubs even sought to work toward the vote. Since most women were denied a college education, women gathered in the domestic sphere of the parlor where they could develop their organizational skills, learn how to speak to a group, and improve themselves in the company of other women. Some elite women had an additional motivation to support suffrage—to keep the upper classes in power. Giving wealthy and educated women the vote would help offset the large influx of lower-class immigrant men that were granted voting privileges with citizenship.

As suffrage slowly became a growing issue, Political Equality Clubs were established across the state. These clubs organized at the local and county level and fed into the larger New York State Woman Suffrage Association. By 1910, clubs varied in size from thirteen members in Binghamton to almost four hundred members in Geneva. Political Equality Clubs distributed leaflets, discussed equal suffrage, hosted suffrage lectures, sent literature and reports to the press, and recruited new dues-paying members.

Annual Convention of the Western New York Federation of Women's Clubs, ribbon, ca.1899.

The Western New York Federation of Women's Clubs was a regional umbrella organization for women's clubs. Suffrage was one of many topics women's groups sought to reform. Courtesy of the Collection of Ronnie Lapinsky Sax.

Annual Convention of the New York State Federation of Women's Clubs, ribbons, Binghamton 1914 and Syracuse 1915.

The New York State Federation of Women's Clubs held their annual convention in Binghamton in 1914 and in Syracuse in 1915. The Syracuse convention was held on November 9–12, 1915, just a week after the defeated suffrage referendum vote. Club organizers immediately began advocating for the next vote two years later. Courtesy of the Collection of Ronnie Lapinsky Sax.

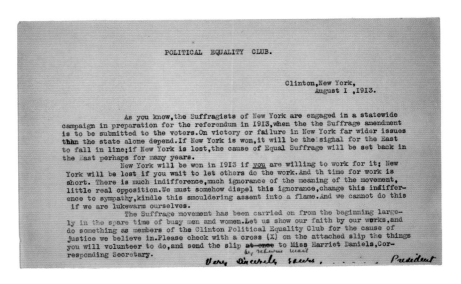

Letter, president of the Political Equality Club of Clinton, August 1, 1913.

Courtesy of the Clinton Historical Society.

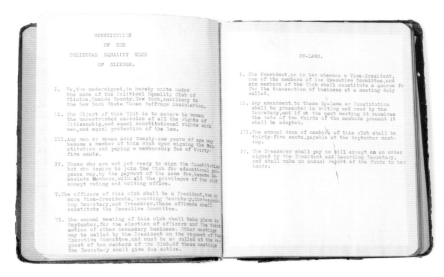

Political Equality Club of Clinton, minutes book, 1910, open to Constitution of the Political Equality Club of Clinton.

There was a proliferation of political equality clubs by the end of the nineteenth century. In 1896, Harriet May Mills and Isabel Howland wrote a manual for establishing political equality clubs with advice on how to have productive meetings. Topics for meetings included, "Our Work, How the People Govern, the Value of the Ballot, Eminent Opinions, Reasons for Woman Suffrage, and Objections Answered." Courtesy of the Clinton Historical Society.

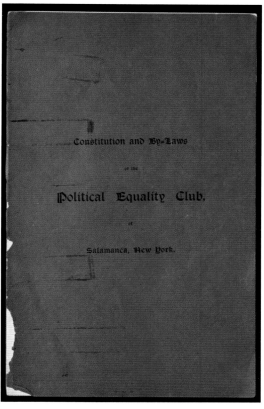

Political Equality Club of Salamanca (NY) Constitution and By-Laws, 1893.

Courtesy of the New York State Library, Manuscripts and Special Collections, N324.623P769 216-2051.

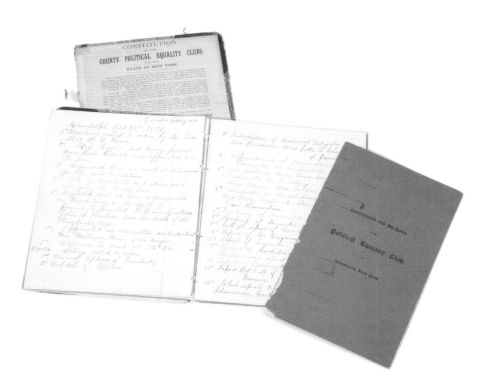

Political Equality Club of Cattaraugus County, minutes book, 1891–1896.

The Political Equality Club of Cattaraugus County included members, mostly women and a few men, from Little Valley, Salamanca, Randolph, and Conewango. Meetings usually opened with members singing together and a prayer. In 1894, this group "Resolved that we thankfully appreciate the actions by the Prohibitionists, the Democrats, and the Populists, in this State Convention, in their endorsement of woman's suffrage. And that we appreciate with equal thankfulness, the practical help of the Republicans of Catt Co, in nominating our P.E. Club Candidate for school Commissioner." Courtesy of the New York State Library, Manuscripts and Special Collections, BD11668.

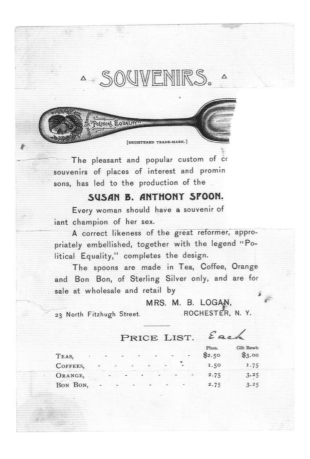

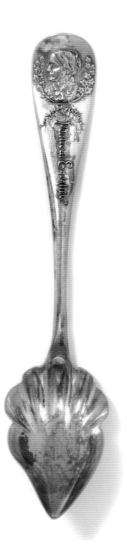

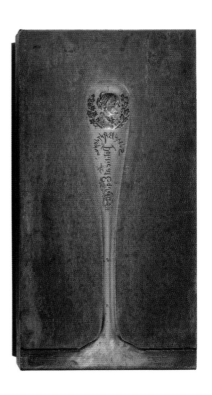

Rochester Political Equality Club spoon, mold, and advertisement, 1891.

This souvenir spoon depicts a bust of Susan B. Anthony and was designed by Millie Burtis Logan, a native of Rochester and distant relative of Anthony, as a fundraiser for the Rochester Political Equality Club in 1891. This is probably one of the earliest minted collector's spoons for the suffrage movement. Florey, *Women's Suffrage Memorabilia*, 172–173. Courtesy of the National Susan B. Anthony Museum & House.

Souvenir spoon advertisement, 1891.

Courtesy of the Department of Rare Books and Special Collections, University of Rochester Libraries.

1903   1904

Rochester *Political* Equality Club

Members and Friends of *Political Equality* are cordially invited to all meetings

Preserve for Reference

OFFICERS

Honorary Presidents
Mrs. Jean Brooks Greenleaf   Mary S. Anthony
President
Miss Mabel A. Clark   Hollenbeck and Norton Streets
First Vice President
Mrs. Amy E. T. Searing   478 Alexander Street
Second Vice President
Dr. Estella Gamble Holdren   650 Powers Building
Recording Secretary
Mrs. Jeannette R. Leavitt   114 South Union Street
Corresponding Secretary
Miss Emogene L. Dewey   54 Gibbs Street
Financial Secretary
Mrs. Emma B. Sweet, 9 Audubon St., or Security Trust Co.
Treasurer
Mrs. Florence D. Alexander   25 Reynolds Street
Auditors
Mrs. Louise Brayer   Mrs. M. D. Fenner
CHAIRMEN OF STANDING COMMITTEES
Foreign Affairs—Home Affairs
Dr. Estella Gamble Holdren   650 Powers Building
Membership
Miss F. A. Reichenbach   36 King Street
Program
Mrs. Florence D. Alexander   25 Reynolds Street
Lectures
Mrs. Emma B. Sweet, 9 Audubon St., or Security Trust Co.

SUNDAY EVENING, JANUARY 3, 1904
LYCEUM THEATER, Eight o'clock
REV. ANNA HOWARD SHAW of Philadelphia :
" *The Awakening of the Civic Conscience.*"

THURSDAY EVENING, JANUARY 21
Eight o'clock
At the home of Mr. and Mrs. Joseph B. Bloss,
334 Oxford Street.
Take Park Avenue car.
In charge of the gentlemen members of the club.
Special Committee—Mr. Howard W. Clark, Mr. George
H. Smith, Mr. C. G. Alexander.

FEBRUARY
(Place and date to be announced later)
COLORADO EVENING. Mrs. Sarah Platt Decker,
Mrs. Ellis Meredith of Denver, and others. To
celebrate their *ten years of political freedom.*

THURSDAY EVENING, APRIL 21
Eight o'clock
At the home of Mr. and Mrs. Frederick Will,
26 Portsmouth Terrace.
Take University Avenue car.
Committee of Arrangements—Mrs. Addie Van Hoesen,
Miss Florence Blackall, Miss Gertrude Watkeys.

THURSDAY AFTERNOON, MAY 19
Two-thirty o'clock
At the home of the President, Miss Mabel A.
Clark, Hollenbeck and Norton Streets.
Annual meeting and election of officers.
Take North Clinton Avenue car to end of route, then
one block east and one block north.

Course ticket for Sunday Evening Lectures including reserved seat, $2.00. General admission, 10 cents ; reserved seat 15 cents additional.

CHARLES MANN PRINTING CO.

Demokraten des 20. Assembly-Dist.
von Kings County
Stimmt nicht für George F. Carew
auf Eurem Stimmzettel, und sorgt dafür,
dass dieser Candidat eine Niederlage erleidet.

Und zwar weil seine Thaten im gesetzgebenden Körper zeigen, daß er keinen Glauben an seine Wähler hat, daß ihm die Interessen Brooklyns nicht am Herzen liegen, und daß er vollständig unter „Boß"-Abhängigkeit steht.

Er mißtraut den Wählern und bemüht sich, dieselben unter die Organisations-Herrschaft zu zwingen:

a) Er stimmte gegen die Förderung der Burd Warren direct nomination Gesetzvorlage und gegen deren Stellvertretung für die irreführende „Blauvelt"-Gesetzvorlage.

b) Er stimmte gegen die Amendments zur „Blauvelt"-Gesetzvorlage, betreffend offizielle Stimmabgabe, und gegen andere wünschenswerthe Veränderungen.

c) Er stimmte, daß die „Hinman-Ferris"-Gesetzvorlage nicht zur Abstimmung gelangen sollte.

d) Er stimmte für die schließliche Annahme der directen Nominations- und Primary-Gesetzvorlage, welche so sehr im Interesse der Organisation und gegen das der Wähler ist, daß dieselbe als privilegierter Despotismus ("Legalized bossism") gebrandmarkt ist.

e) Er stimmte für das schmachvolle „Levy"-Wahlgesetz. Die dem unabhängigen Wähler damit bereiteten Hemmnisse waren so in die Augen springend, daß die höchsten Gerichtshöfe desselbe als unconstitutionell erklärt haben.

f) Er stimmte dafür, die Frauen des Rechtes zu berauben, an den Wahlstellen Beobachtungen anzustellen.

Er lehnt sich dagegen auf, daß den Wählern Gelegenheit gegeben wird, in wichtigen Sachen Beschlüsse zu fassen:

a) Er stimmte gegen den Antrag, dem Aufsichts-Committee über die Gesetzvorlage für Frauenstimmrecht Bericht zu erstatten, und verweigerte damit Schritte zu thun, um die Wähler über die Frage des Frauenstimmrechts entscheiden zu lassen.

b) Er ist dagegen, die Frage des Frauenstimmrechts den Wählern zu unterbreiten. Wir sagen: „Laßt die Wähler entscheiden." Herr Carew sagt: „Ich will entscheiden."

Er hat für Gesetzvorlagen gestimmt, welche gegen das Interesse der Gemeinwohlfaßt sind:

a) Er stimmte für die „Gittins Race Trad"-Vorlage.

b) Er stimmte für die „McClelland-Waller New York West Side Trad"-Vorlage, welche eine fast unbegrenzte Macht verleiht, Wasserfronten der Eisenbahn zu überweisen, ohne daß das Publikum darüber gefragt wird.

c) Er stimmte für alles Salär-Grabichen und für die „Ripper"-Gesetzgebung der Session.

d) Er stimmte für die „Ripper"-Urkunde auf Befehl des demokratischen „Boß" und gegen das Interesse Brooklyns.

Sind dies keine Gründe, um gegen Herrn Carew zu stimmen?

Politische Frauen-Vereinigung,
Centralstelle der Wahl-Campagne :
20th District, Kings County,
Telephone, 2728 Bushwick.   356 Central Avenue, Brooklyn

Rochester Political Equality Club list of officers, 1903/1904.

The Rochester Political Equality Club began at the home of Mary and Susan B. Anthony in 1885 as the Women's Political Club. Mary Anthony and Mrs. Ellen Sully Fray established the club as a women's rights organization. In addition to voting rights, the club pushed to appoint Rochester's first police matron in 1886, demanded that women serve on the local school board, and advocated hiring female physicians on the city's public health staff. Courtesy of the Department of Rare Books and Special Collections, University of Rochester Libraries.

Don't Vote for George F. Carew, broadside, 1911.

This German broadside, created by the Women's Political Organization in Brooklyn, explains that Assemblyman Carew (Democrat) voted against the women's suffrage amendment. It also claims that Carew is controlled by the local "boss." Carew lost his reelection campaign in 1911 by 374 votes. Courtesy of Coline Jenkins, Elizabeth Cady Stanton Family.

Mary Burnett Talbert, photograph, ca. 1901.

Mary Burnett Talbert (1866–1923) was a nationally significant woman's and civil rights advocate. She attended Oberlin College and moved to Buffalo in 1891 after her marriage to William Talbert. Her reform work served as a catalyst for the creation of both the Niagara Movement (1905) and the National Association for the Advancement of Colored People (1910). Talbert was elected president of the Empire Federation of Colored Women's Clubs in 1911 and the NACW in 1916. Courtesy of the Buffalo History Museum.

Phyllis Wheatley Club, Buffalo, New York, photograph, ca. 1910.

In 1899, Mary Burnett Talbert and Susan Evans established a local Buffalo affiliate of the National Association of Colored Women (NACW) called the Phyllis Wheatley Club. Mary Burnett Talbert, standing fourth from left. Courtesy of the Library of Congress.

LIFTING AS WE CLIMB

Since African American women were not allowed to join most clubs, they formed their own, working toward equality for their race and gender. In the 1890s, Ida B. Wells Barnett (1862–1931) began a nationwide reform campaign against lynching. Lecturing widely across the country, she helped to establish several African American women's clubs. In 1896, black women's clubs joined together to form the National Association of Colored Women (NACW) under the leadership of Mary Church Terrell. The NACW adopted the motto of "Lifting as We Climb," which promoted the organization's dual mission of women's rights and community uplift. Colored women's clubs were like those of white women's in composition and the topics they supported. The members of both groups were educated, from the middle and upper classes, and supported temperance, moral purity, education reform, and suffrage. Additionally, the NACW used their groups to work toward race equality for both genders. The NACW saw the struggle for suffrage as the right to vote not just for women, but also for African American men still disfranchised through the political maneuverings of whites.[3]

In 1908, Alice Wiley Seay founded the Empire State Federation of Women's Clubs (ESFWC), an affiliate of the NACW, as the umbrella organization of New York State African American women's groups. In addition to community uplift, the ESFWC had the responsibility of caring for the long-famous and elderly Harriet Tubman at her home in Auburn, New York, until her death in 1913.[4]

"GIVE HER OF THE FRUIT OF HER HANDS"

WOMEN'S SUFFRAGE ACTIVITY ON THE BUFFALO-NIAGARA FRONTIER

Shannon M. Risk

Niagara University

Suffragists on the Buffalo-Niagara Frontier were active in the movement for decades, starting in the late 1800s. Reformers turned their attention toward women's enfranchisement, which corresponded with the growth of the industrial region itself. White suffragists sought to gain the vote as part of their burgeoning roles in shaping their communities, whereas black suffragists labored for basic human dignity and to protect their civil rights and liberties.[i]

Buffalo and Niagara Falls grew along the Erie Canal and Great Lakes business corridor throughout the 1800s. Along with great wealth came well-heeled reformers who forged a Social Gospel by taking their Anglo-Saxon Protestant ideals to the community. Meanwhile, black women sought to uplift women during a time of extremely limited opportunity. Women became more involved in politics, experiencing a metamorphosis in their own lives. Though the climate in this region was unwelcoming to women's political participation, women adopted the maternal approach to assure men that gender roles would not be disrupted. Despite the conservative atmosphere, reform organizations were attracted to this region because it was ripe for political promise in the late 1800s.[ii]

Because women were excluded from formal politics, they created their own parallel organizations to generate change in their communities. Local suffragists like Helen P. Jenkins and Belva Lockwood consistently participated in the New York State Woman Suffrage Association (NYSWSA), the National Woman Suffrage Association, as well as several other organizations.[iii] The Women's Congress met in Buffalo in 1881, bringing dynamic speakers like Mary Livermore, Julia Ward Howe, and Dr. Elizabeth Blackwell, setting the stage for future progressive inroads.[iv] In 1873, the Society for the Advancement of Women met in Buffalo. The organization's goals were to "interest the women of the country in matters of high thought, and in all undertakings found to be useful to society."[v] In October 1884, the NYSWSA came to Buffalo for its annual convention. The *New York Times* noted attendance was small, and the delegates focused on determining whether they already had the right to vote in the US Constitution. They also discussed the debate over female enfranchisement in Great Britain and its implementation in Utah Territory in 1870.[vi]

Women in the region used increasing access to higher education and professional fields to serve as model citizens for those unsure if women could be political beings. Not surprisingly, they were mostly suffragists. Belva Lockwood, from nearby Royalton, earned a law degree and was the first woman to argue a case in front of the Supreme Court. She ran for president in the 1884 and 1888 elections, but the American public was unreceptive. Sarah Lamb Cushing, who earned her medical degree after training with Elizabeth Blackwell, came to Lockport to practice medicine for fifty years. Cushing said, "All pioneers in these movements have been scoffed at, and have borne the heat and the burden of ridicule, through many years." Mary Macaulay, originally from Leroy, who was once Susan B. Anthony's secretary, became a telegraphic operator in Lockport and rose to the vice presidency of the Telegrapher's Union in 1919. Macaulay said the vote would help working women gain the same rights as men, though she was the rare female professional who received equal pay. Another early reformer, Maria Love, however, avoided politics, stayed in the background, and spoke out against the women's vote. Even so, she spearheaded the first daycare in Buffalo that allowed working parents to leave their children in a safe environment during the workday.[vii]

In Buffalo, a chapter of the Women's Educational and Industrial Union formed in 1884. The leaders, Mrs. George Townsend and Mrs. Lily Tifft, tried to steer the group away from suffrage, but member Dr. Sarah Morris pushed the issue. Morris later left the organization and became the first president of the Political Equality League of Buffalo.[viii] Another leader, Charlotte Mulligan, created the Twentieth Century Club in 1896, after a gathering of alumnae from the Buffalo Female Seminary. The club was a place for refined ladies to hold educational and social events. Its members were often suffragists, and the club hosted delegates to a national convention in 1908.[ix] In Buffalo, the Cary and Rumsey families dominated society and reform, running an educational group called "The Class," but they split on the woman's franchise. For example, Evelyn Rumsey, niece of Maria Love, was an ardent suffragist who created one of the iconic posters of the movement in 1910.[x]

Though there was documented interracial interaction among suffragists, black women formed their own groups. Prominent leader and Oberlin College graduate Mary Talbert tied into the women's club movement, forming the Phyllis Wheatley Club in 1899. The black population was small, so combining the talents of the women in her community made sense. Talbert and the club participated in the formation of the National Association for Colored Women (NACW), inviting the NACW to hold its convention in Buffalo in 1901. Talbert's friend Mary Church Terrell led the NACW. They and other black clubwomen and men gathered in 1905 to form the Niagara Movement, which then blossomed into the National Association for the Advancement of Colored People. Early on, the NAACP pursued equality through legal channels, and Buffalo reformers like Talbert, Clara Payne, Susan Evans, and Mrs. C. H. Banks were early shapers of the movement.[xi]

White Buffalo suffragists petitioned the National American Woman Suffrage Association (NAWSA) to host its annual convention in 1901, tying this event to the Pan-American Exposition in Buffalo that year. While they did not gain the convention that year, continuing requests to NAWSA and a promise of $10,000 toward the convention succeeded in 1908. Meanwhile, the Pan Am Exposition offered an opportunity to white and black women to demonstrate their contributions to society. While the Twentieth Century Club hosted visiting dignitaries, black groups pleaded for inclusion in the exposition festivities. Mary Talbert was denied a spot on the planning committee, but the black community did get representation at the exposition, unfortunately, a racist depiction that focused on "slavery and minstrelsy."[xii]

The October 15–21, 1908, NAWSA convention was held in Buffalo's YMCA building, but other groups sponsored separate meeting locations, including: the Buffalo Fine Arts Academy, Central Presbyterian Church, Twentieth Century Club, Lenox Hotel, Star Theater, Larkin Company, Remington Typewriter Company, Shredded Wheat Biscuit Company, and the Albright Knox Gallery. Receptions were hosted by leaders like Mrs. Richard Williams, Mrs. George Howard Lewis, and Mrs. Helen Z. M. Rodgers. There was no evidence that local black women attended this convention, and the NAWSA was influenced by white, Southern suffragists who argued the vote would bolster white supremacy. The key issues at the convention centered on the concerns of white suffragists, including better representation and incorporation of university-educated suffrage groups and labor unions. M. Carey Thomas of Bryn Mawr championed college women, while Harriot Stanton Blatch, daughter of the famous suffrage pioneer, Elizabeth Cady Stanton, coordinated the more diverse group of female laborers. At the end of the convention, the executive committee considered bids for new convention hosts, including Niagara Falls. Though New Orleans won the bid, this did not stifle suffrage momentum.[xiii]

In the same year, the NYSWSA held its convention in Buffalo, two days before NAWSA's, celebrating its fortieth anniversary. Its main discussion was about participating in the commemoration of the sixtieth anniversary of the 1848 Seneca Falls Woman's Rights Convention.[xiv] The organization returned for a convention in Niagara Falls from October 18th to the 21st, 1910. The Shredded Wheat Biscuit Company hosted the convention, and Mayor Peter Porter gave the welcoming address.[xv]

THE LADIES OF THE NEW YORK STATE WOMAN SUFFRAGE ASSOCIATION AT NIAGARA FALLS POSED FOR THIS PICTURE ESPECIALLY FOR THE BUFFALO SUNDAY COURIER.

Niagara Falls NYSWSA, photograph, 1910.

Courtesy of the Library of Congress.

After 1908, Buffalo and Niagara Falls suffragists continued their efforts, traveling to the state legislature with other delegates to argue for the vote, creating districts across the state to better organize suffrage efforts, stumping on street corners, and holding a suffrage parade that traveled down prominent Buffalo streets. A participant of the suffrage parade, Mrs. Springstead, described her cohorts, led by Mrs. Frank J. Shuler, as wearing "white dresses with long, gored skirts, shirt-waists with huge mutton sleeves and stiff, high-boned collars." Springstead said, "it took a great deal of courage, for the public was not at all receptive to this sort of thing. The streets were densely packed. All the women in the parade carried pennants with 'Votes for Women' emblazoned thereon in black letters. Red, white and blue sashes had the same message on them." In addition to parades, women like Springstead went door-to-door encouraging their neighbors to sign petitions.[xvi]

Anti-suffragists also organized in the Buffalo area. The first documented meeting took place when the New York State Opposed to Woman Suffrage Association auxiliary met in 1896 in the Queen City.[xvii] The anti-suffragists did not gather steam until after 1910 when dynamic organizer, Elizabeth Winslow Crannell, editor of *The Anti-Suffragist*, lectured that year at the annual meeting of the Buffalo Association Opposed to Woman Suffrage.[xviii] Buffalo anti-suffragists headed to Albany in 1911 to shore up members of the Joint Assembly and Senate Judiciary Committee during a hearing.[xix] According to historian Susan Goodier, the anti's were having trouble "attracting working class women to their cause, but they appealed to working class men, for example, reaching out to the Snow Steam Pump Works in Buffalo."[xx]

In the final years of the suffrage struggle, white women in the Buffalo–Niagara Falls area continued working with state and national organizations, while black women sought not just the vote, but basic citizenship rights through the NAACP. Historian Lillian S. Williams noted Buffalo's white suffragists "ignored the African American community and focused on 'white' immigrants in their many causes."[xxi] The First World War brought many black and white suffragists into the war effort, capitalizing on their existing organizations. Artist Evelyn Rumsey, for instance, volunteered at Fort Snelling in St. Paul, Minnesota. Meanwhile, Buffalo's wealthy women donated toward the last suffrage campaign in New York in 1917. Some protested with younger, more radical National Woman's Party members on picket lines at the White House, accusing President Woodrow Wilson of fighting for democracy elsewhere while denying it to American women. Buffalo reporter Mrs. Louise Kendall was arrested on that picket line and sent to a work camp at Virginia's Occoquan Prison for "30 days where she was locked up with humanity's worst."[xxii]

After New York women gained the vote, they joined a new organization proposed by NAWSA president Carrie Chapman Catt, the League of Women Voters. This non-partisan organization taught women about the American political system and encouraged them to vote. The Nineteenth Amendment gave all American women the vote in 1920. In 1930, Buffalo's former suffragist Helen Z. M. Rodgers projected that fifty years into the future "men will have entirely overcome their prejudices concerning women in business and the professions. . . . They will wisely realize that the greater number of people employed and producing, the greater opportunities for advancement for everyone are made possible."[xxiii]

Notes

i. Thanks to Melissa Dunlap and Ann Marie Linnabery, Niagara County Historical Society; Cynthia Van Ness, Buffalo History Museum; Lenora Henson, Theodore Roosevelt Inaugural Site; and the librarians at Niagara University Library.

ii. Brenda K. Shelton, *Reformers in Search of Yesterday: Buffalo in the 1890s* (Albany: State University of New York Press, 1976), 23.

iii. Elizabeth Cady Stanton, Susan B. Anthony, and Matilda Joslyn Gage, eds., *History of Woman Suffrage*, Volume 2 (Rochester: Susan B. Anthony, 1882), 538–544; "Women in Council: National Woman Suffrage Association," *New York Times*, May 15, 1874.

iv. "Women's Congress, Buffalo, 1881," *Unity*, Vol. 8, No. 6 (16 November 1881).

v. Susan B. Anthony and Ida Husted Harper, eds., *History of Woman Suffrage*, Volume 4 (Rochester: Susan B. Anthony, 1887), 1050.

vi. "Woman Suffrage Advocates, Their State Convention at Buffalo—A Platform, but No Nominations," *New York Times*, October 9, 1884.

vii. "Mrs. Sarah L. Cushing," March 12, 1919; "Eulogy," by Reverend G. A. Papperman, First Presbyterian Church, Lockport, New York, n.d.; "Miss Mary J. Macaulay," *Commercial Telegrapher's Journal*, n.d., 41; Ann Marie Linnabery, "Lockport Woman Was Early Female Telegrapher and Union Leader," *Niagara Discoveries, 2013–2015: Articles from the Union-Sun & Journal* (Lockport: Kax Solutions & Services, 2015), 19; Thomas C. Jepsen, *My Sisters Telegraphic: Women in the Telegraph Office, 1846–1950* (Athens: Ohio University Press, 2000), 187–188.

viii. Shelton, *Reformers in Search of Yesterday*, 21–22.

ix. Evelyn Hawes, *The Twentieth Century Club of Buffalo: Seventy-Five Years* (Buffalo: Twentieth Century Club, 1994).

x. Mary Rech Rockwell, "'Let Deeds Tell': Elite Women of Buffalo, 1880–1910," PhD dissertation, University at Buffalo, 1999, 343–344; Edwine N. Mitchell, "The Class," *Niagara Frontier News*, ca. 1930s, 5–7.

xi. Lillian S. Williams, "And Still I Rise: Black Women and Reform, Buffalo, New York, 1900–1940," *Afro-Americans in New York Life and History*, Vol. 14, No. 2 (31 July 1990): 7–34; Rosyln Terborg-Penn, *African American Women in the Struggle for the Vote, 1850–1920* (Bloomington: Indiana University Press, 1998), 99–100.

xii. Susan B. Anthony and Ida Husted Harper, eds., *History of Woman Suffrage*, Volume 5 (New York: National American Woman Suffrage Association, 1922), 35–36; Williams, "And Still I Rise."

xiii. "How to Fill the Theater," *Buffalo Express*, 19 October 1908; Anthony and Harper, *History of Woman Suffrage*, 5:43, 213–230, 444; Harriet Taylor Upton, ed., *Proceedings of the Fortieth Annual Convention of the National American Woman Suffrage Association* (Warren: The Association, 1908), 6, 13, 17, 63, 95.

xiv. See Lisa Tetrault, *The Myth of Seneca Falls: Memory and the Women's Suffrage Movement, 1848–1898* (Chapel Hill: University of North Carolina Press, 2014).

xv. Ida Husted Harper, ed., *History of Woman Suffrage*, Volume 6 (New York: National American Woman Suffrage Association, 1922), 447–449.

xvi. Harper, *History of Woman Suffrage*, 6:455–457, 468, 470, 472, 476; *Buffalo Evening News*, 11 October 1930.

xvii. Susan Goodier, *No Votes for Women: The New York State Anti-Suffrage Movement* (Urbana: University of Illinois Press, 2013), 45; "Women at Odds over Suffrage Question," *New York Times*, 22 May 1896.

xviii. Goodier, *No Votes for Women*, 47.

xix. Goodier, *No Votes for Women*, 58.

xx. Goodier, *No Votes for Women*, 84.

xxi. Rockwell, "'Let Deeds Tell,'" 371.

xxii. Harper, *History of Woman Suffrage*, 6:478, 482; Rockwell, "'Let Deeds Tell,'" 416; *Buffalo Evening News*, 11 October 1930.

xxiii. *Buffalo Evening News*, 11 October 1930.

Elizabeth and Anne Miller at Lochland, photograph, ca. 1905.

Courtesy of the Geneva Historical Society.

Gavel from the Geneva Political Equality Club, ca.1905.

This gavel was presented to Anne Fitzhugh Miller by the Geneva Political Equality Club. Miller's initials are on one side of the gavel and P[E]C is on the other—the "E" is missing. Anne's reform activities stretched past local borders. She was the first president of the Ontario County Political Equality Club, a leading member of the Legislative Committee of the New York State Woman Suffrage Association, and a life member of the National American Woman Suffrage Association. Courtesy of the Geneva Historical Society.

ELIZABETH AND ANNE MILLER:
A MOTHER-DAUGHTER SUFFRAGE TEAM

Elizabeth Smith Miller (1822–1911) and Anne Fitzhugh Miller (1856–1912) were a mother-daughter team with reform in their blood. Elizabeth Smith Miller was the daughter of Gerrit Smith, a well-known antebellum reformer in New York State, as well as second cousin to Elizabeth Cady Stanton. In the 1850s, Elizabeth supported dress reform by designing and wearing what would become the Bloomer costume. She advocated for women's rights on both the national and local level long before it was socially acceptable. Her daughter Anne was born in 1856 and soon picked up the quest for women's rights as well. Anne made her first public speech for equal suffrage at the New York State constitutional convention in 1894.

Both mother and daughter were so active in NYSWSA the organization held the 1897 and 1907 conventions in their hometown of Geneva, New York. The success of the first meeting prompted the Millers to establish the Geneva Political Equality Club that same year with a

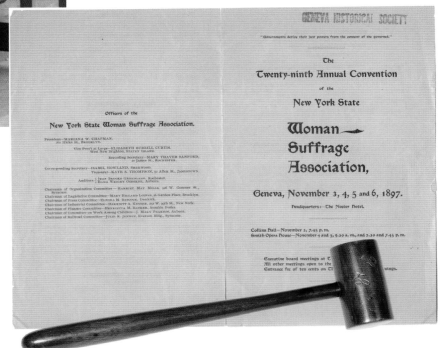

Convention program for the New York State Woman Suffrage Association, Geneva, New York, 1897.

Elizabeth Smith Miller organized this convention and entertained speakers at her home, known as Lochland. The success of this convention spurred the establishment of the Geneva Political Equality Club. Courtesy of the Geneva Historical Society.

focus on equal suffrage, but broader reforms such as improved industrial conditions, world peace, and a general understanding of public affairs were also important to them. The response to the formation of the Geneva PE Club was overwhelmingly positive; fifty people attended the first meeting.[5] By 1907 the club, the largest in the state and with both men and women participants, had 362 members. Elizabeth was named the honorary president and Anne served as president until 1911. Both Elizabeth and Anne remained politically active until their deaths—Elizabeth in 1911, and Anne's sudden death in 1912. The Geneva Political Equality Club continued until 1917 when New York State passed the equal suffrage amendment.

Program for address by Emmeline Pankhurst, sponsored by the Geneva Political Equality Club, 1909.

British suffragist Emmeline Pankhurst spoke in Geneva at the request of Elizabeth and Anne Miller. Pankhurst spoke on the history of the British suffrage movement. The Geneva Political Equality Club printed the program in green, white, and violet, the colors of the Woman's Social and Political Union, Pankhurst's organization. Courtesy of the Geneva Historical Society.

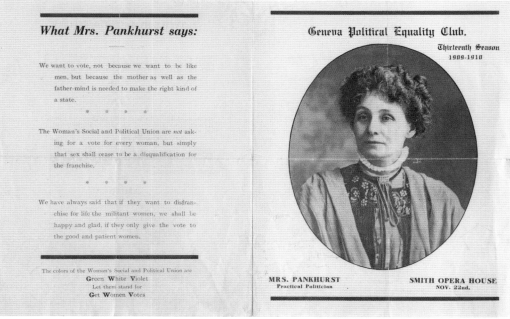

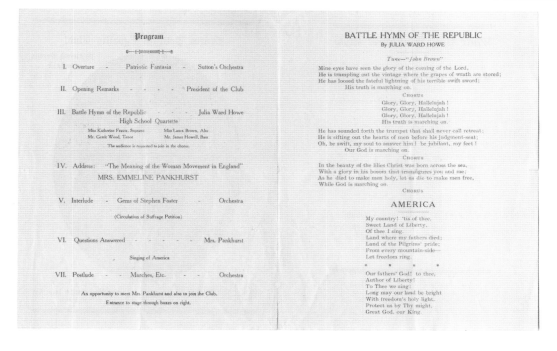

CAMP FOSSENVUE

Elizabeth Smith Miller and her daughter, Anne Fitzhugh Miller, and a group of their friends that included Ruth Lesley Ver Planck, Emily Dilworth Snyder, Anne Palfrey Bridge, James Fowler, and William Fitzhugh Miller established a camp in 1875 on Seneca Lake called Fossenvue. The camp became a place where the Millers and their friends could relax, swim, discuss art and literature, and debate the politics of the day.[6] The Millers' connections to the women's rights movement and the Geneva Political Equality Club drew several activists to Fossenvue, including Susan B. Anthony, Harriot Stanton Blatch, Alice Stone Blackwell, Emily Howland, and Max Eastman.[7] The camp lasted for twenty-six years.

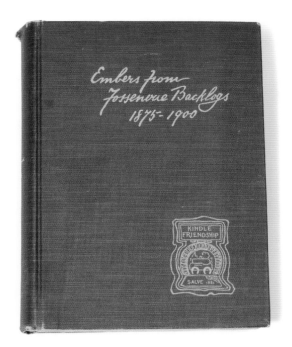

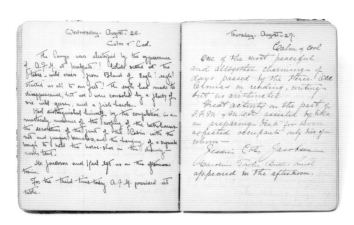

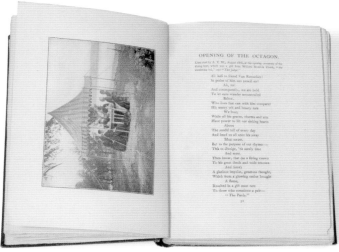

Embers of Fossenvue, book, 1901.

This book records poems, stories, photographs, and every visitor at Fossenvue between 1875 and 1901. It was self-published and given as a present on Christmas by the Millers in 1901. Courtesy of the Geneva Historical Society.

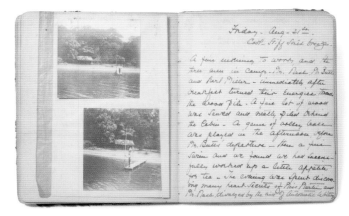

Fossenvue camp journal, 1908.

This camp journal records the weather, happenings, and visitors at Fossenvue in 1908 and was probably penned by the seven founders of the camp. Fossenvue is an anagram for "the seven of us." The journal is part of the Miller Family Collection at the Geneva Historical Society. Courtesy of the Geneva Historical Society.

HARRIET MAY MILLS

Harriet May Mills (1857–1935) dedicated her life to women's suffrage and activism. She was born in Syracuse, New York, into a family of prominent abolitionists. So ardent were her family's abolitionist tendencies, they named her after the prominent local abolitionist Reverend Samuel J. May. She graduated from Cornell University in 1879, shortly after women were permitted to attend there. After graduation, Mills began working toward suffrage in Syracuse and in 1892, founded the Syracuse Political Equality Club. Mills soon found that central New York was an ideal location for suffrage reform work and inspiration since the leading ladies of the state organization, such as Susan B. Anthony (Rochester), Isabel Howland (Sherwood), Elizabeth and Anne Miller (Geneva), and Ella Hawley Crossett (Warsaw) were just a few hours away from Syracuse.

In 1894, Mills began working across New York State in support of the constitutional campaign and was soon elected secretary, vice president, and between 1910 and 1913, president of the NYSWSA. Her home in Syracuse, New York, became the organization's headquarters. Mills campaigned for a suffrage amendment nationwide, giving lectures and organizing meetings. After women gained the vote, Mills became active in the Democratic Party. In 1920, she was the first woman to run for a statewide elective office, secretary of state, on the ticket with Governor Alfred E. Smith. Smith and Mills lost the election, but Mills went on to support him and the Democratic Party in subsequent elections. She campaigned with Franklin Roosevelt to specifically address women voters when he campaigned for governor. In 1932, Mills was a member of the Electoral College that sent Franklin D. Roosevelt to the White House.[8]

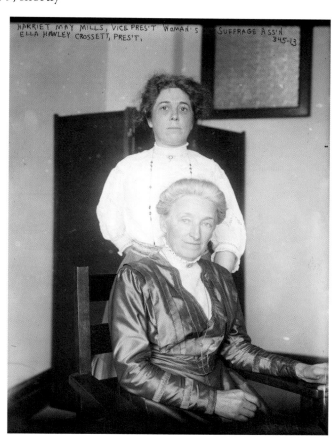

Harriet May Mills (*standing*) and Ella Hawley Crossett (*seated*), photograph, ca. 1905.

Harriet May Mills served as vice president while Ella Hawley Crossett, from Warsaw, New York, served as president of the New York State Woman Suffrage Association between 1902 and 1910. Courtesy of the Library of Congress.

Group of Harriet May Mills personal ribbons, 1898–1917.

These ribbons show the involvement of Harriet May Mills on local, state, and national levels. The "Watcher" ribbon indicates that Mills served as a poll watcher as well. Courtesy of the Collection of Ronnie Lapinsky Sax.

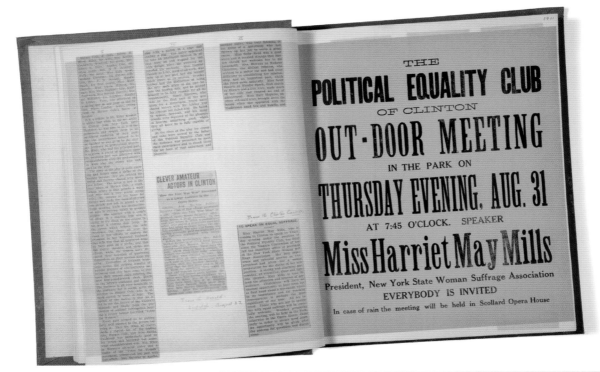

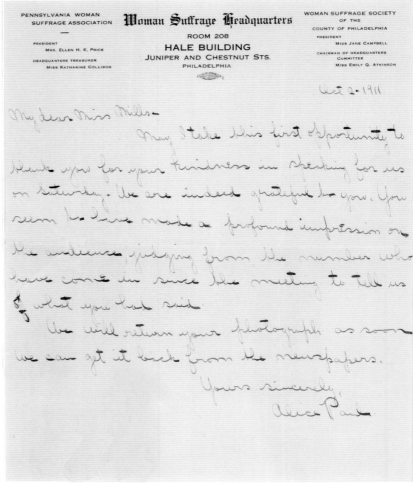

Out-Door Meeting with Miss Harriet May Mills, Political Equality Club of Clinton scrapbook, 1911.

Courtesy of the Clinton Historical Society.

Letter, Alice Paul to Harriet May Mills, October 2, 1911.

Alice Paul writes to Harriet May Mills on October 2, 1911, thanking her for the speech she gave in Philadelphia a few days prior. Mills was then president of New York State Woman Suffrage Association. Courtesy of the Collection of Ronnie Lapinsky Sax.

WOMEN, SUFFRAGE, AND CAPITAL PUNISHMENT:
THE ROXY DRUSE CASE

Women's rights advocates wanted equality between men and women, not just the right to vote. Many of them were against capital punishment, particularly when a woman was on trial. Attendees of the 1859 National Women's Rights Convention submitted a resolution of rights to the New York State Legislature. Its first point, directed toward women on death row, stated, "A citizen can not be said to have a right to life, who may be deprived of it for the violation of laws to which she never consented—who is denied the right of a trial by a jury of her peers—who has no voice in the election of judges who are to decide her fate."[9] Almost twenty years later, women's rights activists were still arguing this point in the case of Roxalana Druse's murder trial.

Roxalana (Roxy) Druse was the last person hanged in New York State. She married William Druse in 1865, and the couple lived on a farm in Warren, New York (Herkimer County), with their two surviving children and a fourteen-year-old nephew. According to neighbors, Roxy was in an abusive marriage. Some accounts claimed that William abandoned his family for long stretches, leaving them with no money or food, and when he was home, he often physically and verbally abused Roxy. However, other accounts later brought out at her trial portrayed Roxy as the transgressor, claiming that she often invited men to their farm for late-night parties and refused to be an obedient wife.[10]

The situation escalated for twenty years until Roxy attacked her husband. According to court testimony and newspaper accounts, a quarrel broke out between the couple at the breakfast table. Roxy retrieved a gun and shot her husband. During this time, Mary, the Druses' nineteen-year-old daughter, placed a rope around her father's neck. When Roxy realized that she had not killed her husband, she made her fourteen-year-old nephew finish the job. Roxy and her daughter then chopped William's head off with an axe, dismantled the body, and burned it in a cookstove. The women disposed of the bones in a nearby pond along with the axe. Roxy threatened to kill the witnesses if they told anyone of this incident.[11] However, her nephew confessed. The axe and remains of the body were found in a matter of weeks. Roxy and Mary were arrested.

Roxy went on trial at the Herkimer County Courthouse in Utica, New York, nearly a year later. She was found guilty and sentenced to death by hanging. Legal maneuvering postponed Roxy's execution date and, ultimately, the case was sent to Governor David B. Hill, who stalled as long as possible because he did not want to make a life-or-death decision.[12] The case made national headlines. Letters and petitions were sent to the governor, both for and against Roxy's death sentence. Women's rights activists came to

Gallows weight, 1887.

This is the counterbalance weight used in Roxy Druse's hanging. It was specifically made for her. Typically, gallows weights were double the weight of the person being hanged. However, this 213-pound weight did not function properly, and Druse, who weighed less than 100 pounds, hung for fifteen minutes before she died. Druse's botched hanging triggered the New York State Legislature to pass a law making electrocution the preferred means of execution. Roxy Druse was the last person hanged in the state of New York. Courtesy of the New York State Museum, H-2011.34.1.

Letter, February 21, 1887.

In this letter from Mary S. Anthony to Governor Hill, Anthony writes in support of commuting Druse's death sentence to life in prison: "If you were a thorough disbeliever in the death penalty for men or women, and were allowed no voice in making the laws, would you consider it fair or just for a class of persons to insist upon making them for you, & hanging you if you disobeyed them?" Anthony ended the letter stating, "Hoping you will be made to see this matter in the light of justice & right." Courtesy of the New York State Archives.

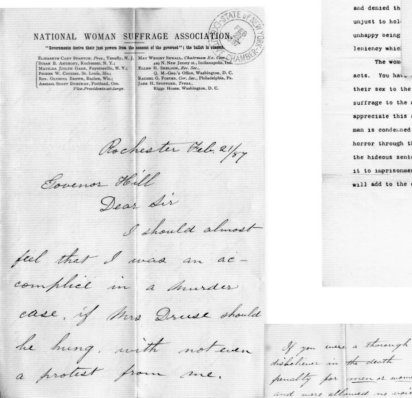

Resolution from the New York State Woman Suffrage Association, December 2, 1886.

This resolution is from the New York State Woman Suffrage Association, led by Lillie Devereux Blake. The NYSWSA unanimously approved the resolution in support of commuting Druse's sentence to life in prison. Blake added to the letter, "So long as women are held incompetent to make or enforce law, and denied the right of trial by jury of their peers, it is surely unjust to hold them to full accountability for their actions. This unhappy being is politically a minor. She ought to receive the leniency which would be shown a minor." Courtesy of the New York State Archives.

Roxy's defense. Many argued that if women did not have input into the laws that govern them, they should not be executed because of those laws.[13]

Ultimately, all attempts to commute Roxy's sentence failed and Governor Hill concluded that he would not interfere with the case. Hill announced, "The law of the state made by men is simply in harmony with the law of the Almighty. . . a commutation would only result in more husband killers."[14] On February 28, 1887, Roxy was hanged behind the Herkimer County jail. Her daughter, Mary, pleaded guilty to murder and spent her life in prison.

Application for Clemency, 1885.

Courtesy of the New York State Archives.

Political Cartoon, 1887.

Roxy Druse was probably the impetus for this political cartoon since it was submitted to the New York State Executive Chamber on February 9, 1887. Courtesy of the New York State Archives.

Frances Willard, photograph, ca. 1885.

The Woman's Christian Temperance Union was so popular that by1890 it had 150,000 members. Courtesy of the Library of Congress.

Onondaga County Woman's Christian Temperance Union, flag, ca. 1890.

At a time when suffrage was still a radical concept, the WCTU offered a more traditional and appropriate organization for women to join. In the 1890s, New York State had over nine hundred WCTU local clubs. Courtesy of the Onondaga Historical Association.

WOMAN'S CHRISTIAN TEMPERANCE UNION: ALLY OR ENEMY TO SUFFRAGE?

Susan B. Anthony knew that if suffrage were ever to be won, at both the state and national levels, large numbers of women and men needed to support the cause. Anthony sought to build partnerships with any organization where suffrage might find an ally. The largest and most powerful organization that sought backing from suffrage advocates was the Woman's Christian Temperance Union (WCTU). The WCTU, founded in December 1873 in Fredonia, New York, after a series of prayer meetings and public demonstrations at local saloons, sought to create a moral world by embracing purity and evangelical Christianity and, more importantly, abstinence from alcohol and tobacco.[15] Suffrage and the WCTU found common ground with the "Home Protection Ballot," which argued that women were the morally superior sex and therefore needed the vote to protect the sanctity of the home.

However, collaborating with the WCTU polarized many of the men in New York State because cities with large immigrant populations tended to promote and advocate for the liquor interests and not suffrage. Buffalo and New York City, the two largest cities in the state and both with large immigrant populations, barely supported suffrage early on. In the 1890s, New York City contained half of the state's population and only 15 percent of the NYSWSA members.[16]

New York State Woman's Christian Temperance Union ribbons and pins, 1900, 1901, 1909, 1928, and 1929.

New York State women were leaders in the establishment of the WCTU. The first state convention took place in Syracuse in October 1874 with the first national convention following a few weeks later in Ohio. In addition to their abstinence from alcohol platform, New York WCTU members worked toward prison reform, social purity reforms, and education reforms. This group endorsed suffrage in 1886, while the entire NYS WCTU supported the 1915 and 1917 suffrage referendums. Longtime NYS and national WCTU leader Ella A. Boole served on Carrie Chapman Catt's Empire State Campaign Committee. The white ribbon was adopted in 1877. Courtesy of the Collection of Ronnie Lapinsky Sax.

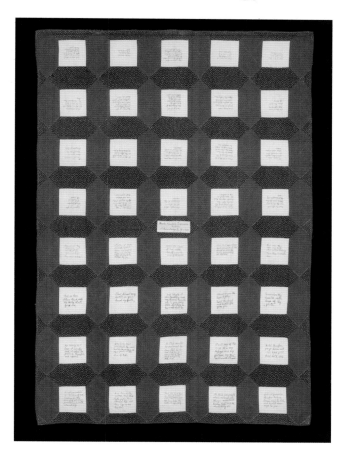

Temperance quilt, 1904.

Each block of this quilt is inscribed with a Bible verse. It was made by the Woman's Christian Temperance Union in Schenectady, New York. Since women dominated temperance organizations' memberships, quilts were an item that could be made and then raffled off for fundraising. Quilts also created a sense of community—often several women worked on one quilt—and then were used to decorate the group's meeting spaces. New York State Museum, H-1984.88.1.

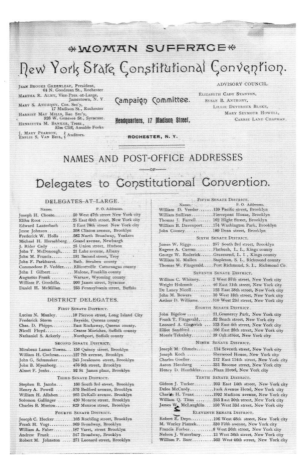

Delegates to the constitutional convention, 1894.

Years before the New York State constitutional convention, women lobbied to be sent as delegates to support the suffrage amendment. Both Governor David B. Hill (in office, 1885–1891) and Governor Roswell P. Flower (in office, 1892–1894) recommended women serve as delegates, and the legislature approved the bill. Jean Brooks Greenleaf was the only woman nominated in the state to serve, but she did not receive enough votes to serve as a delegate. Courtesy of the Library of Congress.

Leaders of the New York State movement from *History of Woman Suffrage*, **1902.**

Courtesy of the New York State Library, Manuscripts and Special Collections, 324.3 S79.

THE NEW YORK SUFFRAGE CAMPAIGN OF 1894

In 1894, New York State held a convention to revise its constitution. Susan B. Anthony led the charge to secure a clause for equal suffrage in the new state constitution by a petition campaign. Ten thousand dollars was raised to mount the campaign, and Anthony's house in Rochester served as headquarters in an effort to save money on renting offices. Jean Brooks Greenleaf, president of NYSWSA, and Mary S. Anthony, the corresponding secretary, worked toward this goal for six months with few breaks. Susan B. Anthony, who was seventy-four years old at the time, spoke in each of New York's sixty counties. Harriet May Mills and Mary G. Hay organized mass meetings across the state, while Lillie Deveraux Blake organized all of New York City and Mariana Chapman led

MARY S. ANTHONY
Rochester, N. Y.

MARIANA W. CHAPMAN,
Brooklyn, N. Y.

JEAN BROOKS GREENLEAF,
Rochester, N. Y.

EMILY HOWLAND,
Sherwood, N. Y.

ELIZA WRIGHT OSBORNE,
Auburn, N. Y.

Brooklyn. The women circulated 5,000 petitions and secured 332,148 individual signatures of which about half were from men. Members from the WCTU, labor organizations, and Granges also signed the petition, which brought the total number of signatures to almost six hundred thousand.

Another tactic the suffragists employed for this campaign echoed the sentiment of revolutionary patriots. Organizers collected information on how much money women in New York State paid in property taxes and presented the information to the state legislature claiming, "*No taxation without representation!*" Despite all their efforts, the amendment was voted down: 98 opposed to 58 in favor.[17]

Petition for Woman Suffrage to the New York State Constitutional Convention, card, 1894.

Courtesy of the New York State Library, Manuscripts and Special Collections, SC13339.

Lillie Deveraux Blake.

Lillie Deveraux Blake, carte de visite, ca.1865.

Lillie Deveraux Blake (1833–1913) was instrumental in organizing New York City for the 1894 campaign. She was an author of fiction and a successful press correspondent in Washington, DC, during the Civil War. She served as president of the New York State Woman Suffrage Association between 1879 and 1890 and as president of the NYC Suffrage League between 1886 and 1900. Courtesy of the Collection of Ronnie Lapinsky Sax.

Constitutional Amendment Mass Meeting, Lowville Opera House, broadside, 1894.

While many of the supporters for the 1894 constitutional amendment were middle- and upper-class women, this statewide campaign signaled the changing tide of the suffrage movement. Various groups began working together toward the suffrage goal and leaders started to organize mass meetings. Courtesy of the New York State Library, Manuscripts and Special Collections, BRO0407+.

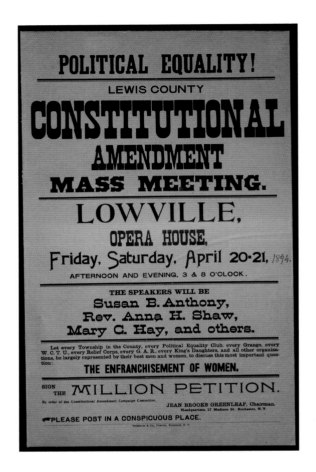

New York State Woman Suffrage Association convention ribbon, Ithaca, New York, 1894.

This convention ribbon was created to celebrate the number of signatures collected for the New York State constitutional convention, which met in the summer of 1894. Even though suffrage was not yet put on the ballot, the movement mobilized, gathering six hundred thousand signatures in support. The next NYS constitutional convention was held in 1915 with suffrage on the ballot. Courtesy of the Collection of Ronnie Lapinsky Sax.

According to a witness at the convention, the delivery of the petitions was quite dramatic.

> The names were enrolled on pages of uniform size and arranged in volumes, each labeled and tied with a wide yellow ribbon and bearing the card of the member who was to present it. At the opening of the sessions, when memorials were called for, he would rise and say: "Mr. President, I have the honor to present a memorial from Mary Smith and 17,117 others (for example), residents of _____ county, asking that the word 'male' be stricken from the Constitution." Often one after another would present a bundle of petitions until it would seem as though the entire morning would be thus consumed. They were all taken by pages and heaped up on the secretary's table, where they made an imposing appearance.
>
> Mrs. Burt, the president of the W.C.T.U., brought in the petitions of her society all at once, many great rolls of paper tied with white ribbons. A colored porter took them down the aisle on a wheelbarrow.[18]

ESSAY

"JUST CAUSE TO FEEL PROUD"

Chautauqua County's Leading Role in Grassroots Suffrage Activism

Traci Langworthy
Jamestown Community College

On the day after Christmas in 1854, Susan B. Anthony presided over a convention at the Chautauqua County, New York, Courthouse to discuss "all the reasons which impel Woman to demand her right of Suffrage."[i] She would lead a multitude of similar public meetings across the state in the years before the Civil War as she and other women's activists "systematized" their efforts to expand the civil rights of women in New York.[ii] Still, the women and men who gathered in the village of Mayville impressed Anthony as especially "earnest" proponents of women's equality. After gathering their signatures on petitions supporting women's suffrage and property rights, Anthony set out the following day for the nearby town of Sherman where she spoke by invitation to a "large" audience. "Never saw more enthusiasm on the subject," she wrote in her diary afterward. "Even the Orthodox Churches vied with each other [over], who should open their doors" to host the proceedings.[iii]

Recent scholarship suggests such enthusiasm for women's equality was not uncommon in the rural reaches of New York State as the cause blossomed.[iv] By the waning years of the nineteenth century, women's suffrage drew some of its strongest support from farming towns where women made vital contributions to the sustenance of their households and communities.[v] And few were better organized for action than the communities surrounding Chautauqua Lake. By 1891, more residents of Chautauqua County were counted among the members of the National American Woman Suffrage Association (NAWSA) than in any other county nationwide. While the area's history of progressive reform nurtured a conducive climate for equal rights within many households, much of the credit for the local movement must be given to the women who marshaled the forces of change. Through the various efforts of their "political equality" clubs, Chautauqua County suffragists built a network of grassroots support that became a model for others to follow.

The roots of their activism first sprouted in Jamestown in November 1887, when thirteen women founded the First Political Equality Club of Jamestown during a visit to town by Mary Seymour Howell of the state suffrage association.[vi] The "First" designation reflects the novelty of the name. Although other local suffrage clubs were in existence elsewhere in the nation—including a "Women's Political Club" founded in December 1885 in Rochester—they only later adopted the moniker "political equality."[vii] The newspaper article announcing the new club said the name "fully explains its objects and purposes." It also noted that the club was open to men.[viii]

Once begun, the movement blossomed very quickly. Before a year had passed, eleven more political equality clubs formed in the area.[ix] Ellen A. Martin wrote to the national *Woman's Tribune* in 1888 to share news of the flurry of activity. A former area resident, she had come home for a visit to find that the prospect of possible enfranchisement was having a "salutary effect" on her old neighbors, "making women assert themselves—'feel their oats,' so to speak." She was on hand when Anthony and Elizabeth Cady Stanton spoke together in Jamestown on August 10, drawing a "packed" house.[x] A little over two months later, on October 31, 1888, the Jamestown club hosted a formal convention at which the Chautauqua County Political Equality Club was born.[xi] In another three years, this group's membership would well exceed one thousand individuals, building on the support of political equality clubs that had formed in twenty-four out of the county's twenty-seven townships.[xii]

The groundswell of activity drew the praise of national leaders. Based on the county's membership rolls, delegates to NAWSA's 1891 convention designated Chautauqua as the "banner county" in the nation for women's suffrage.[xiii] County president Elnora Babcock of Dunkirk beamed over the distinction when she addressed the local army of women who gathered for the county suffrage convention in 1892: "We have just cause to feel proud of the work that has been done . . . in this County, and the honor so justly accorded us of being the banner County of the U.S."[xiv] For her own part, Babcock later assumed a national post superintending all of NAWSA's press work from her residence in Dunkirk.[xv]

Further points of pride were the conventions the county PEC held twice a year to conduct countywide business and host state and national speakers. Their success quickly led to larger affairs at the area's renowned summer venues. Of particular interest was the nearby Chautauqua Assembly (now Institution) where the cofounder, Methodist Episcopal bishop John Heyl Vincent, had made no secret of his opposition to women voting. In 1891, county suffragists convinced the Chautauqua management to host the first-ever "Political Equality Day" on the grounds.[xvi]

Susan B. Anthony at the Cassadaga Lake Assembly in Lily Dale, New York, photograph, probably 1894.

Anthony is seated on the right, second woman from the gentleman standing with the hat. The two stars on the banner represent the states of Wyoming and Colorado where women could then vote. The woman holding the banner is Marion Skidmore, president of the Political Equality Club in Lily Dale. Courtesy of the Chautauqua County Historical Society, McClurg Museum.

The program went on to become an annual event that regularly featured national leaders. Many "equalityites" also made an annual pilgrimage to Lily Dale, New York, where the Spiritualist community at the Cassadaga Lake Assembly welcomed discussion of women's full equality. Anthony wrote of the first "Woman's Day" held there in August 1891: "Every cottage in the camp was festooned with yellow [signifying suffrage support], and when at night the Chinese lanterns on the piazzas were lighted, Lily Dale was as gorgeous as any Fourth of July, all in honor of Woman's Day and her coming freedom and equality."[xvii]

Clearly, such events fanned the flames of the local movement, as did the opportunity for social gatherings with neighbors. But in between the fun and fanfare, Chautauqua County women had other, more practical reasons for committing their energies to the cause. Like women in similar communities across the state, they recognized the power the vote would give them to press for other important reforms, from temperance to equal pay for female teachers.[xviii] Temperance had a particularly robust following in Chautauqua County, as evidenced by the anti-saloon crusade commenced by Fredonia women in December 1873 that touched off events leading to the founding of the Woman's Christian Temperance Union (WCTU).[xix] The desire to participate in matters affecting their children's education was a particularly strong motivator. Since state lawmakers had granted women the right to vote in school elections beginning in 1880, Chautauqua County women had exercised the right enthusiastically and elected twenty-nine women to local boards of education by 1892.[xx]

For local farm women in particular, practical concern for schools and communities could lead to radical assertions. In her annual report to the state convention in 1894, then–county president Ellen Cheney of Poland Center noted that, with the exception of clubs in the more populous locales of Jamestown, Dunkirk, and Fredonia, the majority of the area's equality clubs were based in "country places." She continued,

> The women who make up the membership of these country clubs are mostly women who work; not laboring women in the sense that politicians speak of "laboring men," but women who *do things*. They get meals and wash dishes, and sweep, and wash clothes, and iron, and make bread, and make butter, and tend chickens, and keep a garden, and do the family sewing.[xxi]

Many such women sought the full rights and responsibilities of citizenship as an extension of their equal responsibilities on the family farm. As Carrie E. S. Twing of Westfield stated in 1894, "We believe in married hands, in married heads, in married hearts and married interests. . . . The women of the farm want to be equal, nothing more. They wish to respect their husbands enough to feel they would not do so foolish a thing as to marry their inferior."[xxii] Jamestown's Martha Almy believed that many pro-suffrage farming men were of like mind. "Most of the men and women in this western district have toiled side by side in the accumulation of a competence, and under such circumstances men rarely speak of 'supporting their wives.' They very naturally recognize the dignity of an equal co-partnership," she asserted.[xxiii]

Twing's and Almy's remarks came at a critical moment in the fight in New York State, when the opportunity presented by the 1894 state constitutional convention brought together a variety of constituencies of women as well as men in support of women's suffrage, from unionized workers in New York City to farming men from the Patrons of Husbandry.[xxiv] Expanding upon the gender-inclusive policies of the national Grange, the state Grange actually had come out in support of suffrage as early as 1881, at the urging of member Eliza C. Gifford from the Chautauqua County town of Busti.[xxv] At the Grange's state convention in Utica in February 1894, delegates passed resolutions not only supporting the revision of the state constitution to allow female voters but also "making it the duty of every subordinate Grange in the State" to hold a public meeting about suffrage.[xxvi] Notably, Chautauqua County led the state in Grange membership in the years preceding and also was the home of the current state master, Walter C. Gifford of Busti (Eliza's husband).[xxvii] In his address to his fellow Grangers, Gifford exhorted: "We cannot afford to be idle or indifferent to the nature of the amendments soon to be made to our State Constitution. Many important ones will be proposed, but none of greater importance than that asking for the enfranchisement of one-half the citizens of this State."[xxviii]

While the support of the Grange for women's suffrage contributed to much of the pro-suffrage sentiment in Chautauqua County by the 1894 campaign, members of the local Political Equality Clubs did the work necessary to turn sentiment into action. As the 1894 proceedings approached, Jamestown's Martha Almy, then serving as vice president of the state suffrage association, worked feverishly in Rochester with Anthony and others on the campaign committee to coordinate presentations and petition drives in every county in the state.[xxix] Although small in proportion to the 296,062 signatures of support reportedly collected statewide, the 12,547 signatures canvassed by club members in Chautauqua County were equivalent in number to about 90 percent of the county's voter turnout in the preceding year's election. A similarly remarkable level of support also resulted from petition campaigns in the largely rural upstate counties of Allegany, Cattaraugus, Orleans, Wyoming, and Yates. In Monroe County, suffragists in Rochester and surrounding towns collected enough signatures to exceed the number of men who voted in their county in 1893.[xxx] Although comparisons to voter turnout are somewhat misleading since the petitions were signed by women as well as men, these figures suggest both the strength of support for suffrage within the western counties and the effectiveness of small-town organizing. One Ellington officer's faith in her work shone through in the annual report she filed with the county's leadership: "Our workers are few but faithful," she wrote, "and are strengthened with the thought that great victories have been won by small bands."[xxxi]

When Albany lawmakers finally submitted the question of women's enfranchisement to state voters in 1915, men in Chautauqua County approved the measure by the widest margin in the state.[xxxii] Although it failed that year statewide, the editor of the *Jamestown Evening Journal* held that local women should be proud "in this showing for their own city and county. It shows that they not only represented but helped to mould [*sic*] public sentiment on the suffrage question, and Chautauqua County will go down into history as a leader in the suffrage movement."[xxxiii]

Notes

i. "Woman's Right to Suffrage," *Mayville Sentinel*, 20 December 1854; "Chautauqua County Women's Rights Convention," *Mayville Sentinel*, 3 January 1855.

ii. Elizabeth Cady Stanton, Susan B. Anthony, and Matilda Joslyn Gage, eds., *History of Woman Suffrage, Vol. 1, 1848–1861* (New York: Fowler and Wells, 1881), 619 (https://archive.org/stream/historyofwomansu01stan). The conventions and petition campaigns led by Anthony and others in the years before the Civil War ultimately helped convince lawmakers in Albany to pass an 1860 law that expanded the rights of married women to their property and wages. Anthony's diary and newspaper announcements suggest that Chautauqua County was the site of the first county convention she facilitated as part of this important campaign on behalf of New York State women. See Ann D. Gordon, ed., *In the School of Anti-Slavery, 1840 to 1866*, vol. 1 of *The Selected Papers of Elizabeth Cady Stanton and Susan B. Anthony,* (New Brunswick: Rutgers University Press, 1997), 288–289, 291-295, 301-302.

iii. Anthony diary, 26–27 December 1854, in Gordon, *The Selected Papers of Elizabeth Cady Stanton and Susan B. Anthony*, 1:288–289.

iv. See Lori D. Ginzberg, *Untidy Origins: A Story of Women's Rights in Antebellum New York* (Chapel Hill: University of North Carolina Press, 2005); and Judith Wellman, *The Road to Seneca Falls: Elizabeth Cady Stanton and the First Woman's Rights Convention* (Champaign: University of Illinois Press, 2004).

v. Nancy Grey Osterud demonstrates how rural upstate women might establish a basis for gender equality through their productive labor and participation in both men's and women's organizational activities. See Osterud, *Bonds of Community: The Lives of Farm Women in Nineteenth-Century New York* (Ithaca: Cornell University Press, 1991), especially 286–288. Support for women's suffrage among farming populations is evident in western states, particularly through the advocacy of farmer's organizations. See Rebecca J. Mead, *How the Vote Was Won: Woman Suffrage in the Western United States, 1868–1914* (New York: New York University Press, 2004); Marilyn P. Watkins, *Rural Democracy: Family Farmers and Politics in Western Washington, 1890–1925* (Ithaca: Cornell University Press, 1995); and Michael Lewis Goldberg, *Any Army of Women: Gender and Politics in Gilded Age Kansas* (Baltimore: Johns Hopkins University Press, 1997).

vi. Elnora Monroe Babcock, "Political Equality Movement," in *The Centennial History of Chautauqua County, New York* (Jamestown: Chautauqua History Company, 1904), 1:510; John P. Downs, ed., *History of Chautauqua County, New York, and Its People* (New York: American Historical Society, 1921), 1:351.

vii. For an early summary of the Rochester Women's Political Club, renamed the Rochester Political Equality Club, see Blake McKelvey, "Woman's Rights in Rochester: A Century of Progress," *Rochester History*, Vol. 10, Nos. 2–3 (July 1948): 15–17 (http://www.libraryweb.org/~rochhist/v10_1948/v10i2-3.pdf). Geneva was the home of another particularly active PEC by the late 1890s, as seen in Robert A. Huff, "Anne Miller and the Geneva Political Equality Club, 1897–1912," *New York History*, Vol. 65, No. 4 (October 1984): 325–348.

viii. "Political Equality Club," *Jamestown Evening Journal*, Saturday, 12 November 1887, 4.

ix. Clubs organized in 1888 included those in Kennedy, Mayville, Frewsburg, Ellington, Fredonia, Sinclairville, South Stockton, Gerry, Westfield, Harmony, and Kiantone, New York. See Babcock, "Political Equality Movement," 510; Downs, *History of Chautauqua County*, 351; and Minutes of the Chautauqua County Political Equality Club, 1888–1903, Ms. 29, Special Collections, Fenton History Center Museum and Library, Jamestown, New York.

x. Ellen A. Martin, "The Jamestown Meeting and School Suffrage," *Woman's Tribune*, 13 October 1888, 3. For Anthony's diary account of her visit to Jamestown, see Ann D. Gordon, ed., *Their Place Inside the Body-Politic, 1887 to 1895*, vol. 5 of *The Selected Papers of Elizabeth Cady Stanton and Susan B. Anthony* (New Brunswick: Rutgers University Press, 2009), 132–134. Anthony and Stanton offered two presentations. The afternoon talk drew one hundred women at Anthony's estimation and "the house was packed" for the evening program.

xi. Babcock, "Political Equality Movement," 511; Downs, *History of Chautauqua County*, 351–352.

xii. Babcock, "Political Equality Movement," 515; and the report of then-state suffrage association president Jean Brooks Greenleaf in "The National American Woman Suffrage Convention," *The Business Woman's Journal* [later *American Magazine*] (February 1892): 53.

xiii. "The National American Woman Suffrage Convention," 53. Also see "Woman's Day at Cassadaga Lake," *Woman's Tribune*, 10 September 1892, 172. Babcock reported that the county held this distinction for "several years" ("Political Equality Movement," 515). At the end of 1894, Chautauqua County reported 450 memberships to the state association, which still far surpassed the second highest number of 160 memberships reported by Kings County. See *1894. Constitutional-Amendment Campaign Year: Report of the New York State Woman Suffrage Association* (Rochester: Charles Mann, 1895), 174, 179–216 (https://books.google.com/books?id=gRs5AQAAMAAJ).

xiv. Elnora Babcock, "Annual Address of Mrs. Babcock at Chautauqua Co. Convention" (unpublished manuscript, 1892), 18. A copy of this address was provided to the author from a private collection.

xv. Babcock served in this role for NAWSA from 1899 to 1906. One county history touted her work: "There is scarcely a newspaper in the United States that does not receive suffrage matter either directly or indirectly through the National Suffrage Press Bureau in Dunkirk" (*The Centennial History of Chautauqua County*, 2:474). See also her biography in Frances E. Willard and Mary A. Livermore, *A Woman of the Century: Fourteen Hundred-Seventy Biographical Sketches Accompanied by Portraits of Leading American Women* (Buffalo: Charles Wells Moulton, 1893), 40–41.

xvi. Babcock, "Political Equality Movement," 514; Evaline Clark, "Woman's Day at Chautauqua," *Woman's Journal*, 15 August 1891. Some commentary from Anthony and Frances Willard about Bishop Vincent's views is offered in Ida Husted Harper, *The Life and Work of Susan B. Anthony* (Indianapolis: Hollenbeck Press, 1898), 2:708–709.

xvii. Harper, *The Life and Work of Susan B. Anthony*, 2:710; Babcock, "Political Equality Movement," 514–515.

xviii. Demonstrating the diversity of reforms the local clubs supported, attendants at a county PEC meeting in Bemus Point, New York, in 1889 adopted resolutions advocating full suffrage, government pensions for women who served as nurses during the Civil War, equal child custody rights, the appointment of female police matrons to protect "the unfortunate women of our cities," and equal pay for female teachers ("Basket Picnic at Bemus Point Saturday June 1," *Fredonia Censor*, 29 May 1889).

xix. See Jacqueline Trace, "Fighting the Demon Drink in Fredonia: The Women's Temperance Crusade," *Western New York Heritage*, Vol. 17, No. 4 (Winter 2015): 28–35; and Douglas H. Shepard, "The Temperance Movement in Fredonia," Chautauqua County, New York, July 2009 (http://app.chautauquacounty.com/hist_struct/Pomfret/Shepard-TemperanceMovement2009. html).

xx. Babcock, "Political Equality Movement," 516.

xxi. *1894. Constitutional-Amendment Campaign Year: Report of the New York State Woman Suffrage Association*, 186. The italics are her own.

xxii. *1894. Constitutional-Amendment Campaign Year: Report of the New York State Woman Suffrage Association*, 56. A resident of Westfield in Chautauqua County, Twing offered these comments during a hearing held on women's suffrage as part of the constitutional convention proceedings in 1894. She spoke on behalf of the New York State Grange in addition to the residents of her legislative district.

xxiii. *1894. Constitutional-Amendment Campaign Year: Report of the New York State Woman Suffrage Association*, 43. Almy's comments also came during an 1894 hearing on suffrage.

xxiv. In addition to the Grange, pro-suffrage memorials were sent to the convention from affiliates of the American Federation of Labor and various other labor and reform organizations. See *1894. Constitutional-Amendment Campaign Year: Report of the New York State Woman Suffrage Association*, 141. As Susan Goodier explores, the 1894 suffrage debate also mobilized the opposition. See Goodier, *No Votes for Women: The New York State Anti-Suffrage Movement* (Champaign: University of Illinois Press, 2013), chap. 1.

xxv. Osterud, *Bonds of Community*, 259–260; Babcock, "Political Equality Movement," 518–519. For further discussion of the Grange and women's rights, see Donald B. Marti, "Sisters of the Grange: Rural Feminism in the Late Nineteenth Century," *Agricultural History*, Vol. 58, No. 3 (July 1984): 247–261.

xxvi. Martha R. Almy, "Woman Suffrage in N.Y. Grange," *Woman's Journal*, 10 March 1894, 75.

xxvii. "The State Grange," *Fredonia Censor*, 12 February 1890. Also notable, the first chapter of the Grange in the nation formed in Fredonia, New York, in 1868.

xxviii. Almy, "Woman Suffrage in N.Y. Grange."

xxix. Anthony diary, 1–7, 12 January 1894, in Gordon, *The Selected Papers of Elizabeth Cady Stanton and Susan B. Anthony*, 5:563–565, 572. Almy eventually moved to the campaign's headquarters in Albany and, after the convention, assumed management of all the state association's legislative work (Gordon, *The Selected Papers*, 5:563–564n).

xxx. *1894. Constitutional-Amendment Campaign Year: Report of the New York State Woman Suffrage Association*, 139–141.

xxxi. Minutes of the Chautauqua County Political Equality Club.

xxxii. Downs, *The History of Chautauqua County*, 356; "Woman Suffrage Defeated in Three of the Eastern States," *Jamestown Evening Journal*, 3 November 1915, 1.

xxxiii. "Woman Suffrage Defeated in Three of the Eastern States," *Jamestown Evening Journal*, 3 November 1915, 4.

THE NEW WOMAN: CHANGING WOMEN, CHANGING LEADERS, AND CHANGING STRATEGIES

The new century ushered in the "New Woman" and, thus, different leaders and strategies for the suffrage movement emerged. At the beginning of the twentieth century, more women worked outside the home than ever before. Women were slowly gaining access to a college education and a few were even entering professional fields of work. This generation of women did not seek the vote to uplift society and make it better; the "New Woman" sought the vote because she felt she was equal to men. Women across New York State embraced these new ideas about womanhood. Harriot Stanton Blatch and Carrie Chapman Catt incorporated this new ideology by working to change the political scene in New York State and the nation.

New Woman Wash Day, stereo card, ca. 1897.

Courtesy of the Library of Congress.

Jean Brooks Greenleaf and Susan B. Anthony, photograph, 1900.

This photograph was taken in 1900 shortly after women were admitted into the University of Rochester. Women began petitioning the university in the 1880s to admit female students. However, the Board of Trustees agreed only if the petitioners could raise $100,000. Almost $50,000 was raised. Not to be defeated, as a last-ditch effort, Susan B. Anthony pledged her life insurance policy. In the fall of 1900, women were finally admitted to the University of Rochester. *Susan B. Anthony: Celebrating "A Heroic Life,"* online exhibition, University at Rochester River Campus Libraries. The caption on the back of this photograph says, "The Girls are in." Courtesy of the Department of Rare Books and Special Collections, University of Rochester Libraries.

Inez Milholland, photograph, ca. 1913.

Inez Milholland (1886–1916) embraced the "New Woman" ideology. She attended Vassar College and New York University Law School and was involved with several reform activities, including labor reform, civil rights, prison reform, pacifism, and women's suffrage. She spent time in London, where she was involved with the radical British suffrage movement. She brought the techniques she learned in London home to the American movement. Because of Milholland's beauty and status in society, her suffrage activities were often reported in the news and she became a celebrity for the cause. In 1916, she toured the western United States with the National Woman's Party. While touring, she became ill and died shortly after collapsing on a stage. She is buried in Lewis, New York, where she spent summers with her family each year. Courtesy of the Library of Congress.

Lock of hair and photographs of Mildred Clark Pryor, ca. 1923.

Women embraced the new era in hundreds of different ways. Mildred Clark Pryor (1902–1997) from Hornellsville, New York, began working when she was sixteen years old at the Erie Railroad dispatcher's office. Later, she took a job as a bookkeeper for a local store. She "bobbed" her hair around 1923. According to family members, Pryor asked both her husband and father their opinions before she decided on the new style. After her haircut, she saved her long locks of hair. The framed photograph above shows Pryor before and the photograph on the left shows Pryor with her new hairstyle seated in the center (with dark sweater). Courtesy of Coreen Hallenbeck.

Madam C. J. Walker (*driving*) with (*left to right*) her niece Anjetta Breedlove; Madam C. J. Walker Manufacturing Company factory forelady (manager) Alice Kelly; and Walker Company bookkeeper Lucy Flint, photograph, 1911.

Courtesy of the Schomburg Center for Research in Black Culture, New York Public Library.

MADAM C. J. WALKER

Madam C. J. Walker (1867–1919) was a successful African American entrepreneur, businesswoman, philanthropist, and social and political activist during a time when both African Americans and women were not common in the world of business. Born as Sarah Breedlove on the same Louisiana plantation her parents were enslaved, she worked as a farm laborer and laundress. In the late 1880s, Walker moved to St. Louis to join her four brothers already established there as barbers. After ten years in St. Louis, Walker began to suffer from hair loss and sought relief from homemade and commercial remedies. Thus, began her interest in hair products.

In 1905, she married Charles Joseph Walker and moved to Denver, Colorado, where she sold hair products made by Annie Malone. She soon decided to start her own hair product business and changed her name and the name of her company to Madam C. J. Walker. The product line was directed specifically at African American women. Walker traveled the country for eighteen months promoting her products and recruiting local women to sell them. In 1910, she settled in Indianapolis where she opened a factory, a hair-care training school, and a salon. By 1916, the company had expanded to Central America and Walker

turned over the day-to-day operations of the company and moved to Harlem, New York.

Even though Walker continued as head of the company, she became politically active. She donated generously to the NAACP and other community groups and was an outspoken proponent of anti-lynching laws. She encouraged her workers to get an education and get involved in community activism. When Walker passed away in 1919, her daughter, A'Lelia, took over the company which remained in business until 1981.

Madam C. J. Walker's Glossine hair paste and advertisement, ca. 1920.

Courtesy of the New York State Museum, H-2010.45.30-31.

HARRIOT STANTON BLATCH

Harriot Stanton Blatch (1856–1940) helped to revolutionize and shape New York State's suffrage movement from a nineteenth-century movement of upper-class, white women to a modern twentieth-century reform movement involving women from more classes and ethnic backgrounds.

Blatch was the second daughter and sixth child of Elizabeth Cady Stanton. She was born in Seneca Falls and attended Vassar College. Upon graduation in 1878, she traveled the suffrage lecture circuit with her mother and helped author the *History of Woman Suffrage*, Volume 2. After living in Europe for a year, she met Englishman William Henry Blatch Jr. The couple married in 1882 and moved to England for twenty years. While in England, Blatch worked with women-focused reform groups and was heavily influenced by the power of the organized working classes and the British suffragists with their militant tactics.

When she returned to the United States in 1902 with her family and settled in New York City, she expected to jump into the suffrage movement,

THE LID IS OFF AGAIN.

"The Lid Is Off Again," political cartoon, 1904.

The premise of the New Woman was not totally embraced by society. This illustration by Samuel D. Ehrhart (1862–1937) depicts a devil taking the lid off a box labeled "Society," allowing fumes to escape that show the liberation of women, such as being granted divorces, horseback riding, driving automobiles, gambling, and smoking in social situations. The illustration appeared in *Puck* on March 30, 1904. Courtesy of the Library of Congress.

but she was shocked to find it clinging to nineteenth-century tactics. She and a small group of women wanted to modernize the movement and soon realized that they had to abandon the traditional NYSWSA and create their own group. In January 1907, Blatch and a group of forty women met in lower Manhattan to create a new kind of suffrage organization—one that was dramatic, political, and included working industrial and professional women. The result was the formation of the Equality League of Self-Supporting Women, which would later become the Women's Political Union (WPU).[19]

Harriot Stanton Blatch, framed photograph, 1912.

Courtesy of Coline Jenkins, Elizabeth Cady Stanton Family.

Suffrage parade in New York City, photograph, 1912.

Harriot Stanton Blatch was inspired by the work of the British suffragists and embraced public demonstrations such as open-air meetings and parades. She is pictured here on the right in her cap and gown. Courtesy of Coline Jenkins, Elizabeth Cady Stanton Family.

Blatch was well versed in politics and used this to her advantage when organizing suffrage workers and dealing with politicians. Her work was critical for both of New York's referendum campaigns in 1915 and 1917. After New York won the vote, Blatch remained active in women's rights, working for passage of the Nineteenth Amendment and later promoting the Equal Rights Amendment, which was never ratified by the states and died.

> The suffrage movement was completely in a rut in New York State at the beginning of the twentieth century. It bored its adherents and repelled its opponents. Most of the ammunition was being wasted on its supporters in private drawing rooms and in public halls . . .
> —Harriot Stanton Blatch and Alma Lutz,
> *Challenging Years: The Memoirs of Harriot Stanton Blatch*

"Give Her of the Fruit of Her Hands,"
Woman Suffrage, poster, 1905.

This poster was based on a painting by Evelyn
Rumsey Cary, a native of Buffalo, New York. The
image depicts a woman emerging from the
earth like a tree. In the background is a classical
building, possibly the Albright Knox Art Gallery
(originally built for the Fine Arts Pavilion for the
Pan-American Exposition in 1901 but not opened
until 1905). "Give her of the fruit of her hands
and let her own works praise her in the gates" is
also printed on the foreground of the image. This
poster was used widely in the suffrage movement. Courtesy of the New York State Library,
Manuscripts and Special Collections, US GEN 236.

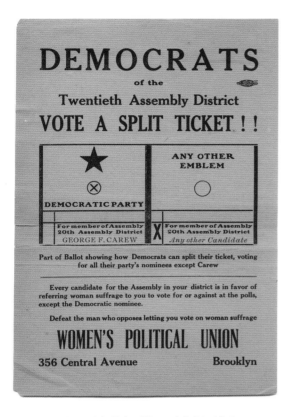

Vote a Split Ticket, Women's Political Union, handbill, ca.1911.

Courtesy of Coline Jenkins, Elizabeth Cady Stanton Family.

Votes for Women New York pin, 1915.

Courtesy of the National Susan B. Anthony Museum & House.

Votes for Women bag, ca. 1915.

Harriot Stanton Blatch purposefully chose the Women's Political Union's name and colors in solidarity with the Women's Social and Political Union (WSPU), the militant British organization. Both organizations' colors were white, purple, and green.

Courtesy of the Sophia Smith Collection, Smith College.

WPU Votes for Women pennant, ca.1915.

Courtesy of the Onondaga Historical Association.

WOMEN'S POLITICAL UNION

Traditional suffrage organizations ignored working women because of class and nativism. However, championing the rights of working women brought great results and new life into the New York movement. In 1907, Harriot Stanton Blatch and a group of New York City women founded the Equality League of Self-Supporting Women. By 1908, the league had a membership of over nineteen thousand and continued to try new tactics such as outdoor meetings and street parades—both attracted attention from the public and newspapers. Mirroring the politicians, the league organized members by political districts that helped suffragists send their message out faster and allowed for local control, better communication, faster reaction time, and the ability to put pressure on elected officials, particularly the ones opposed to suffrage. Some of the older and more conservative suffrage leaders feared the new methods,

but they could not argue with the results. In 1910, the league's name changed to the Women's Political Union and the focus shifted to the politics of the movement. In 1916, the Women's Political Union merged with the Congressional Union (later called the National Woman's Party) under the direction of Alice Paul.

Woman Suffrage Party, sash, ca. 1913.

Courtesy of the Geneva Historical Society.

CARRIE CHAPMAN CATT

Carrie Chapman Catt (1859–1947) was one of the key organizers for women's suffrage in New York State and at the national level. Her "Winning Plan" for suffrage ultimately helped New York State women win the vote in 1917.

Catt grew up in Iowa, where she worked as a teacher to pay for her college tuition. In 1885, she married newspaper editor Leo Chapman, who died shortly after the couple wed. She soon became interested in suffrage, establishing Political Equality Clubs and serving as the state's group organizer and secretary. Catt became involved with the NAWSA, working at both the state national levels. Susan B. Anthony took notice of her organizational and public speaking skills and tapped Catt to succeed her as president of the NAWSA in 1900. After one term in office, she stepped down to care for her ailing second husband, George Catt, who died in 1905.

Catt traveled internationally on behalf of woman suffrage and then settled down in New York City, where she became active at the local level. In 1907 she formed the Interurban Woman Suffrage Council, which brought together most of the suffrage groups in the city under one umbrella organization. This organization served as the model for Catt's New York City Woman Suffrage Party, which she organized in 1909. The Woman Suffrage Party was the basis for the Empire State Campaign Committee, which launched the unsuccessful campaign for a state constitutional amendment in 1915. This same year Catt returned as president of the NAWSA with what she called the "Winning Plan" to secure the vote in New York State and, in turn, use New York's win to propel the federal amendment forward.

Carrie Chapman Catt, photograph, ca. 1920.

Courtesy of the Library of Congress.

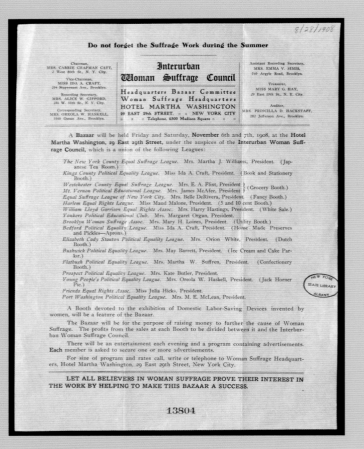

Notice of suffrage bazaar from the Interurban
Woman Suffrage Council, August 28, 1908.

Courtesy of the New York State Library,
Manuscripts and Special Collections, SC13804.

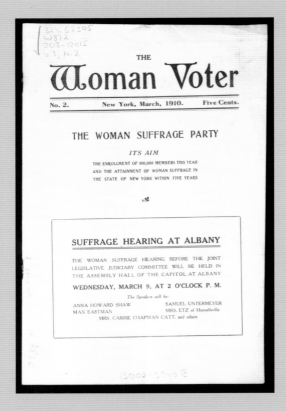

The Woman Voter, No. 2, March 1910.

Courtesy of the New York State Library,
Manuscripts and Special Collections, N324.62305
W872 203-12015.

To the men and women of all the
Boroughs of Greater New York

HELP THE DISTRICT ORGANIZATION:

Sign name and address and mail this Post Card.

Name..

Address...

You will be invited to the meetings of the District in
which you live. 13804

Help the District Organization card, ca. 1912.

Courtesy of the New York State Library,
Manuscripts and Special Collections, SC13804.

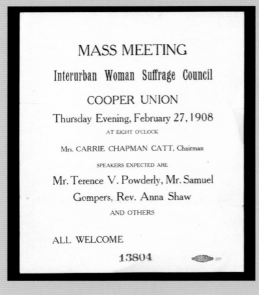

Mass meeting at Cooper Union, February 27,
1908.

Courtesy of the New York State Library,
Manuscripts and Special Collections, SC13804.

BY
CARRIE CHAPMAN CATT.

PERHAPS, if you paused to think that the laws under which you live, and which control the whole environment of your life, are the direct or the indirect results, of the averaged opinions which are put into the ballot box, you would incline to study the questions which pertain to the right of voting.

PERHAPS, If you realized that law guarantees, or restricts your own personal liberty; protects or jeopardizes your health, your home, your happiness; regulates the food you eat, the clothes you wear, the books you read, the amusements you enjoy; in fact permits, or prohibits, your every act, you would feel a serious obligation to inquire into the nature of such authority over you.

PERHAPS, if you paused to think that law will never represent the highest intelligence or morality since intelligence and morality must always be averaged at the ballot box with ignorance and immorality, you would perceive that whenever intelligence and morality predominate over ignorance and immorality, the trend of civilization *must* be upward, and you would search for such factors.

"Perhaps," by Carrie Chapman Catt, ca. 1912.

Courtesy of the New York State Library, Manuscripts and Special Collections, SC13804.

New York State Woman Suffrage Party banner, ca.1915.

Courtesy of the New York State Museum, H-1935.4.23.

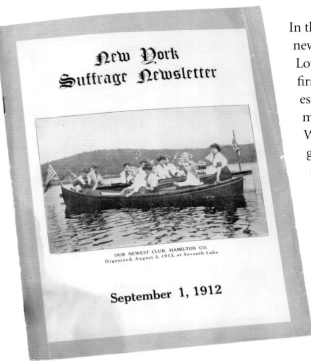

New York Suffrage Newsletter, September 1912.

Courtesy of the Collection of Ronnie Lapinsky Sax.

COURTING WORKING WOMEN AND IMMIGRANTS: LILLIAN WALD, HENRY STREET SETTLEMENT

In the early twentieth century, settlement houses were created to help newly arrived immigrants adapt to living in a new modern city. The Lower East Side of Manhattan was often the place where immigrants first found homes in New York City. Several settlement houses were established in the area, but none was as important to the suffrage movement as the Henry Street Settlement. Established by Lillian Wald in 1893, the Henry Street Settlement served the poor immigrant community by offering home health care on a sliding fee scale. In addition to offering educational opportunities and a community center, the Henry Street Settlement also worked to educate immigrants about the suffrage movement.

As the Henry Street Settlement expanded, Wald established a Visiting Nurse Service that reached out to all sections of the city. Many of the nurses who worked for Wald believed in the New Woman and advocated for suffrage. By 1913, there were ninety-two nurses making over two hundred thousand visits per year to the newly arrived citizens and the poor. Visiting nurses were trusted members of the community and served as an important link between the suffrage movement and new immigrants.

Typically, nativism kept suffragists from cultivating the immigrant vote. Many middle- and upper-class women did not want to ask newly arrived immigrant men for the vote. However, if the referendum were to be won, support from the large numbers of immigrants was crucial. During the 1915 and 1917 referendum campaigns, the state was organized into political districts down to the local level with the goal to canvass

Visiting nurse's bag from Schenectady Visiting Nurses Association, ca. 1920.

The Schenectady Visiting Nurses Association was established in 1919 with financial support from the Schenectady Women's Club and the City Federation of Women's Organizations. These visiting nurses offered countywide service to anyone with public health needs. In the early years, the agency primarily offered nurses for maternity care and delivery. By the 1920s and 1930s, the association offered care for the sick in their homes and taught hygiene and sanitation classes. Courtesy of the Bellevue Alumnae Center for Nursing History Archive, Center for Nursing at the Foundation of New York State Nurses, Guilderland, New York.

Visiting nurse going over the rooftop, photograph, 1915.

From *The House on Henry Street*, by Lillian Wald.

Lillian Wald, photograph, ca. 1910.

In 1903, Wald also helped to establish the Women's Trade Union League (WTUL), which was a combination of wealthy reform women and working women, with the goal of organizing women into unions. Wald firmly believed that the vote would help empower working women. Courtesy of the Library of Congress.

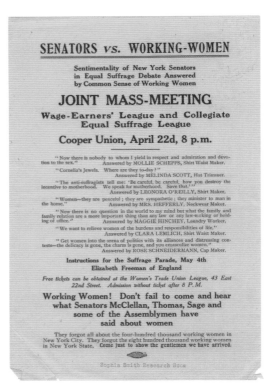

Joint Mass Meeting between the Wage-Earners' League and Collegiate Equality Suffrage League, handbill, 1912.

The Wage-Earners' League was established in 1911 because working women were underrepresented in NAWSA. Thousands of working women attended this rally at Cooper Union to hear working women respond to the arguments senators made for not granting women the vote. Courtesy of the Sophia Smith Collection, Smith College.

Wage Earning Women, STOP! THINK! REASON!, anti-suffrage broadside, ca. 1913.

Anti-suffrage organizations targeted working women for support of their cause. Courtesy of the Clinton Historical Society.

each area and influence each male voter. In both campaigns, the areas with settlement houses had a higher percentage of men voting for suffrage. Lavinia Dock was one of the Henry Street Settlement nurses and an ardent suffragist. According to Wald, "Miss L.L. Dock, a resident of many years, has mobilized Russians, Italians, Irish, and native-born, all the nationalities of our cosmopolitan community, for the campaign."[20] In the 1917 campaign, the New York City vote for suffrage was so large it offset the loss of votes upstate.

SHIRTWAIST WORKERS:
THE UPRISING OF 20,000 AND THE DEATH OF 146

New York City's garment industry mostly employed Jewish and Italian immigrant women between the ages of sixteen and twenty-five years old. Conditions were horrible for the workers. The factories were in old, dilapidated buildings with little light and no ventilation, wages were low ($6 a week for many), exits were frequently locked to prevent theft and unauthorized work breaks, and work hours were long. Since most of these workers were new immigrants who spoke little English, there was little recourse for them. However, in September 1909 workers in the two largest shirtwaist shops in New York City, Leiserson Company and the Triangle Company, went on strike.

Clara Lemlich, a twenty-three-year-old Jewish immigrant from the Ukraine and member of the International Ladies' Garment Workers' Union, led the strike and rallied the cause. Approximately twenty thousand workers (mostly women) went on strike for three months. Most shops acquiesced and offered some kind of union contract or improvements for the workers, but there were no overall institutional changes in conditions. The Triangle Company offered nothing to its workers and was the site of a factory fire in 1911 where 146 workers, mostly young immigrant women, burned to death because the doors were locked and they could not escape when a fire broke out.

Both the strike and the fire reinforced the fact that women workers needed suffrage if they wanted legislators' help to improve working conditions. Many women like Clara Lemlich, Rose Schneiderman, Leonora O'Reilly, and thousands of other women worked toward both labor reform and suffrage in New York.

Sewing machine, ca. 1911.

This sewing machine was collected as evidence after the Triangle factory fire. Most of the workers at the Triangle factory were teenage girls who worked twelve hours a day. Courtesy of the New York State Department of Labor.

Rose Schneiderman, photograph, ca. 1900.

Rose Schneiderman's own experience in sweatshops resulted in her efforts to recruit more women to labor reform. Courtesy of the Kheel Center, Cornell University

International Ladies' Garment Workers' Union Local 25, photograph, 1909.

International Ladies' Garment Workers' Union Local 25 was formed in 1906. Clara Lemlich (*top row, third from left*), who tried to organize shirtwaist workers in the Triangle and Leiserson Companies, was a member. Courtesy of the Kheel Center, Cornell University.

The Women's Trade Union League, photograph, ca. 1900.

The Women's Trade Union League played a critical role in the organization of the shirtwaist strike. In addition, they also worked to pass legislation regarding an eight-hour work day, safer working conditions, and a minimum wage. Courtesy of the Kheel Center, Cornell University.

"Going Out for Better Conditions," photograph, ca. 1909.

Shirtwaist strikers "Going Out for Better Conditions" marched through cold winter streets, waving and cheering, demonstrating courage and tenacity that surprised and impressed many who saw or read about their struggle. Courtesy of the Kheel Center, Cornell University.

Sewing machine operators, photograph, 1909.

Courtesy of the Kheel Center, Cornell University.

Firefighters from Ladder Company 20 arrived at the Triangle Company, photograph, March 25, 1911.

Courtesy of the Kheel Center, Cornell University.

April 5th funeral procession for the seven unidentified fire victims, photograph, 1911.

Members of the United Hebrew Trades of New York and the Ladies' Waist and Dressmakers Union Local 25, the local that organized Triangle Company workers, carry banners proclaiming, "We Mourn Our Loss." April 5, 1911. Courtesy of the Kheel Center, Cornell University.

Suffrage parade, New York City, photograph, 1912.

Parades were often organized by groups. In this photograph, the sweatshop workers marched together. Courtesy of the Sophia Smith Collection, Smith College.

NEW YORK STATE WOMAN SUFFRAGE PARTY
INDUSTRIAL SECTION
MARY E. DREIER, Chairman
303 FIFTH AVENUE   NEW YORK CITY

WOMEN NEED THE VOTE,—to help solve such problems as unemployment, hours of work, fire prevention, compensation, health insurance and old age pensions; to secure pure food, good homes, schools and playgrounds, low rents and protect other interests of the home.
¶ These questions vitally affect working women equally with working men,—therefore, give the women the vote.
Membership:—
     Open to all men and women who are workers or home makers.
Dues :—
     Twenty-five cents a year, which entitles member to a vote in the Woman Suffrage Party of his or her Assembly District.

     Please enroll my name as a member of the Industrial Section of the New York State Woman Suffrage Party; for which I enclose twenty-five cents.

     Name
     Street
     City
     Occupation
                    Date
     If you want to be enrolled as a Voting member of the Party check here.

Mail to MISS JANE OLCOTT, Executive Secretary Industrial Section
303 Fifth Avenue,   New York City

New York State Woman Suffrage Party Industrial Section, enrollment card, ca. 1915.

The Woman Suffrage Party actively recruited working women and worked for equal wages and better working conditions. Courtesy of the Clinton Historical Society.

FRANCES PERKINS

As the result of the Triangle factory fire, New York City created a Committee on Public Safety and tapped Frances Perkins to lead it and identify problems in other factories. Perkins was already working as the executive secretary of the New York City Consumers League, where her work focused on improving the conditions and safety for workers in factories. State senate majority leader Robert Wagner and Assemblyman Alfred E. Smith both proposed legislation to establish a state commission to investigate problems and make legislative recommendations. The New York State Factory Investigating Commission mandate included fire safety and the overall health and well-being of industrial workers. Perkins assisted the commission by writing a report about fire hazards in factories. By 1915, she was a leading expert in the field of industrial policy and lobbied the legislature to create laws to keep workers safe. Perkins took the tragedy of the Triangle factory fire to heart and worked to make New York the leading state in progressive industrial reforms so it would never happen again.

In 1919, Governor Al Smith appointed Perkins to the New York State Industrial Commission. She was the first woman to serve in an administrative position in New York State government and the highest paid woman in New York State government with an annual salary of $8,000.[21] Smith and Perkins worked to enforce the laws that the factory commission created. When Smith unsuccessfully ran for president in 1928, Perkins went to work for the new governor, Franklin D. Roosevelt. In 1929, Roosevelt appointed Perkins the commissioner of labor,

Francis Perkins behind President Roosevelt as he signs the Social Security Act, photograph, 1935.

Frances Perkins examplified what a woman could achieve with an education and the vote. Perkins served in both the state and national government and successfully advocated for progressive changes that helped people. Courtesy of the Library of Congress.

serving the workers of New York State through the initial years of the Great Depression.

In 1933, when Roosevelt went from Albany to Washington, DC, he asked Perkins to serve in his cabinet as secretary of labor—the first women to serve in any cabinet in the White House. She agreed to the appointment, but only if she were able to pursue her own agenda that included a forty-hour work week, unemployment and workers' compensation, minimum-wage earnings, Social Security, direct federal aid to the states for unemployment relief, and a revitalized federal employment service for all workers. Many of these ideas would soon become the backbone of the New Deal program. When the Depression hit workers hard, Perkins advocated for the establishment of a massive public works program to help the county get back to work.[22] Perkins pushed to make the New Deal a reality, helping millions of Americans during a difficult time. She served in FDR's administration until his death in 1945.

SUFFRAGE GOES PUBLIC

By 1910, there were still only four "free" states that allowed women the right to vote: Wyoming (1869), Utah (1870), Colorado (1893), and Idaho (1896). Change was on the horizon; suffrage was on the verge of passing in several western states. Progress in the West combined with the rise of progressive reform movements (labor reform, civil rights, temperance, and government reform) and press coverage of the British suffrage

Harriot Stanton Blatch (*backseat*), Nora Blatch (*driving*), and other Equality League members at a demonstration at the polls in New York City, photograph, 1908.

Courtesy of Coline Jenkins, Elizabeth Cady Stanton Family.

Wagon, ca. 1840.

In 1913, this wagon was covered in suffrage banners and hand-painted signs. One read: "If taxation without representation was tyranny in 1776, why not in 1913?" Suffragists equated their cause with that of our nation's founders. This wagon helped them drive that point home. Claiming it was built in 1776 and belonged to patriots, suffrage activists used the wagon as both a prop and a speaker's platform. On a hot summer day in 1913, Edna Kearns and Irene Davison drove the horse-drawn wagon from New York City to Long Island dressed as minutemen. They passed out leaflets and delivered lectures along the way. Eight-year-old Serena Kearns accompanied her mother, costumed as "little Liberty." Courtesy of the New York State Museum, H-2007.21.1.

movement inspired women to adopt new and more public methods to garner support for suffrage.[23] Suffragists moved away from meeting in home parlors and other private spaces and into public spaces with street parades, open-air meetings, hikes, tents at fairs, theaters, automobile tours, and whatever else would capture the public's attention and, more importantly, that of the press.

PARADES

The first suffrage parade to take place in New York City occurred in February 1908. It was organized by Dr. Anna Mercy, a socialist who organized a branch of the American Suffragettes on the Lower East

Edna Kearns and her daughter Serena, photograph, ca.1914.

Courtesy of Marguerite Kearns.

Edna and Serena Kearns with Irene Davidson, photograph, 1913.

Despite the 1776 claim, wagons were not likely made in this style before 1820. This "pleasure wagon" performed light-duty transport. It was pulled by horses, most likely two, but one horse could have been used. It was owned for many years by the I. S. Remson Manufacturing Company in Brooklyn, which traded in carriages and automobiles. They used the wagon in local parades and for advertising. Company president Andrew Wilson donated this wagon to the suffragettes in 1913. Courtesy of Marguerite Kearns.

Side of Manhattan. The group was denied a permit and only twenty-three women marched, but the event was considered a success.[24] The first major suffrage parade took place in New York City two years later, on May 21, 1910, to protest Albany's legislators for not voting the suffrage amendment out of committee. Harriot Stanton Blatch and the Equality League of Self-Supporting Women organized the event. Over four hundred women marched, while other women drove cars down Fifth Avenue to Union Square where a group of ten thousand listened to speeches.[25] Parades grew in popularity leading up to the suffrage votes in 1915 and 1917.

The Suffrage Hike

On December 16, 1912, twenty-six women left the 242nd Street subway station in the Bronx heading north on a "suffrage hike" to Albany to call on governor-elect William Sulzer. "General" Rosalie Jones, a radical suffragist from Oyster Bay, New York, who planned the event to gain suffrage support from the rural people along the 170 miles to Albany, led the group. Various supporters and newspaper reporters filed in and

Matilda Joslyn Gage banner, ca. 1913.

This banner was carried in a parade in Syracuse in 1913 by Blanche Weaver Baxter, Matilda Joslyn Gage's niece. Baxter was active in the New York State Woman Suffrage Association, president of the League for Political Equality, and a life member of the League of Women Voters. Courtesy of the Onondaga Historical Association.

Palm card with directions for marching in a parade, 1915.

This card created for the Women's Political Union parade in Newark, New Jersey, on October 25, 1915, lists the expected behavior for women marching in the parade. Organization was key to a successful parade. Courtesy of Coline Jenkins, Elizabeth Cady Stanton Family.

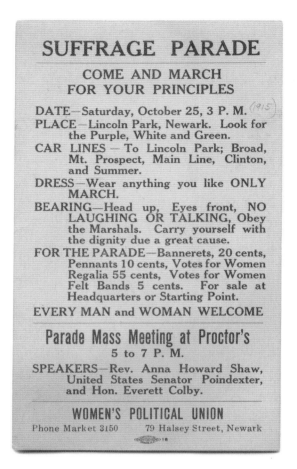

out along the way, but there was a small, devoted number of women who walked with Jones every step of the way—Ida Augusta Craft of Brooklyn, Lavinia Lloyd Dock (a trained nurse, settlement house worker, and editor of the *American Journal of Nursing*), Sybil Wilbur of Boston (an investigative journalist and author), and Katharine Stiles of Brooklyn.

The women walked for thirteen days, camping or staying with supporters along the way, and made as much of local publicity as possible. On December 28 at 4:00 p.m. they walked into Albany straight to the Capitol with much fanfare. Three days later the group was received by the governor at the Executive Mansion where they presented him with a decorated petition urging "the speedy passage of the woman suffrage amendment." Sulzer answered: "All my life I have believed in the right of women to exercise the franchise with men as a matter of justice. I will do what I can to advance their rights."[26]

The hike resulted in such a swell of publicity for women's suffrage that Rosalie Jones and Ida Craft organized another pilgrimage that traveled from New York City to Washington, DC, starting in February 1913. This time their arrival coincided with a large suffrage march held to draw attention from President Woodrow Wilson's inauguration.

Rosalie Jones, photograph, March 1913.

Rosalie Jones shown here wearing a hiking cape and carrying a walking stick covered with yellow roses. Yellow roses were a symbol of suffrage. *Women of Protest: Photographs from the Records of the National Woman's Party*, Manuscript Division, Library of Congress.

Votes for Women pilgrimage petition, 1912.

This petition was carried to Governor Sulzer on the first "suffrage hike" from New York City to Albany. Rosalie Jones hand-decorated the petition in ink and watercolor. It is signed by presidents of the New York State suffrage organizations: Harriet May Mills (president of the NYSWSA), Nora Blatch de Forest (first woman admitted to the American Society of Civil Engineers and granddaughter of Elizabeth Cady Stanton), Helen C. Mansfield (president of the Equal Franchise Society of New York), Katrina Ely Tiffany (recording secretary for the Woman Suffrage Party of New York), James Lees Laidlaw (president of the Men's League for Woman Suffrage), and Mary Garret Hay (president of the New York State Federation of Women's Clubs and League of Women Voters in New York City). Courtesy of the New York State Library, Manuscripts and Special Collections, 1046.

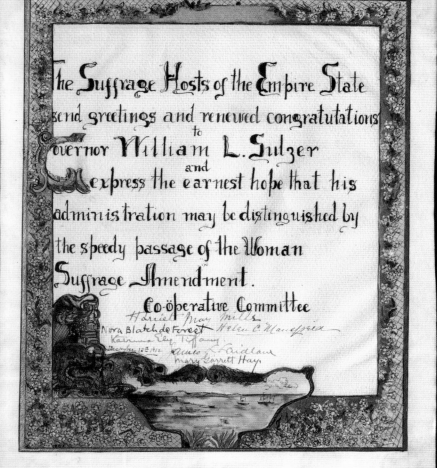

ATTENTION! ATTENTION!—MORE PUBLIC TACTICS

Nora Stanton Blatch, photograph, 1917.

Nora Stanton Blatch (*right*) during a horseback campaign across upstate New York in support of suffrage. Both women wore bifurcated skirts to ride astride. Nora Stanton Blatch was the daughter of Harriot Stanton Blatch and granddaughter of Elizabeth Cady Stanton. Courtesy of Coline Jenkins, Elizabeth Cady Stanton Family.

Votes for Women hood ornament, ca.1910.

Women used the automobile to gain attention for the vote. In 1910, it was uncommon for women to drive a car. Alva Belmont and Inez Milholland loved to drive their cars around to exercise their independence and promote suffrage. In addition, automobile tours had the added benefit of being able to reach rural voters. Courtesy of the Howland Stone Store Museum.

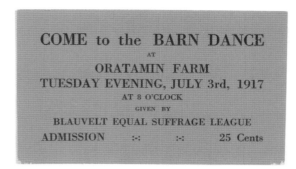

Ticket to the barn dance, July 3, 1917.

The Blauvelt Equal Suffrage League sponsored this dance as a fundraiser in support of suffrage shortly before the final vote in November 1917. Courtesy of the Collection of Ronnie Lapinsky Sax.

"Visit the Suffrage Tent at the State Fair, Syracuse, September 8–13," broadside, ca. 1915.

The New York State Fair was an area where both suffrage and anti-suffrage advocates informed the public. In 1934, the women's building at the fair was named after New York State suffrage leader Harriet May Mills. Courtesy of the Howland Stone Store Museum.

SUFFRAGE FOR SALE

In addition to new public tactics for gathering support for the cause (parades, hikes, open-air meetings, etc.), suffragists also embraced mass merchandising techniques and American consumer culture to sell suffrage to the masses. Suffrage shops and tents at fairs sold hats, sashes, banners, and ribbons for parades and gatherings. Department stores sold playing cards, dishes, dolls, calendars, sewing kits, and board games. Suffrage advertisements appeared on trolley cars, trains, buildings, and in newspapers and magazines. In the years leading up to the 1915 and 1917 referendums, suffrage material was everywhere, which helped the movement to become mainstream.[28]

"On Saturday, Come to our Food Sale at the North Street Suffrage Headquarters," broadside, ca. 1915.

Courtesy of the Howland Stone Store Museum.

"Open Air Meeting" with Frances M. Björkman, broadside, ca. 1915.

This meeting took place at the Cayuga County Political Equality Club, located in Auburn, New York. Frances Björkman was active in the New York City and national suffrage movements and a member of the Heterodoxy women's group, which was a feminist debating group located mostly in Greenwich Village. The one criterion for admission into the Heterodoxy group was that the applicant "not be orthodox in her opinion" (Judith Schwartz, *Radical Feminists of Heterodoxy: Greenwich Village, 1912–1940* [Norwich, VT: New Victoria Publishers, 1986], 123). Courtesy of the Howland Stone Store Museum.

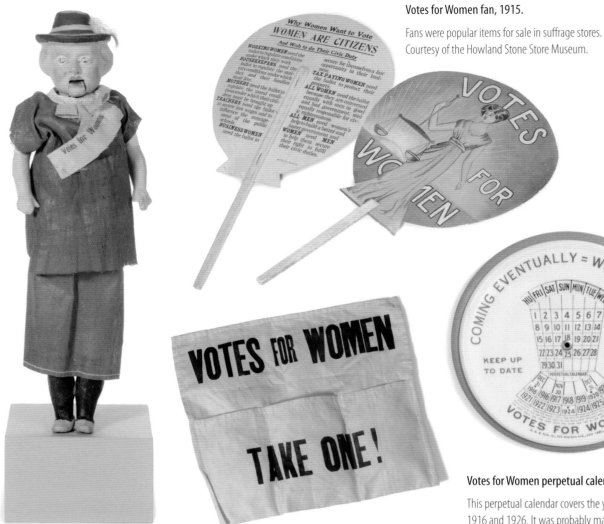

Votes for Women fan, 1915.

Fans were popular items for sale in suffrage stores. Courtesy of the Howland Stone Store Museum.

Votes for Women doll, ca. 1915.

Courtesy of the Elizabeth Cady Stanton Trust.

Canvas bag, ca. 1915.

Courtesy of the Howland Stone Store Museum.

Votes for Women perpetual calendar, ca. 1915.

This perpetual calendar covers the years between 1916 and 1926. It was probably made for the 1915 Empire State Campaign. There is a hand mirror on the reverse. Courtesy of the Collection of Ronnie Lapinsky Sax.

Anti-suffrage parade, postcard set, 1912.

This postcard set published by the Woman Suffrage Party depicts a parade of anti-suffrage proponents. Courtesy of the Clinton Historical Society.

Votes for Women embroidered stockings, ca. 1912.

Courtesy of the Elizabeth Cady Stanton Trust.

Votes for Women 1915, rubber stamp.

This rubber stamp could be used for marking sashes or other suffrage items. Courtesy of the Collection of Ronnie Lapinsky Sax.

Votes for Women hat, ca. 1915.

Courtesy of the Elizabeth Cady Stanton Trust.

Votes for Women ceramic plate, tea cup, and saucer, ca. 1913.

This stoneware dinnerware by the John Maddock Company of England was commissioned by Mrs. Alva Belmont, president of the Political Equality Association, to support the cause. The known pieces from this set include a creamer, a celery plate, a cup and saucer, a salad plate, a luncheon plate, and a soup bowl. The creamer was sold for 25 cents at Mrs. Belmont's Political Equality Association Headquarters in New York City. The service was also probably used for the Council of Great Women Conference in 1914, held at Marble House, Belmont's estate in Newport, Rhode Island. Courtesy of the Collection of Ronnie Lapinsky Sax.

Certificate from Women's Political and Social Union, 1912.

This certificate was given to Alice Wright in honor of her time spent imprisoned at Holloway Prison in London. Courtesy of the Sophia Smith Collection, Smith College.

The Fist, Alice Morgan Wright, plaster, 1921.

The Fist is one of Wright's largest and most accomplished works. It was completed and exhibited shortly after the passage of the Nineteenth Amendment and is likely symbolic of the long struggle for women's suffrage. Wright aligned herself with the militant suffragists because of her time in Great Britain. Courtesy of the Albany Institute of History & Art.

ALBANY'S ARTIST AND SUFFRAGIST

Alice Morgan Wright (1881–1975) grew up in Albany, New York. She attended St. Agnes School in Albany and Smith College in Northampton, Massachusetts. She became interested in art at a young age, particularly in sculpture. After college, she moved to New York City to pursue sculpture at the Art Students League under Hermon Atkins MacNeil and James Earle Fraser and in 1909 moved to Paris to continue her studies. She was fairly successful in Paris as an artist but also found an intense interest in the British suffrage movement, organizing meetings in both Paris and London.

In 1912 she met Emmeline Pankhurst, leader of the militant British suffrage movement, and a close friendship developed between the two women. Wright joined Pankhurst's Women's Social and Political Union (WSPU) and started attending demonstrations. She was arrested with a group of women, including Pankhurst and Emmeline Pethick-Lawrence, who smashed windows during a demonstration. Wright received a two-month sentence for "willful damage" and was sent to Holloway Prison despite claiming she broke nothing.[27] As an American prisoner in a British jail, the newspapers covered the story in detail. In 1914, Wright returned to the United States, continuing both her artwork and her suffrage activities. She was the recording secretary for NAWSA and a member of the New York State Woman Suffrage Party. After women won the vote in New York State and nationwide, she continued her reform work and was a founding member of the League of Women Voters in New York State.

Wright devoted the remainder of her long life to her artwork and advocating for the humane treatment of animals, particularly through the National Humane Education Society. She died in Albany in 1975.

Alice Morgan Wright at art school (*front row center with apron*), Paris, photograph, ca. 1912.

Courtesy of the Sophia Smith Collection, Smith College.

Emmeline Pankhurst, Alice Morgan Wright, plaster, ca. 1912.

While she was imprisoned in London after being arrested for participating in a suffrage demonstration, Wright worked on the study for this sculpture of suffrage leader and friend Emmeline Pankhurst. Courtesy of the Albany Institute of History & Art.

Alice Morgan Wright (*left*) wearing suffrage sash, photograph, ca. 1914.

Courtesy of the Sophia Smith Collection, Smith College.

Holloway brooch, 1912.

This brooch, designed by Sylvia Pankhurst, was presented to Alice Morgan Wright on March 4, 1912, on her release from prison. Morgan participated in a hunger strike but was not force-fed like some of her prison mates. The medal's design is of the portcullis symbol of the House of Commons; the gate and hanging chains are in silver, with a superimposed broad arrow in purple, white, and green enamel (WSPU's colors), representing the image used on prison uniforms in Britain. *Keynoter: Journal of the American Political Items Conservators*, Vol. 2008, No. 2-4. Courtesy of the Sophia Smith Collection, Smith College.

Miss Leila Usher, sculptor with bas-relief of Susan B. Anthony, photograph, ca. 1922.

Sculptor Leila Usher created this portrait for the National American Woman Suffrage Association. Courtesy of the Library of Congress.

Susan B. Anthony, National American Woman Suffrage Association medallion, Leila Usher (1859–1955), bronze, ca. 1906.

Suffrage organizations, like the National American Woman Suffrage Association, employed female artists for a variety of projects, including the design of medallions, sculptures, monuments, and posters. Courtesy of the Collection of Ronnie Lapinsky Sax.

Glass plate slides for movie theaters, ca. 1915.

Suffragists embraced new technology to get their message to a wide audience. These slides were probably made for the 1915 referendum campaign in New York and projected at movie houses to gain support for the vote. Courtesy of the Collection of Ronnie Lapinsky Sax.

ALICE PAUL AND
THE FEDERAL AMENDMENT

Alice Paul (1885–1977), a member of the Quaker faith, grew up in New Jersey. She attended college and then went to work in a settlement house on the Lower East Side of New York City. Because of her work in New York, Paul went to England in 1907 to pursue graduate studies in social work and while there, she became involved with the Women's Social and Political Union (WSPU), a militant suffrage organization founded by Emmeline Pankhurst. Paul soon participated in WSPU demonstrations and was arrested and imprisoned multiple times. She even endured forced feedings after going on hunger strikes while incarcerated. Despite these hardships in London, Paul learned how to generate interest and publicity for a cause and, in turn, how to capitalize on it.

Upon return to the United States in 1910, Paul continued her graduate work, earning a PhD in Sociology from the University at Pennsylvania. In 1912, she became involved with suffrage work full-time and was convinced the best tactic to win suffrage was through a constitutional amendment, known as the Susan B. Anthony Amendment. Working through NAWSA, Paul and Lucy Burns, a young woman from Brooklyn who was also involved with the militant British

Alice Paul sewing the National Woman's Party Flag, photograph, ca. 1916.

Alice Paul worked only for suffrage under the idea that until women could vote, they had no business working toward any other reforms. Paul believed that to force change one must put total pressure on the political party in power. After President Wilson and the Democrats won the election in 1913, Paul pressed them to make women's suffrage a national issue. At the same time, the referendum campaign was raging in New York State. Harriot Stanton Blatch and most of the other New York suffragists urged Paul to stay away from their state campaign because the Democrats were emerging as the more supportive party and the moderates did not want to put the Democratic support in jeopardy. Paul ignored them and went about her business. Dubois, *Harriot Stanton Blatch*, 187. Courtesy of the Library of Congress.

Picketing in all sorts of weather, photograph, 1917.

New York Day Picket, January 26, 1917, Silent Sentinels. Courtesy of the Library of Congress.

Official program Woman Suffrage Procession, Washington, DC, March 3, 1913.

Women from all over the county attended this parade, but there were problems when delegations from the National Association of Colored Women and Howard University's Delta Sigma Theta sorority arrived to march. Since Southern women refused to march with African American women, parade organizers tried to segregate them. According to *The Crisis* magazine, "The woman's suffrage party had a hard time settling the status of the Negroes in the Washington Parade. At first the Negro callers were received coolly at headquarters. Then they were told to register, but found that the registry clerks were usually out. Finally an order went out to segregate them in the parade, but telegrams and protests poured in and eventually the colored women marched according to their State and occupation without let or hindrance." *The Crisis*, Vol. 5, No. 6 (April 1913). Courtesy of the Library of Congress.

suffragists, were asked to head NAWSA's Congressional Committee. Paul and Burns arrived in Washington, DC, in 1913 and went right to work. They quickly found other women who also believed in a suffrage amendment (the other option was winning suffrage at the state level first), and within two months the small group organized a parade of five thousand people. With dramatic flair, Paul picked President Woodrow Wilson's inauguration day for the parade since the Capital would be filled with thousands of visitors. The parade produced a near-riot because there was little help with crowd control from the DC police. Public opinion after the parade sided with the women, and NAWSA received a great deal of attention from the event.

Fearful that militant techniques would alienate many voters, NAWSA leaders were uneasy with Paul and Burns' tactics.[29] In 1913, Paul and Burns created the Congressional Union (later called the National Woman's Party (NWP), dedicated to seeking a constitutional

Alva Vanderbilt Belmont, photograph, 1911.

New York socialite, suffragist, and multimillionaire Alva Belmont was the largest donor to Alice Paul's efforts. Courtesy of the Library of Congress.

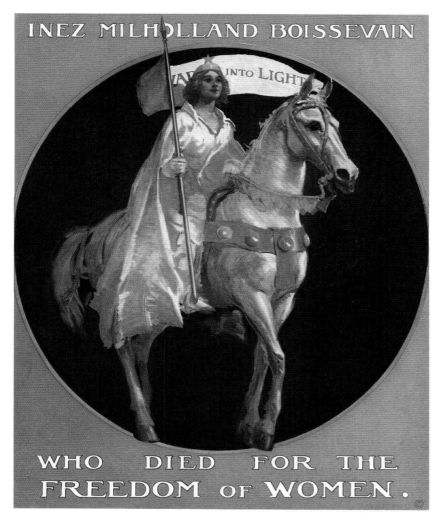

INEZ MILHOLLAND BOISSEVAIN

WHO DIED FOR THE FREEDOM OF WOMEN.

Inez Milholland, poster, 1916.

Inez Milholland was active in the National Woman's Party. When she suddenly passed away in 1916, at the age of thirty, on a suffrage tour in California, she became a martyr for the cause. The National Woman's Party and the Congressional Union immortalized Milholland on this poster, which depicts her when she led the large 1913 Washington, DC, parade. Her banner reads: "Forward, out of darkness, leave behind the night, forward out of error, forward into light." This verse was on the banner she carried at her first parade in 1911. Courtesy of the Division of Political History, National Museum of American History, Smithsonian Institution.

The National Woman's Party: What it is, What it has done, What it is doing, pamphlet, ca. 1913.

New York State Library Manuscripts and Special Collections, 324.3 N277 97-15204.

amendment at any cost. The NWP campaigned against President Wilson and other Democrats during the 1916 elections for not supporting suffrage. In 1917 they began picketing the White House—something that had never been done before. When the nation entered World War I, the NWP leaders escalated tactics to get more attention. Members of the group set banners on fire in front of the White House, climbed statues, and chained themselves to fences and a myriad of other publicity stunts. Paul and her followers were imprisoned on several occasions and subjected to police brutality, but they kept the pressure on until 1919 when the Senate passed the suffrage amendment.

After the Nineteenth Amendment, Paul continued her efforts. She was the author of and proponent of the Equal Rights Amendment in 1923, which never passed, and played a major role in ensuring women were part of the 1964 Civil Rights Act.[30] She passed away in New Jersey in 1977 at the age of ninety-two.

Some of the anti-suffrage leaders who took 1,200 people up the Hudson for their Decoration Day picnic, photograph, May 30, 1913.

(*Left to right*) Mrs. George Phillips, Mrs. K. B. Lapham, Miss Burnham, Mrs. Everett P. Wheeler, Mrs. John A. Church. Courtesy of the Library of Congress.

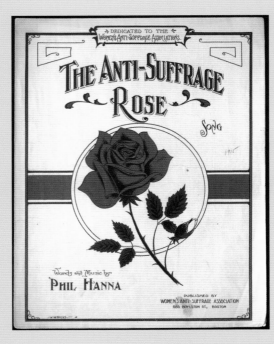

"The Anti-Suffrage Rose," sheet music, 1915.

Anti-suffragists adopted the red rose in an effort to counter the sunflowers and other yellow flowers used by the suffragists. Courtesy of the New York State Library, Manuscripts and Special Collections, SCO SC12607-130.

"Special Privileges New York Women Have Secured Under Male Suffrage," handbill, 1915.

Courtesy of the New York State Library, Manuscripts and Special Collections, SC13339.

SPECIAL PRIVILEGES
NEW YORK WOMEN HAVE SECURED UNDER MALE SUFFRAGE

Married woman not required to contribute to support of family.

Woman may work, earn money, and spend it as she pleases.

May own real and personal property and dispose of it or sell it without her husband's knowledge or consent.

Husband cannot dispose of real estate without wife's consent.

Wife cannot be required to pay husband's bills even if contracted for support of family.

Husband must pay wife's bills whether for the family or for her own personal expenses.

If wife obtains divorce, husband must pay alimony. If husband obtains divorce even through wife's fault, she pays nothing.

Wife may have millions and cut her husband off without a cent. Husband cannot cut off wife without dower right.

If husband owns home, he cannot sell or mortgage it without wife's consent. If wife owns it, she may do as she pleases with it, and without consulting him at all.

If husband fails to support wife, he may be arrested and prosecuted criminally. Wife cannot be compelled to support husband under any circumstances no matter how rich she may be, nor how poor he may become.

A father cannot by will appoint a guardian for minor children against the wishes of the mother.

All women are exempt from military service.

All women are exempt from jury duty.

WOMAN IS NOT DISCRIMINATED AGAINST BY ANY NEW YORK STATE LAW.

Vote NO on Woman Suffrage

NEW YORK STATE ASSOCIATION OPPOSED TO WOMAN SUFFRAGE,
35 West 39th Street　·　·　·　New York City

WOMEN OPPOSED TO SUFFRAGE

As long as there were women working to get suffrage passed, there were also women working to prevent it. In the mid-to-late nineteenth century, anti-suffragists or remonstrants, as they were sometimes called, based much of their reasoning on the ideology of separate spheres for men and women. Men operated in the public sphere of politics, commerce, law, and economics while women operated in the private sphere of domestic duties, child rearing, and religious education. With this line of thinking, suffrage would diminish a woman's purity and potentially harm family life. Anti-suffragists believed that the men in their life (husbands, fathers, brothers, and sons) would look out for their best interests when they went to the polls.

New York State had the most active and organized anti-suffrage activity of any state in the Union, creating the New York State Association Opposed to Woman Suffrage in 1895 and the National Association Opposed to Woman Suffrage (NAOWS) in New York City in 1911.[31] Ironically, the anti-suffrage movement followed a trajectory similar to the suffrage movement with meetings moving from parlors to larger venues; lectures on the speakers' circuit; lobbying legislators; mass-producing pamphlets, pins, and banners; and even creating publicity stunts for newspapers' attention.

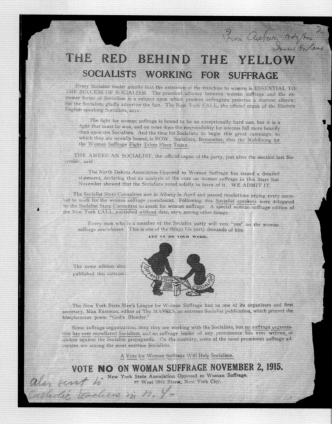

The Red Behind the Yellow, handbill, ca. 1915.

Courtesy of the New York State Library, Manuscripts and Special Collections, SC13339.

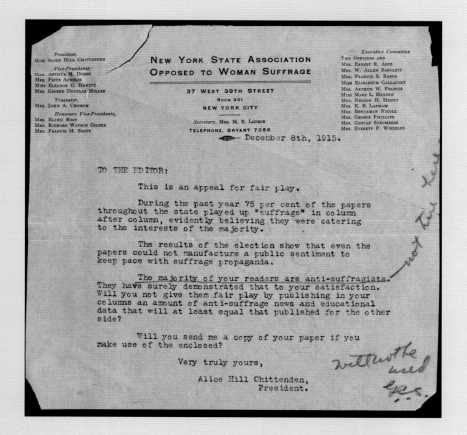

Letter to editor from Alice Chittenden, December 8, 1915.

Courtesy of the New York State Library, Manuscripts and Special Collections, SC13339.

IT MUST BE DEFEATED.

Times, February 5, 1915

The legislators of both houses in Albany, having rushed through the woman suffrage amendment in the easiest way, the question as to whether or not the women of New York State shall hereafter possess the right to vote must be decided by the male electors at the polls next election. No evasion of duty in this matter is possible. No man of voting age may shirk responsibility by ignoring the constitutional amendment ballot. A grave issue faces the men and they must meet it squarely. **The proposal is to transform the whole political and social fabric.** The position of THE TIMES on the question of woman suffrage has long been known. It is totally opposed to the extension of the suffrage on the grounds that **it would not benefit the women in any single way and would tend to disorganize society.**

Men, by their own heedlessness, have precipitated the present crisis. They must meet it. Nothing is to be gained by condemning the hasty and foolish action at Albany. Sooner or later the electorate would have been compelled to take the matter in their own hands. Now is always a good time to perform a duty. **The amendment should be defeated by an overwhelming vote.**

ISSUED BY
The New York State Association Opposed to Woman Suffrage.
37 WEST 39TH STREET,
NEW YORK CITY.

"It Must Be Defeated," NYS Association Opposed to Woman Suffrage, handbill, 1915.

Courtesy of the New York State Library, Manuscripts and Special Collections, SC13339.

After realizing a state suffrage campaign would not go away, a group of anti-suffragists (antis) from across the state convened at Sarah Amelia Cooper Hewitt's home in New York City in April 1895 and established the New York State Association Opposed to Woman Suffrage. Opposing the shenanigans of political machines, the group felt that women could serve and influence society better without getting dirty with politics and the vote. Lucy Parkman Scott served as the organization's first and longest president from 1895 to 1910, followed by Josephine Jewell Dodge (1910–1911, leaving to lead the NAOWS), Carolyn Putnam (1911–1913), and Alice Hill Chittenden (1913–1917). Antis founded auxiliary organizations across the state and worked to get their message out to men and women in the same vein as the suffragists. The antis' efforts were reaffirmed in 1915 when men across the state voted down the referendum on woman suffrage. After New York State's women won the vote in 1917, some antis went on to block the federal amendment, while some embraced the vote and became politically active.

Anti-suffrage pennant and pin, ca. 1915.

The pennant and pin presented here belonged to Charles S. Fairchild (1842–1924) and his wife, Helen Krumbhar Lincklaen (1845–1931) and are part of the Lorenzo State Historic Site collections. Fairchild was a prominent politician and the secretary of the treasury under President Grover Cleveland. He also actively worked against woman suffrage as a member of the Man Suffrage Association. Fairchild served as president of the American Constitutional League (formerly known as the Men's Anti-Suffrage Association), and in 1920, he sued US Secretary of State Charles Evans Hughes and the District of Columbia, alleging that the Nineteenth Amendment was unconstitutional. After two years of litigation, the case of *Fairchild v. Hughes* reached the United States Supreme Court, which found Fairchild had no standing to sue the government; the validity of the Nineteenth Amendment was upheld in a separate case. When Fairchild died in 1924, a leading anti-suffrage publication of the day, *The Woman Patriot*, published his eulogy. Courtesy of Lorenzo State Historic Site, Cazenovia, NY/Office of Parks, Recreation, and Historic Preservation, pennant, LO.1986.2934, pin, LO.1974.1105..

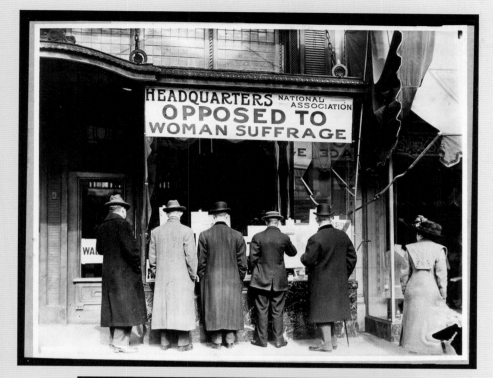

National Anti-Suffrage Association Headquarters, New York City, photograph, 1911.

Courtesy of the Library of Congress.

"Think Over These Facts," broadside, 1915.

This broadside was probably made for the Massachusetts 1915 campaign. Courtesy of the New York State Library, Manuscripts and Special Collections, SC13339.

ANTI
SUFFRAGE

BASE BALL SCHEDULE BOOK

1915

Published by
Women's Anti-Suffrage Associa[tion]
37 WEST THIRTY-NINTH ST[REET]
NEW YORK.

Miss Alice Hill Chittenden, President.
Mrs. M. E. Loomis, Secr[etary]

WOMAN SUFFRAGE
SHOULD BE DEFEATED
BECAUSE—

1. The ballot is not a right, but a privilege that may be granted or withheld as the State deems for its best interests.

2. Wherever woman suffrage has been tried it has resulted in a loss to women and a loss to the State.

3. The granting of the franchise to women forces women into politics, and the political woman has proved herself a menace to society, to the home and to the State.

4. No electorate has existed, or ever can exist, which cannot execute its own laws.

5. Men and women were created and designed by nature to work in different spheres for the common good.

6. The ballot would deprive woman of her non-partisan power through which she is able to do for the State what man is unable to do because of political party ties.

7. The demand for the ballot for women in America comes from a very small proportion of American womanhood, artificially stimulated by women from other countries.

8. The temperamental difference between men and women makes an equal footing in political life an impossibility.

2

JOHN M[cGRAW]
Manager N. Y. Nationa[l]

GIANTS A[T HOME]

April 14, 15, 16..........
April 17, 19, 20, 21......
April 27, 28, 29, 30......
May 11, 12, 13, 14.......
May 15, 17, 18, 19.......
May 20, 21, 22, 24.......

GIANTS AT HOME.
(Continued)

May 25, 26, 27, 28	St. Louis
May 29, 30, 31	Brooklyn
June 22, 23, 24	Philadelphia
June 25, 26, 28, 29	Boston
July 8, 9, 10, 12	Cincinnati
July 13, 14, 15, 16	Chicago
July 17, 19, 20, 21	St. Louis
July 22, 23, 24, 26	Pittsburgh
August 17	Brooklyn
August 18, 19, 20	Cincinnati
August 21, 23, 24	St. Louis
August 25, 26, 27	Chicago
August 28, 30, 31	Pittsburgh
September 1, 2, 3, 4	Philadelphia
September 6, 6, 7	Boston
September 29, 30, October 1, 2	Brooklyn

DO YOU BELIEVE IN WOMEN WHO HOLD THIS VIEW?

Dr. Anna Howard Shaw, president of the National American Woman's Suffrage Association, in a signed statement in the New York *Evening Post* for February 25, 1915.

"I believe in woman suffrage whether all women vote or no women vote; whether all women vote right or all women vote wrong; whether women will love their husbands after they vote or forsake them; whether they will neglect their children or never have any children."

4

CHRISTY MATHEWSON,
"Matty," "Big Six," with "Giants."

GIANTS ABROAD:

April 22, 23, 24, 26	Brooklyn
May 1, 3, 4, 5	Philadelphia
May 6, 7, 8, 10	Boston
June 1, 2, 3	Boston
June 5, 6, 7, 8	Philadelphia
June 9, 10, 11, 12	St. Louis
June 13, 14, 15, 16	Cincinnati
June 17, 18, 19	Pittsburgh
June 30, July 1, 2, 3	Brooklyn
July 5, 6, 7	Philadelphia
July 27	Pittsburgh

(Over)

5

Anti-Suffrage Baseball Schedule Book, 1915.

Courtesy of the New York State Library, Manuscripts and Special Collections, SC13339.

GIANTS ABROAD.
(Continued)

July 28, 29, 30, 31	Chicago
August 1, 2, 3, 4	St. Louis
August 5, 6, 7	Cincinnati
August 8, 10, 11, 12	Pittsburgh
August 13, 14, 15	Brooklyn
September 8, 9, 10	Philadelphia
September 11, 12, 13, 14	Cincinnati
September 16, 17, 18	Pittsburgh
September 19, 20, 21	Chicago
September 23, 25, 26	St. Louis
October 4, 5, 6, 7	Boston

WOMAN'S PRIVILEGES IN NEW YORK STATE

Married women not required to contribute to support of family.

Woman may work, earn money and spend it as she pleases.

May own real and personal property and dispose of it or sell it without her husband's knowledge or consent.

Husband cannot dispose of real estate without wife's consent.

Wife cannot be required to pay husband's bills even for support of family.

Husband must pay wife's bills, whether for the family or for her own personal expenses.

If wife obtains divorce husband must pay alimony; if husband obtains divorce, even through wife's fault, she pays nothing.

Wife may have millions and cut husband off without a cent; husband cannot cut off wife without dower right.

If husband owns home he cannot mortgage or sell it without wife's consent; if wife owns it she may do as she pleases without consulting him.

If husband fails to support wife he may be arrested and prosecuted criminally; wife cannot be compelled to support husband under any circumstances, no matter how rich she may be or how poor he may become.

A father cannot by will appoint a guardian for minor children against the wishes of the mother.

All women are exempt from military service and jury duty.

6

GEORGE BURNS,
Left Field, "Giants."

NATIONAL LEAGUE CLUB
RECORDS, 1914.
BATTING.

Club.	G.	AB.	R.	H.	T. B.	PC.
Brooklyn	154	5,162	622	1,386	1,831	.269
New York	156	5,146	672	1,363	1,793	.265
Philadelphia	154	5,110	651	1,345	1,846	.263
Boston	158	5,206	657	1,307	1,745	.251
St. Louis	157	5,046	558	1,249	1,681	.248
Chicago	156	5,050	605	1,229	1,699	.243
Cincinnati	157	4,991	530	1,178	1,496	.236
Pittsburgh	158	5,145	503	1,197	1,557	.233

(Over)

7

NATIONAL LEAGUE CLUB.
RECORDS, 1914.
(Continued)
FIELDING.

Club.	G.	PO.	A.	E.	PC.
Pittsburgh	158	4,211	2,085	223	.966
St. Louis	157	4,271	2,056	239	.964
Boston	158	4,222	2,162	246	.963
New York	156	4,165	2,032	254	.961
Brooklyn	154	4,112	1,924	248	.961
Cincinnati	157	4,157	2,097	314	.952
Chicago	156	4,150	1,918	310	.951
Philadelphia	154	4,120	2,016	324	.956

SOME VIEWS OF SUFFRAGE.

Hon. Elihu Root—"I am opposed to the granting of suffrage to women because I believe that it would be a loss to women, to all women and to every woman, and because I believe it would be an injury to the State and every man and woman in the State."

Cardinal Gibbons—"I am unalterably opposed to woman suffrage, always have been and always will be. I will continue to urge that nothing be done which will take woman out of her proper sphere."

Senator Hinman—"I have not changed my mind upon the merits of this question. It is, in my judgment, a part of the propaganda of today, which is a fundamental error, that all things can be accomplished by law instead of by the development of individual character, the improvement of the integrity of the family and the moral status of the community."

Miss Ida Tarbell—"The best laws in regard to women and children have been passed in States where there is no woman suffrage. I don't like to see our women get mixed up in politics because they're just the same old partisan politics. Women can do something better."

8

"WILD BILL" DONOVAN,
Manager N. Y. Americans ("The Yankees.")

YANKEES AT HOME.

April 22, 23, 24, 26	Washington
May 1, 3, 4, 5	Philadelphia
May 6, 7, 8, 10	Boston
June 1, 2, 3	Boston
June 4, 5, 7, 8	Detroit
June 9, 10, 11	Chicago
June 12, 14, 15, 16	St. Louis
June 17, 18, 19	Cleveland

(Over)

9

"Mr. Voter, You Do Not Want Woman Suffrage," Association Opposed to Woman Suffrage, Utica Auxiliary, handbill, ca. 1912.

Anti-suffragists often printed their handbills on pink paper. Courtesy of the Clinton Historical Society.

"Woman Suffrage Has Been Defeated," handbill, 1917.

Courtesy of the New York State Library, Manuscripts and Special Collections, SC13339.

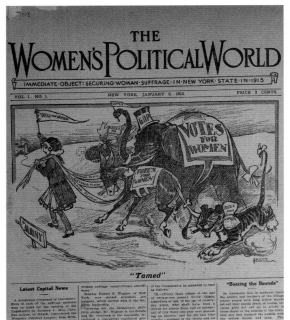

Women's Political World, newspaper, vol. 1, no. 1, January 8, 1913.

Harriot Stanton Blatch and her Women's Political Union began publication of the *Women's Political World* in January 1913. The biweekly newspaper focused on politics but also reported on suffrage events, labor activities, and other issues of the day. Courtesy of the New York State Library, Manuscripts and Special Collections, 324.3 fW872 1913-1914.

Harriot Stanton Blatch in Albany, photograph, 1912.

Harriot Stanton Blatch (*left*), Mrs. Townsend (*right*), and the Women's Political Union delegation marching up the New York State Capitol steps in Albany on March 12, 1912. Blatch and the WPU were in Albany to obtain signatures from a majority of assemblymen in an effort to bring the suffrage measure to the assembly. The *New York Times* quoted Blatch the evening before the signature deadline: "We now lack only thirteen of the Constitutional majority of seventy-six . . . and we'll get those before we go to sleep or we'll make the lives of these people miserable." Courtesy of Coline Jenkins, Elizabeth Cady Stanton Family.

GEARING UP FOR THE NEW YORK STATE REFERENDUM: THE POLITICS OF SUFFRAGE

Holding meetings and conventions gained support from women, but if suffrage was to win in New York State, politicians needed to support it, too. Beginning in 1910, Harriot Stanton Blatch and her Women's Political Union (WPU) began a campaign to force the state legislature to pass a bill authorizing a referendum on suffrage. Blatch set up offices in Albany, hired a lobbyist, and worked with a small group of women to put pressure on legislators. By the end of 1912, the WPU had persuaded the three major parties (Democrats, Republicans, and the Progressives) to adopt a suffrage plank. On January 27, 1913, both houses of the legislature signed legislation eliminating the word "male" and enfranchising "every citizen of the age of twenty-one years . . ." However, even more difficult than persuading the politicians to favor suffrage was organizing a movement that would convince the men of New York State to vote for suffrage.

Despite the longevity of the suffrage fight in New York, it was considered a difficult state to win. The geography worked against unification as there were many rural areas that were sparsely populated and several large cities, including New York City, which had more people than many states. It had a foreign population of 2.5 million out of a total of 9 million people. Traditionally, foreign-born men did not favor suffrage. Owners of large industries in the state did not want women

to vote so they could keep wages low. Additionally, the state had several "political" machines—both Republican and Democrat—that held a huge influence over its voters and were tepid about suffrage.[32]

> In the next two years we must convert the voters to the fundamental ideals of democracy, to a belief in the basis of a republican government. . . . In New York we have a far bigger population to reach. In New York we have a far older civilization, with its deeply rooted prejudices to move. We have the biggest German city in the nation, the biggest Jewish city to convert from its Germanic and Hebraic attitude toward women. We have the biggest corporations of the United States, with their fears of ideals of women, to overcome. We have the most highly developed political machines of any state, and bipartisan agreements and distrust of new voters to outweigh. If New York can be won for democracy, any state can be won.
>
> —Harriot Stanton Blatch, *Chicago Tribune*, March 13, 1913

Blatch and the WPU escort a New York State legislator to a referendum vote, photograph, 1911.

Harriot Stanton Blatch's Women's Political Union embraced more militant tactics and sought the support of upper-class women in New York City and immigrant and working women in upstate New York. In addition, the WPU had a huge war chest to support the cause. One of the chief fundraisers for the WPU was Vira Whitehouse, who was adept at raising large sums of money quickly. This image from 1911 depicts a bold move by Blatch (*on the left*) leading a NYS legislator, by the arm, to a vote on the suffrage referendum. Courtesy of Coline Jenkins, Elizabeth Cady Stanton Family.

These letters are from leaders in New York State suffrage groups to the Constitutional Convention Suffrage Committee chairman, Patrick Cullinan. Amendments to the New York State Constitution must be passed by two consecutive legislatures. The measure is then placed on the ballot in the next general election. Courtesy of the New York State Archives.

Letter, Harriot Stanton Blatch
to Patrick Cullinan, June 29, 1915.

VOTES FOR WOMEN
EMPIRE STATE CAMPAIGN COMMITTEE

CHAIRMAN: MRS. CARRIE CHAPMAN CATT

SECRETARY: MRS. CHARLES P. HOWLAND   TREASURER: MRS. CHARLES L. TIFFANY

NEW YORK STATE WOMAN SUFFRAGE ASSN.   WOMAN SUFFRAGE PARTY   EQUAL FRANCHISE SOCIETY
MRS. RAYMOND BROWN, PRESIDENT   MISS MARY GARRETT HAY, CHAIRMAN   MRS. HOWARD MANSFIELD, PRESIDENT

COLLEGIATE LEAGUE   MEN'S LEAGUE FOR WOMAN SUFFRAGE
MRS. CHARLES L. TIFFANY, PRESIDENT   JAMES LEES LAIDLAW, PRESIDENT

CHAIRMEN OF SECTIONS
ART PUBLICITY: MRS. JOHN W. ALEXANDER   ORGANIZATION: MRS. CARRIE CHAPMAN CATT   LITERATURE: MRS. HOWARD MANSFIELD
PRESS: MRS. SIMON FLEXNER   FINANCE: MRS. WARNER LEEDS   PUBLIC HEARINGS: MISS HARRIET MAY MILLS

CHAIRMEN OF CAMPAIGN DISTRICTS
2ND: MRS. RAYMOND BROWN   6TH: MRS. HELEN B. OWENS, ITHACA   9TH: MRS. CARL OSTERHELD, YONKERS
3RD: MISS LEILA STOTT, ALBANY   7TH: MRS. A. C. CLEMENT, ROCHESTER   10TH: MRS. GORDON NORRIE, STAATSBURG
4TH: MRS. F. G. PADDOCK, MALONE   8TH: MRS. F. J. SHULER, BUFFALO   11TH: MRS. GEORGE NOTMAN, KEENE VALLEY
5TH: MISS HARRIET MAY MILLS, SYRACUSE   12TH: MISS LUCY C. WATSON, UTICA

MAIN HEADQUARTERS
303 FIFTH AVENUE
NEW YORK

TELEPHONE MADISON SQUARE 6370

May 11, 1915.

Hon. Patrick W. Cullinan,
Chairman Suffrage Committee,
Constitutional Convention,
Albany, New York.

My dear Sir,

    I enclose a copy of a letter which I am sending to all members of the Suffrage Committee, and which speaks for itself. I was sorry not to have seen you after the hearing, but I did not want to take more time of a busy man.

    I believe the Parsons resolution will clear the field so far as our question is concerned, provided at the end of the session the order is given which Mr. Root suggested and said he would endorse.

    We saw several members of the convention, among them Mr. Hinman and Senator Wagner, and while they were unfamiliar with the Parsons resolution, they both said they wanted to do everything possible to get the measure clearly before the voters, and I believe the resolution will pass the convention unanimously if recommended by the Suffrage Committee.

    I understand that Mr. Louis Marshall is proposing today an amendment to the Constitution which he believes will cover the exigencies of the case. It, however, in no wise conflicts with the Parsons resolution. We therefore hope that the Suffrage Committee will recommend the Parsons Resolution and will give the Convention an opportunity to pass upon it.

    I will esteem it a very great favor if you will advise me if any matter comes up which makes it seem desirable for any of us to be present in Albany. Some of our women will come up this week in any case. A letter or telegram can always find me at 303 Fifth Avenue, or someone who represents me.

Yours truly,

Carrie Chapman Catt

Letter, Carrie Chapman Catt
to Patrick Cullinan, May 11, 1915.

Votes for Women
Women's Political Union

OFFICERS
HARRIOT STANTON BLATCH, PRESIDENT
DORA G. S. HAZARD, VICE-PRESIDENT
EUNICE DANA BRANNAN, TREASURER

Telephones { Bryant 7754 / Bryant 7755 }

HEADQUARTERS
25 WEST FORTY-FIFTH STREET
NEW YORK CITY

EXECUTIVE BOARD
LOUISE BEIDERHASE
ANNA CONSTABLE
NORA BLATCH deFOREST
FRANCES F. EINSTEIN
ROSE PERKINS HALE
FLORENCE KELLEY
CAROLINE LEXOW BABCOCK
ALICE J. G. PERKINS
ETHEL R. PEYSER
MARGARET WILSON REEVE
ELIZABETH SELDEN ROGERS

ALBERTA M. HILL
EXECUTIVE SECRETARY

June 29, 1915.

Hon. Patrick W. Cullinan,
    Albany, N.Y.
My dear Mr. Cullinan:

    After consultation, Mrs. Carrie Chapman Catt and I have concluded that the Suffrage Committee has already given us so much time and attention that there is no need of our appearing at the suffrage hearing on Wednesday to discuss further the Franchot and Eisner amendments. It is quite clear to the committee, I am sure, what problem they have to solve. Without exception, I am sure every member of the Suffrage Committee wishes to fulfill the pledges of the Republican and Democratic parties in regard to putting an unequivocal suffrage amendment before the voters on November 2nd. We would object, of course, to Mr. Eisner's amendment, as it in no way solves the difficulty that confronts the relation of woman suffrage to the Constitutional Convention and would result in placing two amendments on woman suffrage before the voters at the autumn election. You yourself, and every other leader in the Constitutional Convention, fully recognize that this would be extremely unfair, as it would confuse and divide our forces.

    The solution which the Franchot amendment offers, now that Mr. Franchot has amended his proposal so that the legislative wording is not used, is as satisfactory to us as the Marshall amendment. If the choice lay between the Franchot and Marshall amendments I myself would incline to a preference for the Marshall amendment. The difficulty in our case is caused by Section 3 Article XIV, and as Mr. Marshall attacks the difficulty at its very source, his amendment seems the better and the more logical of the two. However, as the principle of both the amendments is the same and as their wording is absolutely satisfactory to us in that it will cause no misunderstanding among the voters, we feel that we can leave in the hands of the Suffrage Committee the decision in this very important matter.

    Believe me,

HSB/L
Dictated but not read

Respectfully yours,

Harriot Stanton Blatch

Result of Suffrage Canvass.
Watkins, N.Y., May 29, '15.

Election Districts and Streets.	Total Canvassed		For Suffrage		Opposed or Unconverted		Per Cent in Favor	
	Men	Women	Men	Women	Men	Women	Men	Women
Dis No. 2. 1st, 2d, 3d, 4th, 5th, 9th & 10th. Streets between Decatur & Magee St.	36	68	22	45	14	23	61⅕%	66+%
Dis No. 3. 9th & 10th. Streets between Franklin and Decatur.	14	27	10	20	4	7	71⅗%	74+%
Dis No. 1. 1st, 2d, 3d, 4th, 5th, between Franklin and Decatur	16	26	12	16	4	10	75%	61.5%
Other Election Districts and Duplicates. (Had signed before)	13	5	10	5	3	0	76%	100%
Total for the Day	79	126	54	86	25	40	68⅗%	68.25%

More opposition was discovered than usual to the fact that First, Second and Third extend into a section of the village occupied [...]ions and other poor people who do little reading.
J. Norton. Sec.

Results of suffrage canvass, Watkins, New York, May 29, 1915.

Residents of Watkins Glen, New York (Schuyler County) were canvassed on May 29, 1915, about suffrage. The majorities of both men and women were in favor of suffrage, however only 42.4 percent of the male voters in Schuyler County voted for suffrage at the polls in November that year. Courtesy of the New York State Archives.

214 Madison Ave., Watkins, N.Y., June 7, '15.

Suffrage Committee,

Constitutional Convention,

State Capitol, Albany, N.Y.

Gentlemen. -- Understanding that a letter, or letters, have been sent you containing the unproved assertion that "women do not want to vote", I respectfully submit for your consideration, the inclosed statement of one day's canvass for suffrage in this village.

The record for this one day is given because heretofore no exact count of those opposed and unconverted has been kept and also because we had a larger force of women making the canvass. We are usually much more successful. For instance, in one day's trip in the country from Watkins to Hector and Logan and return, eighty-seven people out of about one hundred signed the suffrage slips.

We now have a total enrollment of 1665 in the county. Three of the election districts have about thirty per cent of the registered voters.

If an attempt to side-track this issue and trick the women should be contemplated by any of the gentlemen of the Convention, this tendency should be offset by the fact that such an attempt would likewise trick the voters for our record indicates that a majority of the men are in favor as well as a majority of the women.

We ask that your Convention take such action as will make the suffrage amendment, when ratified, a part of the NEW Constitution.

Very respectfully,

Jessie Norton

Sec.

Assembly District League for Woman Suffrage, Schuyler

Letter, Jessie Norton to Suffrage Committee Constitutional Convention, June 7, 1915.

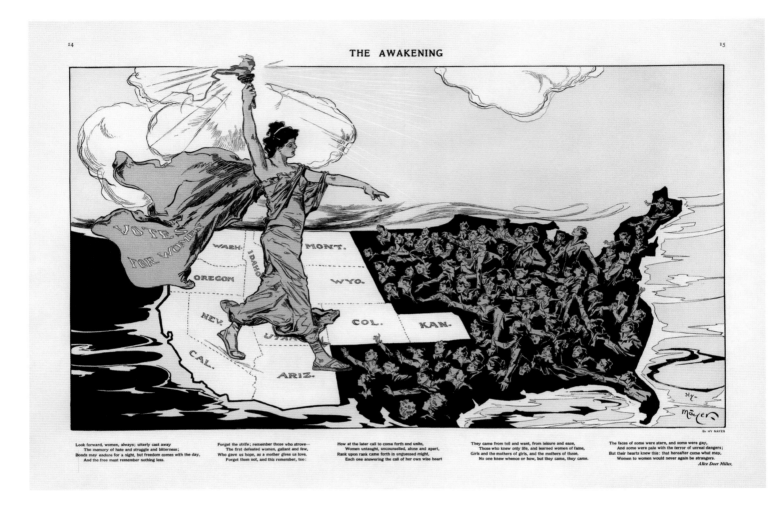

"The Awakening," illustration, Henry Mayer (1868–1954), in *Puck*, v. 77, no. 1981, February 20, 1915.

The cartoon appeared in *Puck* magazine during the 1915 New York State suffrage referendum campaign. The illustration shows a torch-bearing female with a cape labeled "Votes for Women" moving from the West, where women already had the vote, to the East, where women were still in the dark but reaching out toward the light and freedom. Printed below the cartoon is a poem by Alice Duer Miller. Courtesy of the PJ Mode Collection, Cornell University Library.

"THESE MODEL FAMILIES"

ROMANCE, MARRIAGE, AND FAMILY IN THE NEW YORK WOMAN SUFFRAGE MOVEMENT

Jessica Derleth

Binghamton University

In a 1914 interview published by the *New York Times*, William T. Sedgwick, a professor of biology and public health, warned Americans to beware of the "very masculine women, these mistakes of nature, aided and abetted by their counterparts, the feminine men, who are largely responsible for the feminist movement." Particularly insidious, Sedgwick warned, was the way in which "these 'half-women'" proposed the "total destruction of wifehood and the home" by demanding the right to vote.[i] Although many opposed the expansion of the franchise for a variety of reasons, anti-suffragists joined Sedgwick in arguing that the "paramount function of woman is motherhood" and the responsibility of the ballot would distract women from the private sphere.[ii] This lack of respect for the "natural" roles of the sexes, anti-suffragists insisted, indicated a level of sexual deviancy that jeopardized the health of the nation—rooted in marriage, reproduction, and child-rearing.[iii] By the turn of the twentieth century, suffragists in New York (and around the nation) began to acknowledge and directly combat these charges of sexual deviancy, abnormality, and danger. Suffragists redirected the public dialogue on sexuality and female enfranchisement by arguing that they were, by and large, happily married, monogamous, and proud to bear and raise children. Thus, many suffragists embraced normative understandings of romance, marriage, and family to prove their fitness for enfranchisement and full citizenship.

Suffrage proponents and opponents were frequently embroiled in debate about the relationship between voting women and sexual morality. Anti-suffragists, for instance, argued that the "masculine women" and "feminine men" who supported female enfranchisement were childless and barren, unhappy in their marital lives, advocated polygamy, and practiced free love. Worse yet, anti-suffragists predicted, the expansion of the franchise would ultimately destroy manly chivalry and feminine modesty, increase divorce, and lower the quality and prevalence of marriage on a national level. In a 1909 sermon at Carnegie Hall in New York City, for instance, preacher Charles Parkhurst referred to prominent local suffragists as members of the "migratory sisterhood" who committed "tandem polygamy" by divorcing one husband then quickly marrying another.[iv] These "little creatures" and "freaks," a disgusted Parkhurst argued, were allowed to sit on suffrage platforms even though they thought nothing of changing husbands, moving from one lover to the next.[v] Anti-suffragists also warned that suffrage posed a threat to all women, claiming states that enacted female enfranchisement suffered from broken homes, degraded women, demoralized men, low marriage rates, high divorce rates, and an overall decline in monogamy.[vi] Suffragists at both the national and state level directly refuted these "loathsome untruths."[vii] In a 1915 pamphlet published by the Empire State Campaign Committee, for example, Carrie Chapman Catt argued that "no leader of a suffrage association" had ever "expressed opinions not in accord of established codes of morals."[viii] In fact, Catt insisted, any officer found supporting free love or the abolition of marriage "would be promptly voted out of office." The suffrage movement, she argued, "has been instituted and furthered by the desire of women to dignify the home, to strengthen the family ties, [and] to uplift the standard of morals."[ix]

New York suffragists directly confronted charges of sex radicalism and marital discord by using their own lives as practical examples: they testified to the happiness of their marriages, avowed deep commitment to monogamy, and explained why several suffragists remained unmarried. Some suffragists opened their personal lives to scrutiny, pointing to their own homes as evidence that romantic harmony could coexist with women's rights activism. Mary Coleman, a resident of New York City, testified that she refused to force her fiancé to "promise to uphold the suffragette doctrines" because she was opposed to "trying to henpeck a man." Instead Coleman admitted she would "marry him anyhow, and take chances on converting him afterward," because she was "too strong an advocate of marriage" to do "anything that would militate" against it.[x] Suffrage organizations also publicly promoted the image of marital harmony within suffrage households. In 1915, for instance, the "Fifth Avenue Suffrage Shop" in New York City hosted its first ever "Married Couples' Day," where four sets of husbands and wives made speeches "to prove that they were happy though married and suffragists." Eugen Boissevain, husband of Inez Milholland Boissevain, took to the podium on "Married Couples' Day" to demonstrate that women who wanted to vote made good life partners: " 'How do I like being married to a suffragist?' he asked, 'I like it so much that I am sorry for a man married to an anti.' "[xi] Joining him on the platform was Everett Colby, James Lees Laidlaw, and William Curtis Demorest, who offered themselves as evidence of content suffrage husbands. Suffrage spouses also went on tour together, demonstrating

"Suffrage Babies and 'Movie' Teas Arrive," *New York Tribune*, May 17, 1914.

their commitment to one another as well as the expansion of the franchise.[xii] Thus, even though some suffragists offered pointed critiques of marriage and the family—especially women's rights to property, wages, and child guardianship—many insisted that the clear majority of suffragists were strong advocates of marriage.[xiii]

Along with demonstrating their commitment to marriage, suffragists pledged their devotion to bearing and raising children. Such assurances were made necessary by claims that voting was antithetical to motherhood. Emblematic of this was a pamphlet issued by the New York State Association Opposed to Woman Suffrage that said that the "paramount function of woman is motherhood" and "the influence of political life cannot be useful in developing" the "special function of motherhood."[xiv] New York suffragists responded to anti-suffrage claims about the incompatibility of motherhood and politics through such popular mediums as speeches and pamphlets. Yet they also developed a sensational display of suffrage reproduction, the suffrage baby show. Noticing such events in 1911, the journalist Ethel Lloyd Patterson asked readers, "What is a suffrage baby? Maybe you think the answer is, 'A cross between a paradox and a myth.'" Patterson further predicted that many readers "picture[d] the suffrage baby as a whimpering, uncared-for little mite, hungry enough to eat suffrage buttons off his mama's necktie." Patterson happily reported, however, that the Woman Suffrage Party in New York City was "going to show you what a suffrage baby really is" with the "real Suffrage Baby Show."[xv] Prizes and competitions—such as one for the finest sets of twins and another for the mother with the largest family—publicly celebrated the reproductive capacity of suffragists. A Kansas newspaper reporting on the event promised that the baby show would "refute the arguments of the antis that the suffragists do not give to the commonwealth the due number of babies."[xvi] Such baby shows were not unique to New York. Suffrage babies in Virginia, for example, "bore off all the honors in the Better Babies Contest."[xvii] Suffragists in Illinois planned baby shows to "prove they can raise children" and that they had "large families."[xviii] Pennsylvania suffragists also hosted a similar show to prove "how well suffrage babies are taken care of."[xix] And suffragists were also quick to display children in states where women already had the vote, arguing that women with the ballot had more children and were able to care for them better because of their ability to directly influence legislation.[xx]

In addition to baby shows, New York newspapers readily printed pictures of local suffrage children, often furnished by suffragists eager to prove their success as wives and mothers. Sometimes suffrage children caught the attention of newspapers because of their presence at parades and speaking events. Newspapers in 1910, for example, reported with anticipation on a suffrage parade planned for New York City that included carriages and floats with " 'suffrage babies' to show that suffragists do not neglect rearing families."[xxi] By 1914, the *New York Tribune* remarked on the number of "suffrage babies, big and little, [who] are not unaccustomed to appear[ing] in parades," from Sheellagh Stone, who traveled the parade route in her mother's arms at six weeks old, to Serena Kearns, who "march[ed] with all the dignity of her seven years."[xxii] Even when there was not a parade or public spectacle, newspapers printed the names and images of suffrage children. The *Brooklyn Daily Eagle*, for example, printed eighteen pictures of suffrage children in 1915 after Long Island suffragist Edna B. Kearns publicly refuted the argument that "suffragists were too busy trying to convert voters to have children or to pay much attention to the few they have." To prove that suffragists did, indeed, bear children, Kearns arranged for the newspaper to print pictures of suffrage babies: "Those shown on this page are only a few of those she sent in," the newspaper reported, "For several days in *The Eagle* office it fairly rained pictures of all sorts of chubby 'suffrage babies.'"[xxiii] A similar article, printed in the *New York Tribune* in 1914, sought out suffrage children to test the veracity of anti-suffrage claims about "free love, the downfall of the home and no babies." The resulting images and lists of children supported suffragist arguments that "the votes-for-women ranks not only believe in babies but [also] possess large families of them."[xxiv] By furnishing the names and images of their children, suffragists declared that they possessed "these model homes" and were happy to bear and raise children. With such public displays of their fruitful marriages and families, suffragists worked to dispel the image of the free lover or spinster, proving that female enfranchisement was not inimical to traditional understandings of child-rearing and family.

Whether they focused on free love, spinsters, or henpecked husbands, anti-suffragists and suffragists were embroiled in discussions about gender, sexuality, and citizenship at the turn of the twentieth century. Anti-suffragists warned that women's rights were a disruption to the proper relationship between the sexes and spearheaded by men and women who did not abide by socially acceptable understandings of sex, reproduction, or marriage. In defending themselves, many suffragists embraced normative understandings of sex and gender to prove their fitness for enfranchisement and their right to full citizenship. In doing so, suffragists claimed that female enfranchisement would result in a more balanced electorate where husband and wife worked cooperatively for the betterment of the home and the nation.[xxv] They also argued that industrialization and urbanization removed many of the duties of wives and mothers from the home and placed them under government control. Thus, embracing maternal rhetoric allowed suffragists to insist that women had natural expertise in such areas as education, child care, sanitation, and food production. Building on popular ideas about sex, reproduction, and marriage, suffragists argued that women needed to vote alongside their husbands because they worked together to rear a family, nourish the home, promote good morals, and strengthen the nation.[xxvi]

Notes

i. George MacAdam, "Feminist Revolutionary Principle Is Biological Bosh," *New York Times*, 18 January 1914. For reactions, see "Indignant Feminists Reply to Prof. Sedgwick," *New York Times*, 15 February 1914.

ii. Mrs. William Forse Scott and Bertha Lane Scott, *Woman's Relation to Government* (New York State Association Opposed to Woman Suffrage, 1904).

iii. Many of these anti-suffrage arguments about violating natural roles reflected beliefs about women and men existing in separate spheres: men had a natural, God-given duty to work in the public sphere, while women had similar obligations to the private realm of home and children. The separate spheres ideology was exactly that, an ideal that some Americans upheld as the ideal way for men and women to live in relation to one another. Historians have increasingly understood separate spheres to be a rhetorical construction, a metaphor for complex gendered class, rhetorically constructed, racially varied, and reciprocally constructed power relations.

iv. "Society Outside the Capital," *Washington Post*, 29 November 1909.

v. "They're So Unkind to Men," *Kansas City Times*, 26 November 1909; "Sex Relations Merely Animal Under Suffragettes' Creed," *Detroit Free Press*, 26 November 1909. Though Parkhurst did not appear to reference a suffragist by name, some newspapers claimed his remarks were directed toward Alva Belmont. See "Women Angered: Mrs. O.H.P. Belmont Replies to Parkhurst Attack: Calls Doctor Uncharitable: Denounces Sermon against Woman Suffrage, in Which Preacher Spoke of Her Having Secured a Divorce," *Lebanon Daily News*, 26 November 1909. For a direct suffrage response to Parkhurst, see Henry Frank, *A Plea for Woman Suffrage* (New York: unknown publisher, 1911).

vi. Charles Edwin Tibbles, *Doctrines of Woman Suffrage and Monogamous Marriage Antagonistic* (unknown publisher, 1913).

vii. "Suffrage," *Berkshire County Eagle*, 14 July 1915, Susan B. Anthony Ephemera Collection, Clippings, Vol. 19, Huntington Library.

viii. Carrie Chapman Catt, *To the Men and Women of New York* (New York: Empire State Campaign Committee, 1915), 1, National American Woman Suffrage Association Records, 1894–1922, Box 6, New York Public Library. Though Catt maintained that "free love is not and never has been the tenet of suffragists . . . [and] I have met no 'free lovers' among the ranks of the suffrage movement," she also acknowledged that some individuals who supported suffrage also had contrary views about "future morals" (in other words, some persons who supported suffrage also supported free love). See "Society Won't Lose Decency by Suffrage," *Lincoln Daily News*, 21 July 1914.

ix. Catt, *To the Men and Women of New York*, 2.

x. "Suffragette Won't Henpeck Husband Who Will 'Do Her Voting' for Her," *Evening World*, 8 December 1908. Though suffragists pointed to their own lives as proof that suffrage and marriage could coexist, they often downplayed how their relationships were unique. Carrie Chapman Catt, for example, "set as a precondition for accepting George Catt's proposal" that she have the independence to pursue her career in the suffrage movement for at least one-third of each year. See Robert Booth Fowler and Spencer Jones, "Carrie Chapman Catt and the Last Years of the Struggle for Woman Suffrage: 'The Winning Plan,'" in *Votes for Women: The Struggle for Suffrage Revisited*, ed. Jean H. Baker (New York: Oxford University Press, 2002), 132.

xi. "Suffrage Husbands Praise Their Wives," *New York Times*, February 25, 1915. See also: "Novelty in Suffrage Week," *New York Times*, 22 February 1915.

xii. "A Column about Suffrage," *Brooklyn Daily Eagle*, 3 August 1912; "Mrs. James Lees Laidlaw," *Daily Herald*, 20 February 1914; "Members of Franchise Body to Aid Red Cross," *Indianapolis News*, 14 November 1917.

xiii. See Ellen Carol Dubois, *Woman Suffrage and Women's Rights* (New York: New York University Press, 1998), 37, 69–80. Historians have argued that many women's rights activists put aside a broader range of reform concerns under the belief that the ballot would allow women to improve "marital inequality, unfair divorce laws, wage inequality, and intemperance." Alison M. Parker, "The Case for Reform Antecedents for the Woman's Rights Movement," in *Votes for Women: The Struggle for Suffrage Revisited*, ed. Jean H. Baker (Oxford: Oxford University Press, 2002), 23.

xiv. Scott and Scott, *Woman's Relation to Government*, 7–11.

xv. Ethel Lloyd Patterson, "New York to See Suffragette Baby Show to Prove Cause Not Inimical to Family," *Evening World*, 14 September 1911.

xvi. "Suffragist Babies on View," *Evening Kansan Republican*, 23 September 1911.

xvii. "Letters from the Leagues," *Virginia Suffrage News*, Vol. 1, No. 2 (November 1914): 14.

xiii. "Plan Suffrage Baby Show," *New York Times*, 26 November 1911; "Suffrage Baby Show in Chicago," *The Eagle*, 7 December 1911.

xix. "Franchise League Notes," *Indianapolis News*, 24 April 1915.

xx. "Suffrage Babies Best on Earth," *Mount Carmel Item*, 14 June 1915; "Results of Equal Suffrage" (Equal Suffrage League of Virginia, 191–?), Women's Suffrage Ephemera Collection, Folder 1, Bryn Mawr College Library.

xxi. "Women Are to Parade: Suffragists Are to Prove That They Do Not Neglect Homes," *Ogden Standard*, 30 July 1910; "Suffragettes Will Parade," *Pittston Gazette*, 30 July 1910.

xxii. "Suffrage Babies and 'Movie' Teas Arrive," *New York Tribune*, 17 May 1914.

xxiii. "Here Are the Kind of 'Suffrage Babies' They Have on Long Island," *Brooklyn Daily Eagle*, 1 November 1915.

xxiv. "Suffrage Babies and 'Movie' Teas Arrive: Suffragists Refute the Notion That They Believe in Destroying the Home by Pointing to These Model Families: Babies, Too, Believe in Votes for Women," *New York Tribune*, 17 May 1914.

xxv. Suffragists also argued that a minority of men were absent, abusive, or alcoholic. In these instances, they argued, women did not have anyone looking out for their best interest at the voting booth. See Lora S. La Mance, "Two Workings of a Bad Law," *Political Equality Series, National American Woman Suffrage Association*, Vol. 3, No. 3 (1907); Elizabeth Meriwether Gilmer, "Dorothy Dix on Woman's Ballot," *Political Equality Series, National American Woman Suffrage Association*, Vol. 4, No. 6 (1908).

xxvi. On the need for husbands and wives to vote together for the good of the family, see Marguerite Mooers Marshall, "Most Advanced Feminist Wants Husband; Neither Slave nor Master, but a Comrade," *Evening World*, 9 April 1914; Frederic C. Howe, *What the Ballot Will Do for Women and for Men* (New York: National American Woman Suffrage Association, 1912), 5; Pauline Arnoux MacArthur, *Short Talk on Suffrage* (unknown publisher, 1915).

1915 VOTE: THE EMPIRE STATE CAMPAIGN COMMITTEE
VERSUS THE WOMEN'S POLITICAL UNION

The year 1915 brought suffrage referendums in four important eastern states—New York, Massachusetts, Pennsylvania, and New Jersey. These states were politically important because they had large populations. If one of them were to win suffrage, the national situation would be drastically influenced. New York State had two capable women, Harriot Stanton Blatch and Carrie Chapman Catt, and their organizations working toward suffrage, but they were rivals.

Harriot Stanton Blatch and the Women's Political Union worked to successfully lobby the legislature to include a referendum to support a state amendment granting women the vote in the 1915 election. In November 1913, Carrie Chapman Catt and Harriet May Mills organized leaders from suffrage organizations across the state into the Empire State Campaign Committee (ESCC). Catt believed the key to victory was structure and she modeled the ESCC on her own Woman Suffrage Party. As a result, under the ESCC, the state was divided into twelve campaign districts, each with its own chairman. Under each chairman were 150 assembly district leaders, and under these were 5,524 election district captains. Two groups that did not join the ESCC were Harriot Stanton Blatch's Women's Political Union (WPU) and Alva Belmont's Political Equality Association. Blatch considered the ESCC too conservative and continued her political and more militant tactics alongside and in competition with the ESCC.

Victory parade pin and ribbon, November 16, 1915.

This pin was made for the referendum vote in Massachusetts in 1915. Massachusetts, Pennsylvania, and New Jersey all lost their suffrage votes but polled fairly well in favor—Pennsylvania won 46 percent of the vote, New Jersey 42 percent, and Massachusetts 35 percent. Courtesy of the Collection of Ronnie Lapinsky Sax.

Empire State Campaign Committee, crepe-paper banner, 1915.

Empire State Campaign Committee included representatives from New York State Woman Suffrage Association, the Woman Suffrage Party of New York City, the Equal Franchise Society, the College Equal Suffrage League, the Men's Equality League, and other organizations. Courtesy of Coline Jenkins, Elizabeth Cady Stanton Family.

Suffrage parade, New York City, photograph, October 23, 1915.

On October 23rd, ten days before the election, 33,783 women marched up Fifth Avenue in New York City, many of them holding banners and flags in support of suffrage and with record-breaking numbers of spectators. The parade began at 2:00 p.m. and continued well after dark. It was the largest parade ever organized for suffrage in the United States. Courtesy of the Library of Congress.

What came next for both the ESCC and the WPU was the mass mobilization of suffrage workers across New York State. Women (and some men) spread out across the state to educate the male voters about women's suffrage and earn their vote. Furthermore, both Catt and Blatch worked to secure the suffrage plank with each of the political parties. The 1915 campaign culminated with a giant parade of thousands in New York City down Fifth Avenue organized by Catt's Woman Suffrage Party.

Finally, on November 2, 1915, the vote took place. Earlier that week, Tammany Hall declared itself neutral on the question of suffrage, giving Democrats in New York City the option to vote their own conscience and giving suffragists hope. At the end of the day when the votes were tallied, suffrage lost by 194,984 votes. This was the largest vote ever polled for suffrage. Liquor interests and conservatives were primarily responsible for the defeat. However, with 42 percent of the vote in favor of woman suffrage, leaders immediately went back to work.

The day after the election Catt and the leaders of the ESCC announced they would mount another referendum campaign as soon as possible, while Blatch hit the newspapers with anger and disgust. On November 4, 1915, the *New York Times* reported her statements: "No women in the world are so humiliated in asking for the vote as the American woman. The English, the French, the German women all appeal to men of their own nationality. The American woman appeals to men of twenty-six nationalities, not including the Indian."

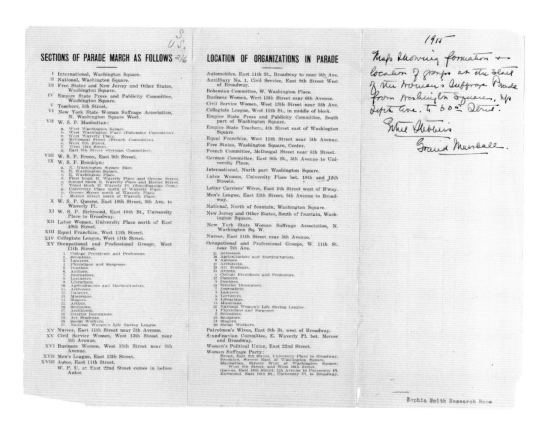

Parade Participant Instructions (*front and reverse*), pamphlet, 1915.

This pamphlet outlines the organization of the October 23, 1915, suffrage parade in New York City. Grand Marshall Ethel Stebbins had the honor of leading the parade. Courtesy of Sophia Smith Collection, Smith College.

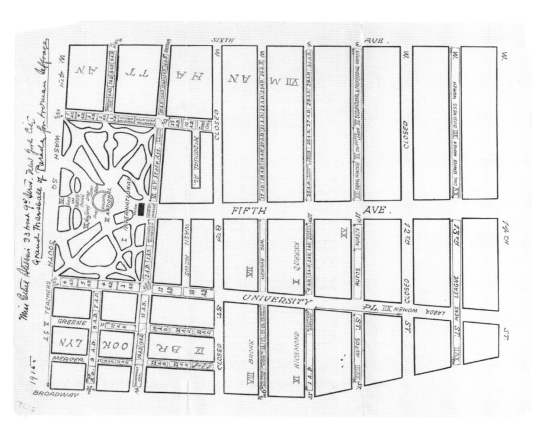

Empire State Campaign Committee, paper drinking cup, 1915.

Courtesy of the Howland Stone Store Museum.

Letter, Carrie Chapman Catt to assembly district leaders, June 4, 1914.

In the lead-up to the 1915 vote, Carrie Chapman Catt and the Empire State Campaign Committee created a sense of unity for the cause. In this instance, Catt is proposing the idea that paper drinking cups could be purchased at the county level and distributed as souvenirs. Courtesy of the Department of Rare Books and Special Collections, University of Rochester Libraries.

THE EMPIRE STATE CAMPAIGN COMMITTEE
303 Fifth Avenue
New York

June 4, 1914.

To Assembly District Leaders:

We have thought it would be helpful and appropriate if the field suffrage workers in each county would give away a cheap souvenir. It is not the intention of the Committee to present these souvenirs to the county workers, but that the county workers should pay for them. Before placing the order we must have some idea of how many are going to be required.

If we are able to order in lots of 50,000 we can supply you with drinking cups upon which is printed in yellow ink in the middle, our

VOTES FOR WOMEN
1915

design, used on our regular envelopes. At the top there will be the following wording in blue ink:

DRINK TO THE SUCCESS OF THE WOMEN
OF THE EMPIRE STATE.

At the bottom:

CAMPAIGN HEADQUARTERS,
303 Fifth Avenue, New York.

These we can deliver to you at $1.75 per thousand postpaid.

Instead of drinking cups we could order tags with the same "Votes for Women 1915" design, printed in blue ink, with a border of yellow and a string attached, ready to be fastened on. These we can deliver to you at the rate of $2.25 per thousand postpaid.

The drinking cups would probably be more attractive as a souvenir, but there is more publicity in the tags, provided people would wear them. We will order the souvenir which receives the majority vote. We would like you to place your order now for the number of souvenirs which you will require for your fair. You need not pay in advance. An immediate reply is essential as the order must be placed in time for the souvenirs to be ready for the season of fairs.

Yours cordially,

Carrie Chapman Catt
Chairman.

According to the printed list of Agricultural Fairs those scheduled for your county are as follows:

Brockport, Sept. 2 - 5

"Before a Forage for Votes, Essex County Suffragists Gathered Before the Suffrage Headquarters," photograph, 1915.

Katherine Notman's house in Keene Valley also served as the Woman Suffrage Party headquarters for Essex County. In 1915, 45.5 percent of the male voters in Essex County voted in favor of the suffrage referendum. Courtesy of the Keene Valley Library.

Women Suffrage Headquarters during the 1915 Campaign, Auburn, New York, photograph.

Isabel Howland (1859–1942, *standing with fur stole*) was the Cayuga County suffrage leader and served as president of the NYSWSA.
Courtesy of the Howland Stone Store Museum.

THE HOWLAND FAMILY

The Howland family was involved with reform movements throughout the nineteenth and twentieth centuries in central New York, including abolition, education reform, and women's rights. Emily Howland (1827–1929) and her niece, Isabel Howland (1859–1942), were both involved with women's rights and suffrage. Emily began working for women's rights in the 1850s and is considered a "pioneer" of the movement. She was also a major financier of NAWSA and NYSWSA. Isabel followed in her aunt's footsteps and worked for women's suffrage. She served as president of NYSWSA and was active on the national level. Both women were among a group of Cayuga County suffragists who marched in the May 1912 suffrage parade in New York City. The posters from the Howland Stone Store Museum were probably purchased and used by Emily and Isabel Howland and other Cayuga County suffragists.[33]

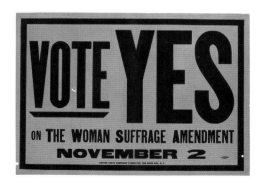

"Vote YES on the Woman Suffrage Amendment"
November 2, poster, 1915.

Courtesy of the Howland Stone Store Museum.

"Votes for Women 1915," poster.

Courtesy of the Howland Stone Store Museum.

The primary operations of the campaign were mobilization and gathering support. Here are some of the overall accomplishments in 1915 leading up to the vote:

- 7.2 million leaflets were printed and distributed
- 657,000 booklets were printed, one sent to each political leader in the state
- 592,000 congressional hearings and speeches were mailed to voters
- 149,500 posters were hung
- 1 million suffrage buttons were distributed
- 200,000 cards of matches with "*Votes YES on the Suffrage Amendment*" were distributed
- 35,000 suffrage fans were distributed
- 10,325 meetings were recorded between May 1915 and November 1915
- Mass meetings were held in 124 cities in New York State (16 in NYC)
- Parades took place in most of the state's cities
- Suffrage speeches were held at moving-picture theaters and vaudeville shows
- Press and Publicity Council worked with 893 newspapers and journals to promote suffrage through the press
- Art shows were organized
- A suffrage game called Coney Island was created
- Stunts were created to get newspaper publicity—suffrage baseball games, a Fourth of July celebration at the Statue of Liberty, telephone and telegraph days when the wires carried suffrage messages to politicians and judges all day, car rallies, and suffrage restaurants were created
- 12,000 New York City school teachers paid fifty-cent dues and gave up their summer vacations to work for suffrage[34]

"Victory 1915, Votes for Women," poster.

Courtesy of the Howland Stone Store Museum.

"Do Not Fail to Hear Carrie Chapman Catt," Sunday, May 16, 1915, handbill.

Courtesy of the Howland Stone Store Museum.

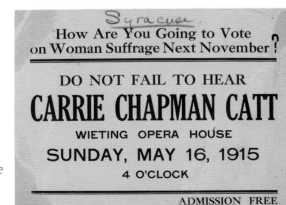

Father Knickerbocker – My Girl! How you have grown!, watercolor, Ditton, ca. 1914.

The artist "Ditton" remains a mystery, but similar images appeared in New York State newspapers as a cartoon titled "Father Knickerbocker—My girl! How you have grown!" in the months leading up to the 1915 vote. Courtesy of the Collection of Ronnie Lapinsky Sax.

Victory 1915 ribbon and yellow flower.

NAWSA adopted yellow as its suffrage color as early as 1876. Courtesy of the National Susan B. Anthony Museum & House.

"Elizabeth Cady Stanton Centennial" at the Johnstown Opera House, October 15, 1915, broadside.

In the final days of the 1915 referendum campaign, Harriot Stanton Blatch used her mother's centennial birthday to garner support for the cause and claim her leadership position for the suffrage cause. Blatch organized a giant birthday campaign in honor of her mother, who would have turned one hundred years old in November. Events took place in Johnstown (where Stanton was born), Seneca Falls, various Stanton sites in New York City, and culminating at the Hotel Astor three days before the election on November 2, 1915. This is a broadside from the events in Seneca Falls. Courtesy of the Howland Stone Store Museum.

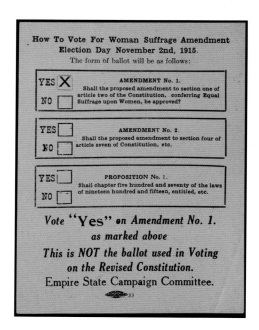

"How to Vote for Woman Suffrage Amendment Election Day, November 2nd, 1915," broadside.

Empire State Campaign Committee. Courtesy of the New York State Library, Manuscripts and Special Collections, SC13339.

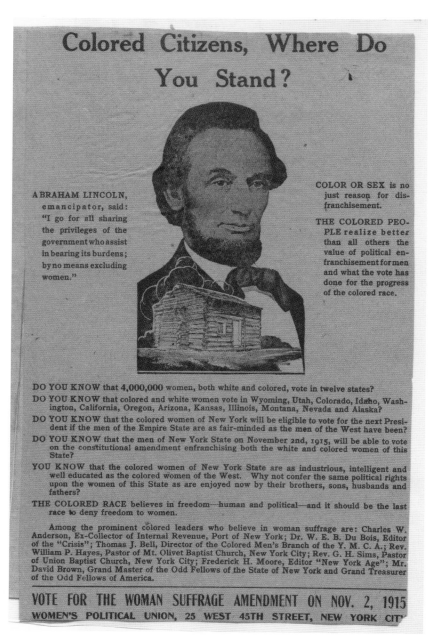

The Crisis, magazine, August 1915.

In addition to civil rights for African Americans, the National Association for the Advancement of Colored People (NAACP) also supported women's suffrage. Some of the founding members of the NAACP, including Mary Talbert, Mary Church Terrell, and Mary White Ovington, were leaders in the women's suffrage movement. Most of the national suffrage groups and many of New York State's suffrage groups did not allow African American women to join, so they started their own groups. Courtesy of the New York State Library, Manuscripts and Special Collections.

"Colored Citizens, Where Do You Stand?," broadside, 1915.

This broadside published by the WPU specifically appealed to New York State's African American voters. It also lists prominent African American men who already supported suffrage including W. E. B. Du Bois and several prominent pastors. Courtesy of the Library of Congress.

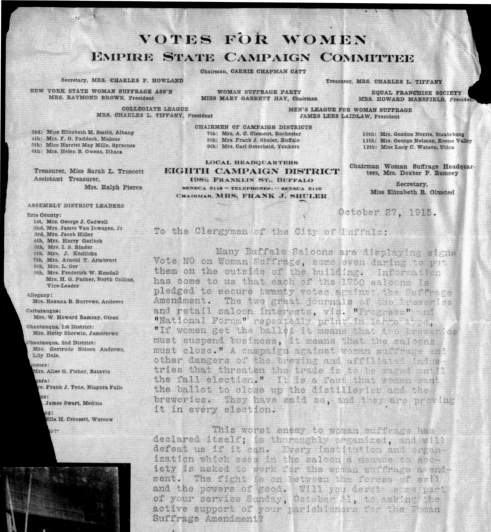

VOTES FOR WOMEN
EMPIRE STATE CAMPAIGN COMMITTEE
Chairman, CARRIE CHAPMAN CATT

Secretary, MRS. CHARLES P. HOWLAND   Treasurer, MRS. CHARLES L. TIFFANY

NEW YORK STATE WOMAN SUFFRAGE ASS'N   WOMAN SUFFRAGE PARTY   EQUAL FRANCHISE SOCIETY
MRS. RAYMOND BROWN, President   MISS MARY GARRETT HAY, Chairman   MRS. HOWARD MANSFIELD, President

          COLLEGIATE LEAGUE   MEN'S LEAGUE FOR WOMAN SUFFRAGE
   MRS. CHARLES L. TIFFANY, President   JAMES LEES LAIDLAW, President

                            CHAIRMEN OF CAMPAIGN DISTRICTS
3rd: Miss Elizabeth M. Smith, Albany   7th: Mrs. A. C. Clement, Rochester   10th: Mrs. Gordon Norrie, Staatsburg
4th: Mrs. F. G. Paddock, Malone   8th: Mrs. Frank J. Shuler, Buffalo   11th: Mrs. George Notman, Keene Valley
5th: Miss Harriet May Mills, Syracuse   9th: Mrs. Carl Osterheld, Yonkers   12th: Miss Lucy C. Watson, Utica
6th: Mrs. Helen R. Owens, Ithaca

                                    LOCAL HEADQUARTERS   Chairman Woman Suffrage Headquar-
Treasurer, Miss Sarah L. Truscott   EIGHTH CAMPAIGN DISTRICT   ters, Mrs. Dexter P. Rumsey
Assistant Treasurer,   198½ FRANKLIN ST., BUFFALO   Secretary,
        Mrs. Ralph Pierce   SENECA 5118 — TELEPHONES: — SENECA 5119   Miss Elizabeth R. Olmsted
                                   CHAIRMAN, MRS. FRANK J. SHULER

ASSEMBLY DISTRICT LEADERS
Erie County: October 27, 1915.
  1st, Mrs. George J. Cadwell
  2nd, Mrs. James Van Inwagen, Jr   To the Clergymen of the City of Buffalo:
  3rd, Mrs. Jacob Hiller
  4th, Mrs. Harry Garlock   Many Buffalo Saloons are displaying signs
  5th, Mrs. I. S. Binder   Vote NO on Woman Suffrage, some even daring to put
  6th, Mrs. J. Kudlicka   them on the outside of the building. Information
  7th, Mrs. Arnold T. Armbrust   has come to us that each of the 1750 saloons is
  8th, Mrs. I. Orr   pledged to secure twenty votes against the Suffrage
  9th, Mrs. Frederick W. Kendall   Amendment. The two great journals of the breweries
     Mrs. H. G. Parker, North Collins,   and retail saloon interests, viz. "Progress" and
        Vice-Leader   "National Forum" repeatedly print in large type,
                                   "If women get the ballot it means that the breweries
Allegany: must suspend business, it means that the saloons
  Mrs. Roxana B. Burrows, Andover must close." A campaign against woman suffrage and
                                   other dangers of the brewing and affiliated indus-
Cattaraugus: tries that threaten the trade is to be waged until
  Mrs. W. Howard Ramsay, Olean   the fall election." It is a fact that women want
                                   the ballot to close up the distilleries and the
Chautauqua, 1st District: breweries. They have said so, and they are proving
  Mrs. Hetty Sherwin, Jamestown   it in every election.

Chautauqua, 2nd District: This worst enemy to woman suffrage has
  Mrs. Gertrude Nelson Andrews,   declared itself; is thoroughly organized, and will
     Lily Dale.   defeat us if it can. Every institution and organ-
                                   ization which sees in the saloon a menace to soc-
Genesee: iety is asked to work for the woman suffrage amend-
  Mrs. Alice G. Fisher, Batavia   ment. The fight is on between the forces of evil
                                   and the powers of good. Will you devote some part
Niagara: of your service Sunday, October 31, to asking the
  Mrs. Frank J. Tone, Niagara Falls   active support of your parishioners for the Woman
                                   Suffrage Amendment?
Orleans:
  Mrs. James Swart, Medina   Very truly yours,

Wyoming:
  Mrs. Ella H. Crossett, Warsaw   Mrs. N. R. Shuler

                                   P.S. Enclosed is a picture of one of the many saloons
                                   displaying Vote NO posters.

"Vote No on Woman Suffrage," poster at local saloon in Buffalo, New York, photograph, 1915.

This photograph was included in the letter written by Mrs. Frank Shuler to the clergymen of Buffalo. Courtesy of the New York State Library, Manuscripts and Special Collections, SC13339.

Letter, Mrs. Frank Shuler to the clergymen of Buffalo, October 27, 1915.

Mrs. Frank Shuler, chairman of the ESCC Buffalo area, explains that the local saloons and breweries waged an outright war against suffrage. This letter requested that the clergymen of Buffalo support suffrage in their sermons on Sunday October 31, 1915, just two days before the vote on November 2nd. Courtesy of the New York State Library, Manuscripts and Special Collections, SC13339.

1917 VOTE

Mina C. Van Winkle of Newark, New Jersey, holding a torch at the front of a tugboat, photograph, 1915.

Harriot Stanton Blatch created the "Suffrage Torch" in the summer of 1915 as a publicity stunt. The torch, based on the Statue of Liberty's, signified liberty and freedom and was carried across the state in support of suffrage. In August 1915, this tug from New York met another from New Jersey and the WPU members passed the torch from one state to another. New Jersey was also in the midst of a suffrage referendum campaign. Courtesy of the Library of Congress.

Two nights after the 1915 referendum defeat, the next campaign began at a mass meeting at Cooper Union in New York City. Soon the Empire State Campaign Committee was consolidated under the New York State Woman Suffrage Party led by Vira Whitehouse (director), Gertrude Foster Brown (chairman of organization), and Harriet Burton Laidlaw (chairman of legislative work). Carrie Chapman Catt was tapped to serve as the president of the National American Woman Suffrage Association (NAWSA), but she remained an advisor throughout the campaign. Women across the state mobilized again and repeated the steps that led to the first referendum. They enrolled members in suffrage organizations, filled petitions with 1,014,000 women's signatures from across the state, gave speeches, held conventions, and organized parades. Two main things were different with the second campaign: many workers were veterans to the cause and the United States declared war on Germany.

World War I presented the women of New York with an opportunity. If women aided the war effort, they could, in turn, demand the vote as a reward for their wartime service. Dedication to the war worked, and President Wilson endorsed suffrage as a war measure. On October 27, 1917, thousands of women marched in the final suffrage parade in New York City.

On November 6, 1917, New York men went to the polls and voted in favor of granting women the right to vote in the state.[35] Suffrage lost in upstate counties by 1,570 votes and won in New York City by 103,863 votes. The win was the result of suffrage work done in immigrant communities.

1,006,503 WOMEN IN NEW YORK STATE ASK YOU TO VOTE FOR WOMAN SUFFRAGE AMENDMENT Nº 1 NOV. 6th

Don't Forget To Vote For WOMAN SUFFRAGE First

Your President asks you to vote for it.
Your Governor is for it.
Your party has endorsed it.
Woman suffrage is coming the world around; don't let New York lag behind.

1. To vote "Yes" make a cross X mark in the square opposite the word "Yes."
2. Mark only with a pencil having black lead.
3. Any other mark, erasure or tear on the ballot renders it void.
4. If you tear, or deface, or wrongly mark the ballot, return it and obtain another.

| Yes | X | Amendment No. 1. Shall the proposed amendment to section one of article two of the Constitution conferring equal suffrage on women be approved? |
| No | ☐ | |

New York State Woman Suffrage Party,
303 Fifth Ave., New York.   154   Printed by N. W. S. Pub. Co.

Banner, 1917.

Ten days before the November 1917 elections, a small band of Orange County women carried this banner up Fifth Avenue in New York City. They were part of a massive suffrage parade. Their banner urged male voters to extend the right of suffrage to women in New York by amending the state constitution. The parade was made up mainly of moderate suffragists. Moderates deplored militant tactics. Some even bore banners criticizing suffragists who picketed the White House. Parade organizers preferred to highlight women's loyalty and patriotism. They encouraged World War I soldiers' wives, Red Cross volunteers, and nurses to join the parade. In 1917, suffrage moderates won the vote in New York. But victory at the federal level would require militant pressure as well as moderate persuasion. Courtesy of the New York State Museum, H-1974.174.1.

"Don't Forget to Vote for Woman Suffrage First," handbill, 1917.

The second referendum was different from the first. In 1915, woman suffrage competed for attention on the ballot with a referendum on a new state constitution. Many believe that this was a purposeful attempt to confuse the two issues and defeat the suffrage measure. In 1917, the suffrage referendum was on the ballot alone. Courtesy of the New York State Library, Manuscripts and Special Collections, BRO3052.

Dr. Anna Howard Shaw and Carrie Chapman
Catt at the last suffrage parade in New York
City on October 27, 1917, photograph.

Courtesy of the Library of Congress.

"President Wilson, Vote for Woman Suffrage,
Nov. 6," poster, 1917.

Women dedicated themselves to the war effort,
and, in return, President Wilson endorsed suffrage
as a war measure. Courtesy of the New York State
Library, Manuscripts and Special Collections.

"A Call: The New York State Woman Suffrage
Party," poster, 1916.

Courtesy of the Howland Stone Store Museum.

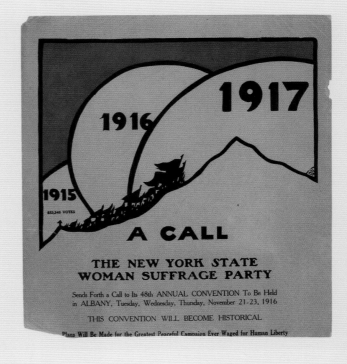

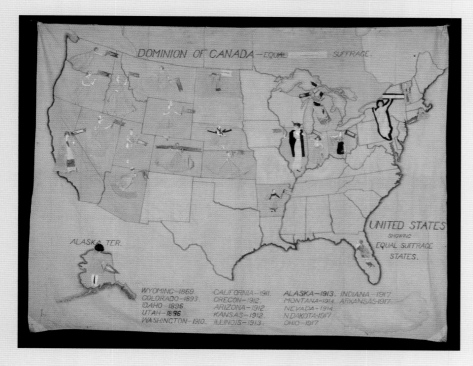

Suffrage banner, ca. 1917.

This banner was probably created in anticipation of New York's suffrage vote in 1917. After 1914, the West was solidly for women's suffrage and over four million women could vote equally with men. Women in the West were instructed to pressure state legislatures for an amendment, while states that had a chance of passing in 1917 were instructed to continue working on the state referendum campaigns. The states that already had the right to vote are indicated with appliqued women in crepe-paper dresses. Courtesy of the Rochester Historical Society.

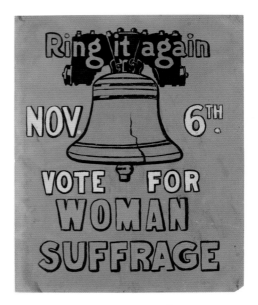

"Ring It Again/Nov. 6th Vote for Women Suffrage," poster, 1917.

This poster showing the Liberty Bell targeted the Pennsylvania 1917 referendum, but it worked for New York State, too. Courtesy of the Howland Stone Store Museum.

The posters on the right were recycled from the 1915 New York State campaign. There is evidence of a "7" patch placed over the "5"—changing the date to "1917."

"Victory in 1917," poster.

Courtesy of the Howland Stone Store Museum.

"There Are One Million Women Taxpayers in New York," poster, ca. 1917.

Courtesy of the Howland Stone Store Museum.

"Women May Vote in Municipal Elections," poster, ca. 1915.

Courtesy of the Howland Stone Store Museum.

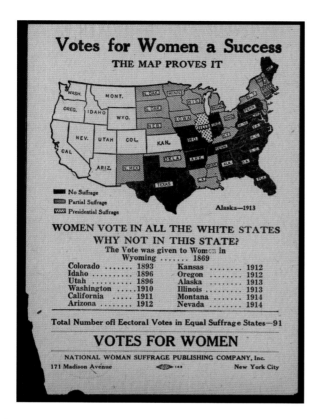

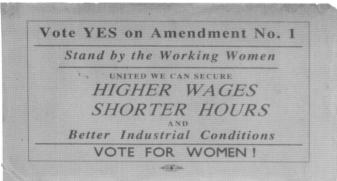

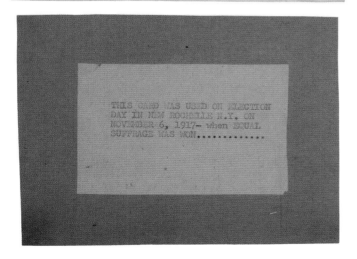

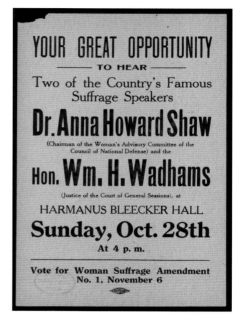

"Votes for Women a Success,"
broadside, ca.1915.

Courtesy of the New York State Library,
Manuscripts and Special Collections, BRO1137.

Lecture by Dr. Anna Howard Shaw and Hon.
William H. Wadhams, broadside, 1917.

Courtesy of the New York State Library,
Manuscripts and Special Collections, BRO1136.

"Vote YES on Amendment No. 1," Higher Wages,
handbill, 1917.

Courtesy of the Collection of Ronnie Lapinsky Sax.

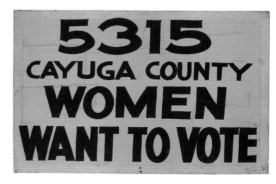

"5315 Cayuga County Women Want to Vote,"
painting, gouache on canvas, 1917.

Courtesy of the Howland Stone Store Museum.

ESSAY

RECOGNIZING RIGHTS

Men in the Woman Suffrage Campaign

Karen Pastorello

Tompkins Cortland Community College, State University of New York

Few realize that male political reformers and religious leaders in upstate New York publicly advocated for woman suffrage at least a decade before the women's rights convention at Seneca Falls. One of the earliest instances of men's support for women came in the form of an 1837 lecture, "On the Political Rights of Women," delivered by northern New York Court of Common Pleas judge John Fine to the Ogdensburg Lyceum. Intending to "discuss the rights of married women in relation to property," Fine "indulged in the hope" that the age he lived in would be made "memorable in promoting the liberties of women" and that the elevation of both men and women would result in "a more just equilibrium of political rights."[i] Fine may have been reacting to the state legislature's lack of response to New York City assemblyman Thomas Herttell's resolution a year earlier suggesting that wives had the right to claim their own property.[ii] In 1848 Governor John Young signed the "Act for the More Effectual Protection for the Property of Married Women" into law, distinguishing New York as the first state in the nation to grant married women rights to their property and wages.[iii] The long-running and heated debates that led to the first "Married Women's Property Act" established an important link between property rights and the broader citizenship rights of women—including suffrage.

As the door to reform for women gradually opened, discussions concerning women's rights spread beyond legislative halls. In November 1846, Unitarian minister Samuel Joseph May became the first clergyman to openly declare his pro-suffrage sentiments in a seminal address on "the Rights and Condition of Women." Speaking to his distinguished congregation from the pulpit of the Church of the Messiah in Syracuse, Reverend May asserted that the "entire disfranchisement of females is as unjust as the disfranchisement of men would be." May envisioned the reach of post-Revolutionary republican motherhood extending past the walls of the home to ensure that "wise, virtuous, gentle mothers of a state or nation" could "contribute to the order, the peace, the thrift of the body politic."[iv] Published in tract form, the sermon circulated across reform circles for years.

Most importantly, men like John Fine, Thomas Herttell, and Samuel May helped to inspire Elizabeth Cady Stanton's call to action culminating in the 1848 Seneca Falls convention where Frederick Douglass stepped forward to eloquently defend woman's right to suffrage as contained in the Declaration of Sentiments. Toward the end of the second day of the convention, on July 21, 1848, thirty-two men, including Douglass, affixed their signatures to the document vowing their support to the nascent movement that promised to attain the recognition of women's rights.[v] When the Civil War ended, women resumed their fight for rights. At the New York State constitutional convention in 1867 the presentation of a woman suffrage petition and a powerful speech by George William Curtis failed to sway legislators to the cause of woman suffrage. During the 1894 constitutional convention, anti-suffrage legislators led by Senator Elihu Root successfully rallied against placing a suffrage referendum before the voters.[vi]

In the half-century following the Seneca Falls convention, increasing numbers of men supported women's suffrage. Some of the first men to advocate for suffrage came out of the abolitionist movement. Other men joined the suffrage movement after being raised by suffrage mothers or marrying women who belonged to one or more reform organizations. Although one *New York Times* reporter suggested that men active in the suffrage cause may have included businessmen or professional men "looking for customers," the majority of empathetic men truly believed in justice for all.[vii] The most ardent male suffragists reasoned that accepting woman's right to the vote would benefit the entire nation. Regardless of men's motivations for suffrage agitation, the majority of male voters had to be convinced to approve a woman suffrage referendum.

By 1907 the New York State Woman Suffrage Association, the largest suffrage organization in the state, began to take a systematic approach to winning suffrage. The association established multiple committees, including a cooperating legislative committee comprised of men charged with petitioning legislators and speaking in favor of suffrage at the legislative hearings in Albany.[viii] Recognizing the value of enlisting men in the women's rights crusade, National American Woman Suffrage Association president Anna Howard Shaw encouraged men to create their own suffrage organization.[ix] Acting on Shaw's suggestion in 1908 *New York Evening Post* owner Oswald Garrison Villard together with his friend and colleague Rabbi Stephen Wise initiated a men's league. They turned to young Columbia University philosophy professor Max Eastman to do the work required to organize the men's league. Eastman, with his mother Annis Ford Eastman's assistance, mailed invitations to join the group to over one hundred influential men on a list that Villard had provided.[x]

By the summer of 1909 newspapers around the state began to cover the activities of the Men's League for Woman Suffrage of the State of New York. At a November meeting held at the City Club, investment banker George Foster Peabody became the men's league's first president, and the membership appointed an executive committee and designated a building on Waverly Place as league headquarters. With annual dues of one dollar, the organization attracted mostly affluent professionals such as writer William Dean Howells and banker and future league president James

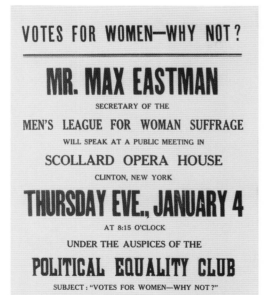

"Votes for Women—Why Not?," speech by Max Eastman, broadside, ca. 1912.

Courtesy of the Clinton County Historical Society.

Max Eastman, photograph, ca. 1912.

Courtesy of the Library of Congress.

Lees Laidlaw.[xi] League men not only helped women seeking the ballot garner publicity, they also donated and raised large sums of money to sponsor lobbying efforts in Albany in an attempt to solicit the support of state legislators.[xii]

As women and men suffrage leaders worked relentlessly to push the woman suffrage referendum through the state legislature, men's league members participated in the rallies, pageants, and parades, and acted in suffrage films, all activities designed and coordinated to enhance the visibility of the campaign. Several men dedicated extraordinary time speaking and organizing across the Northeast. Prior to assuming the editorship of *The Masses*, league secretary Max Eastman traveled extensively, sharing his suffrage sentiments with crowds at campus rallies and in progressive publications.[xiii] After banker James Lees Laidlaw assumed the presidency of the New York City men's league in 1911, he encouraged the establishment of other local men's leagues that soon sponsored their own district rallies, public dinners, and theatrical performances. With the approach of the 1915 election with its woman suffrage referendum, men's leagues devised activities to captivate potential voters' attention. For example, the Kings County Men's League for Equal Suffrage proposed "Flying Squads" of speakers housed in a new building replete with sleeping quarters for the orators and a garage to hold a fleet of automobiles to transport them to speaking engagements.[xiv]

Despite the combined forces of suffragists, New York voters refused to recognize women's right to vote on Election Day in 1915. Suffragists immediately regrouped in the days following the disappointing election, this time concentrating their campaign on winning the votes of the over half a million men who did not vote at all in 1915.[xv] As suffrage workers personally canvassed immigrant men in cities and farmers across rural New York, suffrage leaders worked overtime to ensure that the referendum would come before New York voters again in 1917.[xvi] Since many considered the failure of the referendum to pass in New York City a major obstacle, suffragists welcomed the news that Tammany Hall bosses would assume a neutral stance. Women and men worked at an unrelenting pace to keep suffrage before the public in the wake of the April 1917 entry of the United States into World War I.[xvii]

In October 1917 with the assistance of the New York State Woman Suffrage Association's Men's Advisory Committee and the Men's League for Woman Suffrage, suffragists held a "Men's Experience Meeting" in Carnegie Hall. Prominent men ranging from the governor of Rhode Island to the chairman of the New York State Industrial Commission shared their reasons for supporting woman suffrage with voters.[xviii] New York City judge William H. Wadhams informed the audience that while women were required to obey civil and criminal laws and pay taxes, they lacked political rights. Reasoning that a just government derives its powers from the consent of the governed, Wadhams demanded that women be granted the right to vote.[xix] Over seven decades of suffrage work culminated on November 6, 1917, when male voters approved the woman suffrage referendum granting New York women suffrage and recognizing their rightful place among the governed.

Notes

i. John Fine, "On the Political Rights of Women," in *Lecture: On the Political Rights of Women* (Ogdensburg: Butler and James, 1837), 1–35. William Seward House, Auburn, New York.

ii. Fine, "On the Political Rights of Women," 3–4; Judith Wellman, *The Road to Seneca Falls: Elizabeth Cady Stanton and the First Woman's Rights Convention* (Urbana: University of Illinois Press, 2004), 146.

iii. For the original document, see New York State Archives, "Document Showcase: 'Act for the More Effectual Protection for the Property of Married Women,'" nysed.gov/education/

showcase/201001 (accessed 8 June 2016). A second Married Women's Property Act passed by the state legislature in 1860 went beyond protecting the property women came into marriage with, giving them rights to their own earnings and joint custody of their children. See Faye E. Dudden, *Fighting Chance: The Struggle over Woman Suffrage and Black Suffrage in Reconstruction America* (New York: Oxford University Press, 2011), 29.

iv. Samuel Joseph May, "The Rights and Condition of Women: A Sermon, Preached in Syracuse, November 1846," 2–4, Votes for Women: Selections for the National American Woman Suffrage Association Collection, 1848–1921, Library of Congress. For more on republican motherhood, see Linda Kerber, "The Republican Mother: Women and the Enlightenment—An American Perspective," *American Quarterly*, Vol. 28, No. 2 (Summer 1976): 187–215.

v. National Park Service, "Seneca Falls Women's Rights Convention and the Origins of the Women's Movement," 46 (accessed 8 June 8 2016); Wellman, *Road to Seneca Falls*, 201.

vi. George William Curtis, *Equal Rights for Women: A Speech in the New York Constitutional Convention at Albany July 19, 1867* (Boston: C. K. Whipple. 1869), 1–24, Box 2 Folder 4 Onondaga County Library, Syracuse, New York; Ellen Carol Dubois, *Harriot Stanton Blatch and the Winning of Woman Suffrage* (New Haven: Yale University Press, 1997), 167.

vii. "The Heroic Men," *New York Times*, 3 May 1912.

viii. Oswald Garrison Villard to Anne ("Nannie") Fitzhugh Miller, 3 December 1907. Miller National American Woman Suffrage Association Suffrage Scrapbooks, 1897–1911: Scrapbook 6, p. 25, Rare Book and Special Collections Division, Library of Congress, Washington, DC.

ix. Anna Howard Shaw to Oswald Garrison Villard, February 6, 1908. Oswald Garrison Villard Papers, Houghton Library, Harvard University, bMS Am1323 Item number 3494.

x. Max Eastman, "Early History of the Men's League," *The Woman Voter* (October 1912): 17. (Both Villard and Eastman grew up in suffrage households. Villard was the grandson of abolitionist William Lloyd Garrison and son of Fanny Garrison Villard, noted suffragist. Eastman was the son of Reverend Annis Ford Eastman and the brother of Crystal Eastman, both of whom were staunch suffrage advocates. Eastman also married suffragist Ida Rauh in 1911.

xi. "Men Cry 'Votes for Women,'" *Brooklyn Daily Eagle*, 30 November 1909, 20; "In the Cause of Women," *Times-Herald* (Olean), 21 May 1909, 1.

xii. "To Invade Assembly," unidentified New York clipping (December 1909), Miller National American Woman Suffrage Association Suffrage Scrapbooks, 1897–1911: Scrapbook 8, p. 36, Rare Book and Manuscript Division, Library of Congress, Washington, DC.

xiii. For examples of Eastman's arguments, see Max Eastman, "Is Woman Suffrage Important?" *North American Review*, Vol. 193 (January 1911): 60–71; Max Eastman, "Confession of a Suffrage Orator," *The Masses* (November 1915).

xiv. "Men to Aid 1915 Fight," *New York Tribune*, 27 October 1913, 9.

xv. National American Woman Suffrage Association, *Victory: How Women Won It, 1840–1940* (New York: H.W. Wilson, 1940), 114–115.

xvi. Legislative procedure dictated that the referendum had to pass through both houses of the legislature twice before it was placed on ballot.

xvii. "Suffrage and the War," *Brooklyn Daily Eagle*, 24 October 1917, 25.

xviii. "Men's Experience Meeting at Carnegie Hall," *New York Times*, 3 October 1917.

xix. "Men Urge Vote for Women at Mass Meeting," *New York Tribune*, 4 October 1917.

"The weaker sex?," illustration, Kenneth
Russell Chamberlain, in *Puck*, v. 76, no. 1966,
November 7, 1914.

This illustration was published in *Puck* on November
7, 1914, and shows a Red Cross nurse bandaging
a wounded soldier on a battlefield, with a caption
that reads: " 'Woman's place is in the home'—*Anti-
Suffragists.*" Courtesy of the Library of Congress.

"Why Shouldn't They Be Good Enough Now,"
sheet music, 1919.

Courtesy of the New York State Library,
Manuscripts and Special Collections, SCO13309.

FIGHT FOR THE AMENDMENT

Beginning in 1913, Alice Paul and the militant suffragists were the only dedicated group working to get the suffrage amendment passed. NAWSA worked to pass state referendums in four important eastern states—New York, New Jersey, Massachusetts, and Pennsylvania—all lost in 1915. NAWSA president Anna Howard Shaw stepped down this same year, and Carrie Chapman Catt reluctantly took over the national organization. She wanted to see New York State through to victory and she knew what hurdles lay ahead for the national campaign. NAWSA leadership gave Catt carte blanche to run the campaign as she saw fit and she finally agreed to the presidency. As in her approach in New York State, she coordinated all of the nation's suffrage organizations under the umbrella of NAWSA and put them all to work. The Congressional Union and the Woman's Party were the only groups that did not work within Catt's framework and continued working on their own.[36]

While the Woman's Party continued a militant path toward the amendment, Catt and NAWSA worked to persuade President Wilson to support suffrage. Wilson was anti-suffrage while he was the governor of New Jersey but seemed to be slowly changing his mind and even voted in favor of suffrage in the 1915 New Jersey referendum. NAWSA worked to get Wilson reelected, and by 1917 President Wilson publicly supported the suffrage amendment.

THE "WINNING PLAN"

At the 1916 NAWSA convention in Atlantic City, Carrie Chapman Catt detailed her "Winning Plan" that would lead to a suffrage amendment. The plan laid out in specific detail that the thirty-six state suffrage organizations would work for both state suffrage and federal suffrage at the same time with a concentrated effort on the states more likely to win—all campaigns would have the full support of NAWSA. After a few more states adopted suffrage, NAWSA would then go after the legislatures for a federal amendment. "Some break in the solid 'anti' East should be made too. If New York wins in 1917 the backbone of opposition will be largely bent if not broken."[37] Working at both the state and federal levels allowed for pressure of elected officials. Each of the state suffrage associations had a job to do, and Catt made sure everyone specifically followed the plan even as the nation became involved with World War I.

THE UNITED STATES GOES TO WAR

On April 6, 1917, the United States declared war on Germany. Catt made a controversial decision to support the war effort. She theorized that it would be much harder to deny women the vote if they supported the national war effort. Women, both suffrage and antis, came out in droves to support the war. Women tended gardens, canned food, sold liberty bonds, joined the Red Cross, and filled vacant industrial jobs. The war brought thousands of women out of their homes and into the workforce for the first time. While all this work for the war effort was underway, suffragists continued to pressure legislators, march, write letters, sign petitions, organize rallies, sell buttons, and do anything else they could think of to garner support for the vote. All of this proved successful for nine suffrage wins across the country, but mostly in New York where women were awarded full suffrage in November 1917, the first eastern state to win.

"Better Babies, 'I wish my mother had a vote to keep the germs away,'" poster, ca. 1917.

Courtesy of the New York State Library, Manuscripts and Special Collections, US GEN 219.

Letter pertaining to WWI soldiers, Vira Whitehouse, 1917.

Courtesy of the New York State Library, Manuscripts and Special Collections, BRO1343.

"For Every Fighter a Woman Worker,"
poster, c. 1917

This poster published by the YWCA illustrated the
new role played by women in traditionally male
dominated industries. Courtesy of the New York
State Museum, H-1973.94.1.

"Every Girl Pulling for Victory," poster, c.1917

The importance of women in the war effort was a
common theme in many World War I posters.
Courtesy of the New York State Museum,
H-1973.94.1.

"We Are Ready to Work Beside You," poster, 1917.

Courtesy of the New York State Library, Manuscripts and Special Collections, US GEN 219.

VOTING ON THE AMENDMENT

President Woodrow Wilson supported suffrage in his December 2, 1918, State of the Union address. In May 1919, after an exhaustive lobbying campaign, the House and Senate both barely supported passage of the Nineteenth Amendment with the required two-thirds majority. Next, thirty-six states had to ratify the amendment for passage into the Constitution. By March 1920, thirty-five states had ratified the amendment. Southern states were vehemently opposed to the amendment because they did not want to increase the black vote, and all of them had already voted against it except for Tennessee.[38]

In Tennessee, the vote was tied. This important decision came down to Harry T. Burn (1895–1977), a twenty-four-year-old Republican from McMinn County. Although Burn probably opposed the amendment, he received a note from his mother on the morning of the vote that read: "Hurrah, and vote for suffrage! Don't keep them in doubt. I notice some of the speeches against. They were bitter. I have been watching to see how you stood, but have not noticed anything yet . . . be a good boy and help Mrs. Catt put the 'rat' in ratification."

Harry T. Burn, photograph, ca.1919.

Burn defended his last-minute reversal in a speech to the assembly: "I know that a mother's advice is always safest for her boy to follow," he explained, "and my mother wanted me to vote for ratification." Courtesy of the Library of Congress.

Harry T. Burn reminisces, no date.

Courtesy of the New York State Museum, gift of Elizabeth Meaders, H-2016.45

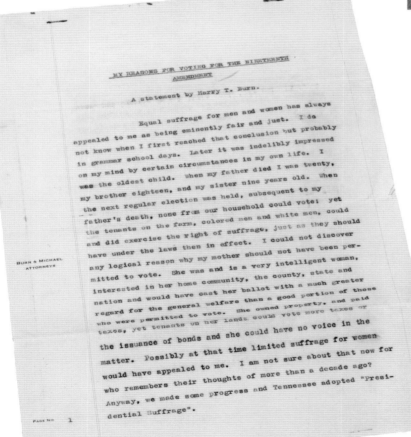

Victory Map, 1919.

Southern states saw the Nineteenth Amendment as a threat to the racial order. If white women were given the vote, then black women would be allowed to vote also. A white man from Mississippi said the following about black women getting the vote: "We are not afraid to maul a black man over the head if he dares to vote, but we can't treat women, even black women, that way. No, we'll allow no woman suffrage" (Stansell, "A Forgotten Fight for Suffrage"). Most of the Southern states waited decades to ratify the Nineteenth Amendment, with Mississippi being the last in 1984. Despite passage of the Nineteenth Amendment, many black women in the South and even in the North would have to wait for passage of the 1965 Voting Rights Act before they were allowed to vote because poll taxes, literacy tests, and overall voter intimidation prevented black women from voting. Even today, the right to vote is in jeopardy in some states where a voter identification card is required. Courtesy of the Library of Congress.

When the roll call reached Burn, he voted to ratify and the suffrage amendment passed. The struggle for democracy that began in Seneca Falls, New York, in 1848 was finally won.

And what shall we say of the women,—of their instant intelligence, quickening every task that they touched; their capacity for organization and cooperation, which gave their action discipline and enhanced the effectiveness of everything they attempted; their aptitude at tasks to which they had never before set their hands; their utter self-sacrifice alike in what they did and in what they gave? Their contribution to the great result is beyond appraisal. They have added a new lustre to the annals of American womanhood. The least tribute we can pay them is to make them the equals of men in political rights as they have proved themselves their equals in every field of practical work they have entered, whether for themselves or for their country. These great days of completed achievement would be sadly marred were we to omit that act of justice.[39]

—President Woodrow Wilson's
State of the Union Address, 1918

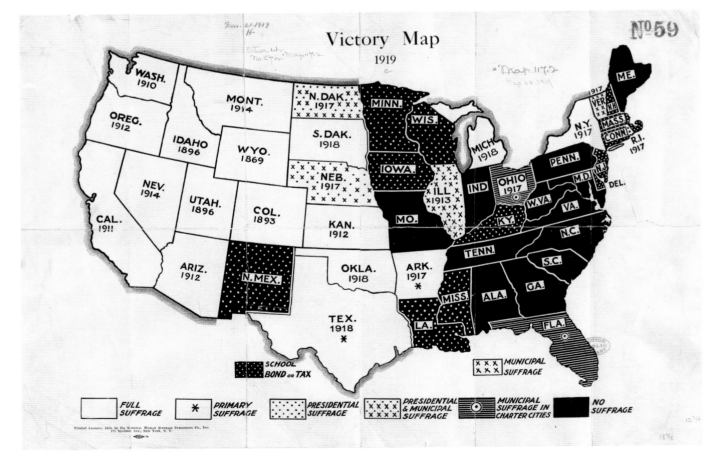

Women at Ballot in New York City (probably at Fifty-Sixth Street and Lexington polls), photograph, 1920.

Courtesy of the Library of Congress.

When Tennessee, the thirty-sixth state, ratified, August 19, 1920, Alice Paul, National Chairman of the Woman's Party, unfurled the ratification banner, photograph.

Courtesy of the Library of Congress.

LEAGUE OF WOMEN VOTERS

In 1920, shortly before the Nineteenth Amendment was ratified, Carrie Chapman Catt established the League of Women Voters (LWV) during the last NAWSA convention as the organization's successor. The purpose of the league was to help twenty million new voters learn to how to participate in and shape the political process. Since its inception, the league has maintained a non-partisan stance so it could help to educate all voters on political issues.

League of Women Voters ribbon, ca. 1940 and button, ca. 1980.

The League of Women Voters of New York State was founded by Carrie Chapman Catt on November 19, 1919. Courtesy of the Collection of Ronnie Lapinsky Sax.

Susan B. Anthony gavel, 1895.

As president of NAWSA, Susan B. Anthony used this gavel at the 1895 annual convention held in Atlanta, Georgia (the date March 3, 1895, is inscribed in ink on the gavel head). At the conclusion of the convention, Anthony gave the gavel to Carrie Chapman Catt. Catt would be Anthony's hand-picked successor as president of NAWSA in 1900. Mrs. F. Warren Green of Larchmont presented the gavel to the New York State League at the Fiftieth Anniversary Convention in 1969. The LWVNY uses the gavel to open its biennial state conventions. Courtesy of the League of Women Voters of New York State.

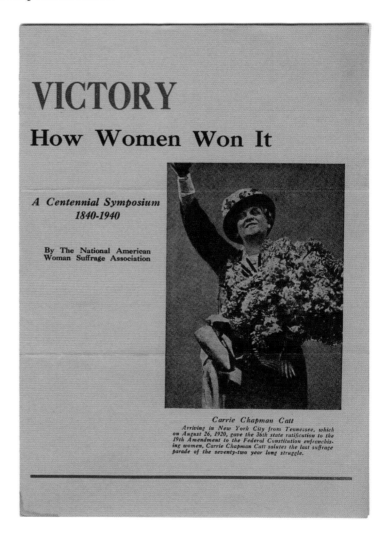

"Victory, How Women Won It," pamphlet, 1922.

This is an image of Carrie Chapman Catt at the victory parade in New York City on August 27, 1920. The NAWSA presented Catt with a star sapphire "Victory Brooch" for all her years of hard work for the cause. Courtesy of the Department of Rare Books and Special Collections, University of Rochester Libraries.

SECTION 3

The Continuing Fight for
Equal Rights, 1920–present

Alice Paul at her desk, photograph, 1913.

Alice Paul and Crystal Eastman, both militant suffragists and members of the National Woman's Party, wrote the text of the original ERA. Courtesy of the Library of Congress.

After the Nineteenth Amendment was ratified, women continued their contributions to society during the twentieth century. They worked to keep food on the table during the Depression, served during World War II in factories and abroad as nurses, and helped African Americans gain their civil rights in the 1950s and 1960s. They naturally assumed that parity with men would follow. Despite the service and the many contributions that women made to American society, this did not happen. Nevertheless, many women, but not all women, continued to slowly chip away at the many disparities in an effort to realize the intent of the Seneca Falls convention, that "men and women were created equal."

EQUAL RIGHTS AMENDMENT

Alice Paul, leader of the National Woman's Party (NWP), realized that suffrage would not guarantee equality between the sexes. To remedy this, on July 21, 1923, Paul presented the Equal Rights Amendment (ERA) to the group of NWP members gathered in Seneca Falls to celebrate the seventy-fifth anniversary of the Seneca Falls convention. Known as the Lucretia Mott Amendment in honor of Mott's work to help organize the original Seneca Falls convention, the amendment stated, "Men and women shall have equal rights throughout the United States and every place subject to its jurisdiction."[1] That same year Susan B. Anthony's nephew, Representative Daniel R. Anthony Jr. (R-Kansas), introduced the ERA to Congress. Since then, the ERA was introduced in every session of Congress between 1923 and 1972.

While Alice Paul and members of the NWP supported the passage of the ERA, many women, even though they may have supported women's suffrage, did not because they felt that it would remove much of the protective legislation that helped women, particularly working women. For example, legislation passed in the 1910s limited women's work hours, banned them from working night shifts, and even gave them a minimum wage. Because of this, Eleanor Roosevelt and Frances Perkins were both against the ERA.[2]

Crystal Eastman, photograph, ca. 1915.

Crystal Eastman Benedict (1881–1928) was a member of the Executive Committee of the Congressional Union for Woman Suffrage and a graduate of Vassar College and New York University Law School. In addition, she was secretary of the New York State Commission of Employee's Liability and Causes of Industrial Accidents, which investigated the employers' liability question, and was an investigator for the Russell Sage Foundation—a philanthropic foundation that sought to improve living conditions for the poor and elderly. She was the sister of Max Eastman, a well-known author, radical activist, and women's rights proponent. Courtesy of the Library of Congress.

In 1943, Alice Paul, who earned three law degrees (LLB, LLM, and DCL) rewrote the language of the ERA to reflect the content of the Fifteenth and Nineteenth Amendments, which stated, "Equality of rights under the law shall not be denied or abridged by the United States or by any state on account of sex."[3] Both Republicans and Democrats supported this language and the amendment, however, many labor supporters and social conservatives still lobbied against the amendment. Contrary to popular belief, women did not vote as a bloc and frequently cast their ballots in the same vein as their husbands or fathers.

The 1960s were marked by tremendous political and social change. The civil rights movement was successful in expanding equality for African Americans. The Civil Rights Act of 1964 was passed by Congress and prohibited discrimination in employment based on race, color, national origin, religion, and sex. In response to this positive legislation, the women's movement gathered supporters. The late 1960s saw women's groups joining forces in support of the ERA and politicians took notice. In 1971, Representative Martha Griffiths (D-Michigan) maneuvered the proposed ERA out of committee and onto the floor for a vote. Both houses passed the amendment, and in March 1972, the proposed Twenty-Seventh Amendment to the Constitution was sent to the states for ratification. Unfortunately, Congress imposed a seven-year time limit for ratification. Twenty-two of the necessary thirty-eight states ratified the amendment right away (New York ratified it on May 18, 1972), but seven years gave the opposition time to gather support.

Conservative and religious groups were against passage, believing that if the amendment were to pass, women would be drafted, mothers would not receive custody of their children, alimony would not be awarded to women, and single-sex bathrooms would be eliminated. A staunch supporter of these beliefs was Phyllis Schlafly, a conservative Republican activist and lawyer from Missouri, who built a grassroots movement of women against the amendment. The anti-ERA campaign worked as public opinion and the Republican Party turned against the passage of the ERA. Since too few states had voted for ratification when the 1979 deadline approached (and some repealed their approval), Congress granted an extension until June 30, 1982. Once again, not enough states supported the amendment. Since 1982, the ERA has been reintroduced to Congress in every session and has yet to be ratified into the Constitution.

I think we ought to start immediately on another campaign similar to that which won suffrage. We should demand a Constitutional amendment of Congress and the President. We are not safe until we have equality guaranteed by the Federal Constitution.

—Alice Paul at the seventy-fifth anniversary of the Seneca Falls convention, 1923

THE CONGRESSIONAL UNION IS REBORN

In 1980, the second Congressional Union (CU) was formed, partially to honor the original militant Congressional Union created by Alice Paul and Lucy Burns and, more importantly, to work toward passage of the Equal Rights Amendment. The original CU organized to promote women's suffrage but split with NAWSA in 1914 over the use of militant tactics and later became the NWP.[4] Using non-violent and direct-action protests, the second CU staged protests that mirrored those of the original CU, which took place sixty-five years earlier—picketing the White House, staging protests the day before the presidential inauguration,

"Women Ask President Harding for ERA," photograph, 1921.

Women ask president for equal rights legislation. Fifty prominent members of the New National Woman's Party called at the White House today to ask the president's aid in passing an "Equal Rights Bill" in the next Congress. The bill would give women full equality in the government service, give married women citizenship in their own right, and make women of the District of Columbia eligible to serve on juries, equal guardianship rights, and equal rights of inheritance and contract. Photograph shows suffragists with President Harding at the White House. Courtesy of the Library of Congress.

ERA bracelet, ca. 1975.

This is the third in a series of four bracelets displaying charms for the states that ratified the ERA. This bracelet's state charms include: Texas, Colorado, West Virginia, Wisconsin, New York, Michigan, Maryland, Massachusetts, Kentucky, and Pennsylvania. Courtesy of the Division of Political History, National Museum of American History, Smithsonian Institution.

Congressional Union demonstration photograph, CU flag, handcuffs, and collateral receipt, January 11, 1982.

On January 11, 1982, Alice Paul's ninety-seventh birthday, members of the CU burned effigies of President Reagan and Marion Callister (a judge who ruled that Congress acted illegally when it extended the deadline for the ERA ratification) in Lafayette Park, Washington, DC. This protest was a recreation of a demonstration that occurred in February 1919 where radical suffragists burned a portrait of President Wilson for his failure to support the Nineteenth Amendment. After burning the effigies of Reagan and Callister, the CU members moved their demonstration to the White House where, like the "silent sentinel" campaigns of 1919, women stood quietly holding signs. Twenty demonstrators were arrested for "incommoding" or blocking the sidewalk. Each woman was released after paying a $50 fine. The demonstration and arrests were covered in the national newspapers the following day. The handcuffs and collateral receipt from the arrest were saved by Pam Elam, one of the event organizers and participants. Courtesy of the New York State Museum, Pam Elam Collection, H-2016.32.

and burning watch fires. These protesters organized demonstrations around historic dates and anniversaries such as November 12, Elizabeth Cady Stanton's birthday. The new CU, making great efforts not to repeat the mistakes of the suffragists, embraced women of color and strove to be a multi-issue group.[5] Unfortunately, after ERA ratification failed, the group slowly lost its impetus.

> All of these actions express our determination that the Equal Rights Amendment will be ratified on June 30, 1982. Equality and justice for women will become a reality—in spite of President Ronald Reagan, in spite of Judge Marion Callister, and in spite of all the right-wing forces of fear in this country that oppose freedom for women.
>
> You will see some fires lit here today. Not just the symbolic and historic watchfire and effigies in the tradition of the suffragists—but feminist fires of the spirit, fires of hope, of activism, of commitment, of sisterhood—fires which, as the suffragists said, represent the "burning indignation of women."
>
> —Pam Elam, Executive Committee of the CU, speech, January 11, 1982, Washington, DC

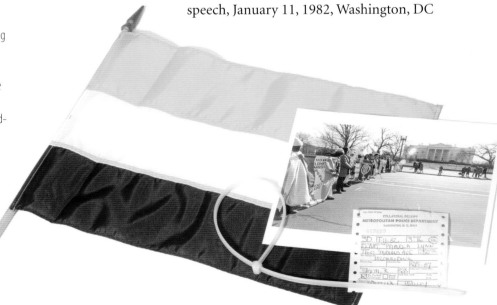

Pam Elam addressing the Congressional Union, January 19, 1981, Washington, DC, photograph.

Pam Elam (*with microphone*), addresses the CU demonstrators at the White House on January 19, 1981. This was the day before President Reagan's inauguration. Courtesy of the New York State Museum, Pam Elam Collection, H-2016.32.

White House pickets of the Congressional Union for Suffrage, photograph, 1917.

The "new" Congressional Union specifically chose similar tactics to the ones used by the radical suffragists leading up to the Nineteenth Amendment. Courtesy of the Library of Congress.

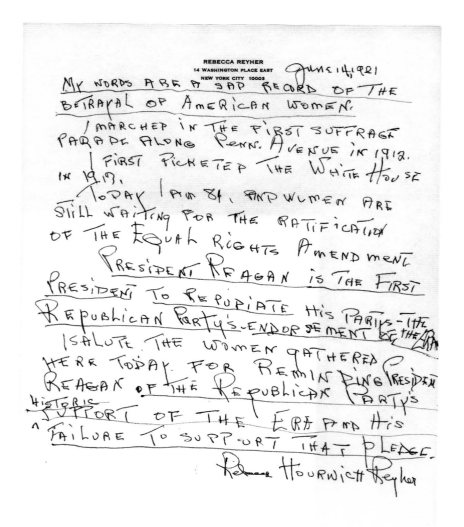

Letter, Rebecca Reyher to a gathering of the new Congressional Union, June 14, 1981.

This letter was written by Rebecca Reyher, a surviving member of the original Congressional Union, to the members of the new Congressional Union. Reyher writes, "I marched in the first suffrage parade along Penn. Avenue in 1912. I first picketed the White House in 1917. Today I am 84 and women are still waiting for the ratification of the Equal Rights Amendment." Courtesy of the New York State Museum, Pam Elam Collection, H-2016.32.

Women's Equality Day, broadside, 1981.

This broadside created to celebrate Women's Equality Day was signed by each of the Congressional Union members. New York State Museum, Pam Elam Collection, H-2016.32.2.

Phyllis Schlafly, photograph, 1977.

Phyllis Schlafly and her supporters at a STOP-ERA demonstration at the White House on February 4, 1977. Courtesy of the Library of Congress.

Stop ERA, button, ca. 1977.

Courtesy of the Collection of Ronnie Lapinsky Sax.

In Honor of Alice Paul, ERA YES, buttons in support of the ERA, ca. 1979 and 1980s.

Courtesy of the Collection of Ronnie Lapinsky Sax.

People of Faith for ERA, ERA YES, buttons, ca. 1980.

While Phyllis Schlafly and the STOP ERA members drew the most media attention; there was also strong opposition against the amendment from conservative religious groups including Roman Catholics, Evangelical Christians, Mormons, and Orthodox Jews. These groups worried that the amendment would guarantee universal abortion rights and legalize gay marriage. Southern whites also opposed the amendment because they worried that the amendment would lead to too much government and less personal freedoms. David W. Brady and Kent L. Tedin, "Ladies in Pink: Religion and Political Ideology in the Anti-ERA Movement," *Social Science Quarterly*, Vol. 56, No. 4 (1976): 564–575. Courtesy of the New York State Museum, H-1984.18.13 and .28.

59¢, button, ca. 1963.

In 1963, working women made 59 cents for every dollar that men earned. In 2010, women made 77 cents for every dollar that men earned. Based on this trajectory, the Institute for Women's Policy Research estimated, in 2015, that women won't receive equal pay until 2059. National Committee on Pay Equity. Courtesy of the New York State Museum, H-1984.18.12.

President Lyndon Johnson signs the Civil Rights Act on July 2, 1964, photograph.

Title VII of the Civil Rights Act of 1964 reads: "It shall be an unlawful employment practice for an employer . . . to discriminate against any individual with respect to his compensation, terms, conditions, or privileges of employment, because of such individual's race, color, religion, sex, or national origin." The word "sex" was added at the last minute by Representative Howard Smith (D-Virginia), who worked with Alice Paul on the addition. Smith's argument for the addition was that if a white woman and a black woman applied for the same job and encountered discrimination, the Civil Rights Act would protect only the black woman. (Some sources claim that Smith introduced gender to the bill because it was so preposterous a notion that the whole bill would be voted down immediately.) Regardless of the motive, the act passed, although the struggle to achieve equal pay for equal work continues today. Courtesy of the Library of Congress.

ESSAY

"AN INFUSION OF HOPE"

New York Women in the Post-Suffrage Era

Robert Chiles
University of Maryland, College Park

"Now having obtained the suffrage, the question is 'What are you going to do with it?'"[i] The query from New York State senator Anthony Griffin, a Tammany Democrat, reflected the trepidations of male politicians across the Empire State in November 1917, just days after the historic referendum to extend votes to New York women. The responses would be complex, featuring an outburst of reforms by panicky politicos, a slow march toward representation for women themselves, and, ultimately, the transformation of the policy priorities of the state.

Instantaneously, Republicans and Democrats statewide scrambled to bring women into their partisan fold. In New York City, Tammany Hall's executive committee voted to double in size, adding a woman for each election district. Like most machine men, Tammanyites had been among the more vociferous opponents of women's suffrage in earlier times; but with varying degrees of pragmatism, opportunism, and conversion, most had changed their tune, so by the fall of 1918, Tammany stalwart and Democratic gubernatorial nominee Alfred E. Smith was leading an aggressive campaign to register women. By the November elections, 1.2 million Empire State women had enrolled in the two major parties.[ii]

Legal changes were also in order. In 1922 Assemblyman Russell Livermore, a Westchester Republican and son of the chair of the state Republican women's executive committee, promoted legislation to grant women equal representation within county party organizations. Assemblyman George Rowe, an Erie County Republican, denounced this as "a sop to the women," while Tammany's Jimmy Walker, the senate minority leader, grumbled that the GOP had "plagiarized" his own earlier proposal; nevertheless, the bill passed with bipartisan enthusiasm and was signed by Republican governor Nathan Miller.[iii]

Meanwhile, five women were elected to the New York State Legislature in the decade following enfranchisement. Ida Sammis, a prominent Long Island suffragist, was elected as a Republican to the state assembly from Suffolk County in 1918.[iv] The same year, Mary Lilly, an accomplished New York attorney, was elected as a Democrat.[v] Both women were defeated for reelection in 1919, but two others were elected that year: Republican Marguerite Smith, a twenty-five-year-old Harlem gym teacher; and Democrat Elizabeth V. Gillette, a Schenectady physician.[vi] While Smith and Gillette would both prove one-termers as well, the next woman elected to the state assembly would enjoy greater longevity. Rhoda Fox Graves was a farmer and educator in St. Lawrence County, where she began working "untiringly" for the Republican Party after women gained the franchise. She ran for the state assembly in 1924, when her male primary opponent taunted her with the cavalier slogan: "There is no sentiment for a woman." Evidently there was, for Graves won overwhelmingly and went on to more than two decades of service in Albany—becoming in 1934 the first woman elected to the state senate.[vii] By the time Graves arrived in the senate, New Yorkers had also elected three women to Congress: Republicans Ruth Baker Pratt (1929–1933) and Marian Clarke (1933–1935), and Democrat Caroline O'Day (1935–1943).[viii]

These New York women in some ways reflected the conflicting agendas of female activists nationwide in the period following ratification of the Nineteenth Amendment. They did not, as many men had feared, gravitate to a single party. Moreover, women who had temporarily coalesced behind suffrage now battled over priorities, with a fundamental schism between those calling for an equal rights amendment to the Constitution and those favoring continued pursuit of social welfare and labor protections (many of which would have been rendered unconstitutional under such an amendment).[ix] Certainly, New York women were not monolithic: Assemblywoman Smith generally opposed "so-called welfare bills," while for Gillette and Lilly such bills were a foremost priority.[x]

Equal Rights Deputation to Governor Smith on 3/5/24, Woman's Party urges legislative program, photograph.

Right to left, front row: Mrs. Lloyd Williams, New York; Mrs. Lieber E. Whittic, state vice chairman, Syracuse; Miss Ethel Barrymore, founder; Governor Smith; Mrs. Theresa Shivarts, New York; Mrs. McKane; *Back row:* Mrs. Abram J. Rose; Mrs. Stephen Pell; Mrs. Robert B. Stearns; Mrs. Josephine Curtis Jenner, life members, all of New York. Mrs. Thomas J. Swanton, Rochester, and Miss Fred Lee Woodson, Washington, are mysteriously invisible in this picture. Courtesy of the Library of Congress.

Another important development growing from enfranchisement was the momentary interest among male politicians in women's welfare agenda. An anxious Congress passed the Sheppard-Towner Act in 1921 to provide federal matching funds for state-level maternal and infant health initiatives—an act widely viewed as an early victory for women. Yet by the mid-1920s, a women's bloc had failed to materialize, political observers dismissively labeled women "indifferent to the franchise," and women's welfare agenda lost its urgency with officeholders. By 1929, Congress allowed Sheppard-Towner to expire.[xi]

In New York, the story was somewhat different. Governor Miller blocked the state from opting into Sheppard-Towner, while former governor Smith, his Democratic rival in 1922, campaigned in favor of participation. Smith won in a landslide. More broadly, Smith's administration (1919–1920; 1923–1928) would gladden women from the progressive social work tradition by pursuing a broadly defined welfare regime. By 1928 Governor Smith could boast: "I have had my strongest and most vigorous support from the women of my State."[xii] This remark, which would have been absurd a mere decade earlier, reflected not only the ways in which women's votes had transformed the *politics* of the Empire State, but also its *policies*: women, led famously by social worker Belle Moskowitz, figured prominently in Smith's administration, and female activists would help the governor achieve a forty-eight-hour week for women and promote a panoply of health, education, housing, and labor reforms. Among the most renowned of these women was Frances Perkins, whom Smith named to the State Industrial Commission in 1919 and made chair of the State Industrial Board in 1926. The credentials Perkins established during her service in New York would lead to her appointment as President Franklin Roosevelt's secretary of labor, in which post she was not only the first female cabinet secretary in United States history but also the architect of revolutionary social welfare and labor reforms.[xiii]

The year that her fellow New Yorkers voted to enfranchise women, social worker Mary Simkhovitch of the Greenwich House Settlement in Manhattan explored the importance of politics to the women of her community. With exposure to the political realm, "women see their own work in its larger aspects," she noted. "They feel new powers, an infusion of hope."[xiv] In the 1920s, women in New York claimed those new powers and ardently pursued their hopes. Conflicting priorities, partisan rivalries, and enduring sexism would beget manifold frustrations, yet by achieving full democratic citizenship, women were equipped to direct a revolutionary shift toward more humane policy priorities in the Empire State.

Notes

i. Anthony Griffin, "Ideals," November 22, 1917, Anthony Griffin Papers, New York Public Library, New York, NY, Box 14.

ii. Anna L. Harvey, *Votes without Leverage: Women in American Electoral Politics, 1920–1970* (New York: Cambridge University Press, 1998), 88–90, 99; "Candidate Smith Talks to Women," *New York Times*, 21 September 1918, 8; John D. Buenker, "The Urban Political Machine and Woman Suffrage: A Study in Political Adaptability," *The Historian*, Vol. 33, No. 2 (February 1971): 264–279.

iii. "Assemblymen Favor Women on Committees," *New York Times*, 15 February 15 1922, 2; "Makes Women Eligible," *New York Times*, 28 February 1922, 20.

iv. Antonia Petrash, *Long Island and the Woman Suffrage Movement* (Charleston: History Press, 2013), 114–117.

v. Doris Weatherford, *Women in American Politics: History and Milestones* (Washington, DC: CQ Press, 2012), 87; "Republicans' Lead Cut in Legislature," *New York Times*, 7 November 1918, 4.

vi "Democrats Lose 18 Assemblymen," *New York Times*, 6 November 1919, 3; "Assemblyman Miss Smith of Harlem," *New York Times*, 9 November 1919, XX1.

vii. James Malcolm, ed., *The New York Red Book* (Albany: J. B. Lyon, 1928), 76; "Mrs. Graves, First Woman in State Senate," *New York Times*, 7 November 1934, 14.

viii. US House of Representatives, *Women in Congress, 1917–2006* (Washington, DC: GPO, 2006), 95, 132, 155–159.

ix. Nancy F. Cott, *The Grounding of Modern Feminism* (New Haven: Yale University Press, 1987), 8; Lynn Dumenil, *The Modern Temper: American Culture and Society in the 1920s* (New York: Hill and Wang, 1995), 104–105.

x. "As Assemblywoman Smith, of New York, Views State Politics," *Literary Digest*, 12 June 1920, 72–75; Don Rittner, "Gillette a Pioneer Schenectady Woman," *Albany Times Union*, 1 July 2009; Weatherford, *Women in American Politics*, 87.

xi. J. Stanley Lemons, "The Sheppard-Towner Act: Progressivism in the 1920s," *Journal of American History*, Vol. 55, No. 4 (March 1969): 776–786; Clarke A. Chambers, *Seedtime of Reform: American Social Service and Social Action, 1918–1933* (Ann Arbor: University of Michigan Press, 1963), 50–51; Robyn Muncy, *Creating a Female Dominion in American Reform, 1890–1935* (New York: Oxford University Press, 1991), 93–123; Dumenil, *Modern Temper*, 107–108.

xii. Alfred E. Smith, "Radio Address at Carnegie Hall, November 5, 1928," in *Campaign Addresses of Governor Alfred E. Smith, Democratic Candidate for President 1928* (Washington, DC: Democratic National Committee, 1929), 309.

xiii. Lemons, "The Sheppard-Towner Act," 782; Lillian Wald, "An Open Letter to Social Workers," Lillian Wald Papers, New York Public Library, Reel 33; Elisabeth Israels Perry, *Belle Moskowitz: Feminine Politics and the Exercise of Power in the Age of Alfred E. Smith* (Boston: Northeastern University Press, 1992), 115–183; Malcolm, *Red Book*, 165; Kirstin Downey, *The Woman Behind the New Deal: The Life of Frances Perkins, FDR's Labor Secretary and His Moral Conscience* (New York: Nan A. Talese, 2009), 75–95, 114–137; George Martin, *Madam Secretary: Frances Perkins* (Boston: Houghton Mifflin, 1976), 141–244.

xiv. Mary Kingsbury Simkhovitch, *The City Worker's World in America* (New York: Macmillan, 1917), 196.

THE BIRTH CONTROL MOVEMENT

At the beginning of the twentieth century, the idea of family limitation reached a new level of awareness in the arena of public discussion. It was not, however, a new idea. For many years, families had recognized the benefits of limiting their family size, and, indeed, after 1800 each subsequent generation reduced its number of children.[6] Once children were not needed for labor on family farms, larger families meant more mouths to feed and bodies to clothe. Women recognized the danger inherent in childbirth as well, and, increasingly in the twentieth century, the impact motherhood had on a woman's career prospects. Early women's rights advocates, including Elizabeth Cady Stanton, had argued for woman's control of her own body, and her right to refuse her husband's advances.

Through the nineteenth and early twentieth centuries, birth control methods remained primitive and unreliable, or prohibitively expensive. As religious views became more conservative about birth control, and federal policy condemned low birth rates, information on birth control options became harder to come by. With passage of the Comstock Act in 1873, which called for the "Suppression of Trade in, and Circulation of, Obscene Literature and Articles of Immoral Use," contraceptives, as well as books and pamphlets covering sex education and family planning, were banned from the mail.[7] In some locations, it became illegal to possess them at all. New York State had its own Comstock laws as well, which did include a provision allowing doctors to provide contraceptive information for the prevention of venereal disease.

Hooked rug, ca. 1910–1940.

Prior to widespread knowledge of birth control, many women worried about how to deal with growing families and questioned how to feed additional mouths and keep up with the extensive demands of housework. This was most true for poor families, who had the least access to birth control. Courtesy of the Sophia Smith Collection, Dorothy Hamilton Brush Papers, Smith College.

MARGARET SANGER
AND THE FOUNDATIONS OF THE MOVEMENT

Margaret Sanger (1879–1966), born in Corning, New York, was one of eleven children and witnessed firsthand the impact of a large family on her family's finances and her mother's health. After training as a nurse, and working among the visiting nurses in New York City, she also saw the tragic circumstances of women who sought illegal and unsafe abortions, and those who remained in poverty due to rapidly growing families. She wrote,

> Ignorance and neglect go on day by day; children born to breathe but a few hours and pass out of life; pregnant women toiling early and late to give food to four or five children, always hungry. . . This state of things became a nightmare with me. There seemed no sense to it all, no reason for such waste of mother life, no right to exhaust women's vitality and to throw them on the scrap-heap before the age of thirty-five.[8]

Sanger felt a strong call to action, to "[a]waken the womanhood of America to free the motherhood of the world!" She set aside her nursing career and "resolved that women should have knowledge of contraception. They have every right to know about their own bodies. I would strike out—I would scream from the housetops. I would tell the world what was going on in the lives of these poor women. I *would* be heard."[9]

Sanger turned first to the pen. From 1912 to 1913, she penned the column "What Every Girl Should Know" in the radical publication *The Call.* The column, later printed as a pamphlet, focused on venereal disease. It was quickly banned by Anthony Comstock.[10] She then developed the concept of a magazine called *The Woman Rebel*, which was intended to challenge Comstock's law and provide information on contraception and sexuality to working women. At a gathering of radicals, Sanger's friend Otto Bobsein coined the term "birth control," as a way to embody Margaret's goals of helping families socially and economically through, as it was generally called in the period, "family limitation." The law quickly caught up with Sanger and her publication, resulting in her arrest in August 1914 and the potential for forty-five years in jail.[11] Before going to trial, Sanger penned the pamphlet *Family Limitation*, which explained forms of birth control and their relative merits, political arguments for using contraception, and a plea, "Women must learn their own bodies."[12] She then fled for Europe under the alias Bertha Watson. *Family Limitation* was distributed after she left the country.[13] In her absence, her husband, William Sanger, was arrested for distribution of the pamphlet. He was eventually sentenced to thirty days in jail. Margaret returned to the United States in October 1915, amid growing media coverage and support for her cause. The charges against her were dropped on February 14, 1916.[14]

On October 16, 1916, Sanger, with the help of her sister, Ethel Byrne, opened the first birth control clinic in the United States at

Margaret Sanger bookplate, Rockwell Kent, ca. 1939–1949.

The idyllic image of a mother and child on Margaret Sanger's bookplate reflects the focus of the early birth control movement on allowing mothers to have the children they truly wanted, giving them the opportunity to better provide for their families. Courtesy of the Sophia Smith Collection, Margaret Sanger Papers, Smith College.

"30 Days in the Penitentiary for this," order form, ca. 1931.

This brochure was an advertisement and order form for Margaret Sanger's 1931 biography, *My Fight for Birth Control: Reminiscences of Margaret Sanger*. The photograph shows the first birth control clinic in the United States, opened by Sanger and her sister, Ethel Byrne, at 46 Amboy Street, in the Brownsville neighborhood of Brooklyn. On the cover of the flyer is an image of a handbill that was distributed by Sanger and her supporters leading up to the opening of the clinic. It includes a call to mothers in English, Hebrew, and Italian to serve the mixed ethnic neighborhood in which the clinic was located. The site was chosen to serve a diverse and poor population, who did not have the access to birth control information that wealthier families had. Courtesy of the Sophia Smith Collection, Margaret Sanger Research Bureau, Smith College.

46 Amboy Street, in the Brownsville neighborhood of Brooklyn. They were aware that distributing information about preventing conception by anyone other than a doctor was illegal. The clinic emphasized prevention of unwanted pregnancies in avoidance of dangerous abortions, and in Sanger's words, "Women of every race and creed flocked to the clinic with the determination not to have any more children than their husbands could support."[15] Ten days into its existence, the clinic was raided by the police. All records and possessions were impounded, and Sanger, Byrne, and Fania Mindell were arrested.

In Byrne's trial, lawyer Jonah J. Goldstein claimed that New York's Comstock Law denied the poor the right to choose their family size, as they could not afford to see private physicians, who were exempted from the ban on disseminating information on contraception. Instead, Byrne faced claims from the prosecution that she was working "to do away with the Jews," the largest ethnic group in the neighborhood. Sentenced to one month in prison, Byrne announced a hunger strike, and prison officials retaliated with forced feedings after four days.[16]

The trials of Sanger and Mindell began on January 29, 1917. The courtroom was packed with a diverse mixture of women, including wealthy supporters from the National Birth Control League and poor mothers from the Brownsville neighborhood, many of whom had been subpoenaed in the trial. Mindell was quickly found guilty of selling

The Birth Control Review, magazine, 1917.

Sanger created *The Birth Control Review* as an alternative means of promoting the cause, outside of work within national organizations like the National Birth Control League. The first issue appeared in January 1917. There was frequent editorial conflict between Sanger's more radical colleagues, who wanted articles on broad social change, and others who felt that the magazine should cover only birth control. Courtesy of the New York State Library, 304.66 qB619 211-658 V.1-2 1917/18.

copies of *What Every Girl Should Know* and was fined $50. The decision was later reversed upon appeal. Sanger was clearly guilty of giving out information on birth control, but the court worked to determine if she had also fitted clients with devices. The female police officer who headed up the raid testified that she found Sanger holding devices in the back room. The question was raised of whether Section 1145 of the New York State Comstock Law, which provided the exemption for medical practitioners, held in the case of prevention of disease. The Brownsville mothers who testified shared stories of poverty, hunger, sickness, infant mortality, and miscarriage, all motivation for obtaining birth control and avoiding unwanted pregnancy.

Ultimately, Sanger was found guilty, and she choose a thirty-day prison sentence over a $5,000 fine. The case went on to the court of appeals, where Section 1145 was interpreted more broadly than before, allowing doctors to prescribe contraception for medical reasons beyond venereal disease. Moving forward, Sanger and others in the birth control movement used a model of delivering family planning services under a physician's supervision.[17]

MARY COFFIN WARE DENNETT (1872–1947)

Mary Coffin Ware Dennett was raised in a family of social reformers in Boston. She became active in the suffrage movement, first through the Massachusetts Woman Suffrage Association, and then as corresponding secretary of the National American Woman Suffrage Association. Dennett was wary of organizations, feeling that they became stagnant. She resigned from suffrage work in 1915, looking for a cause with a broader plan for improving society. That same year, she founded the National Birth Control League (later renamed the Voluntary Parenthood League), along with Jessie Ashley and Clara Gruening Stillman. The league's primary goal was to change the laws that defined printed information about birth control as obscene, causing it to be banned from the mail. Unlike Margaret Sanger, Dennett was against an amendment to the law that would only allow physicians to distribute information on contraception.

What began as Dennett's concern for appropriate sex education for her own family ultimately led to her arrest and a court case that would prompt to changes in the Comstock Law. In 1915, she was disappointed in the printed material that was available to educate her own children, and she authored a pamphlet called *The Sex Side of Life*. The work included information on human biology and transmission of venereal diseases and also talked about the emotional side of sexual relations within marriage. Published in 1918, the pamphlet saw many subsequent editions through the 1920s and was distributed by public and private organizations. In 1922, it was deemed obscene by the Solicitor of the Post Office, and in 1928 Dennett was convicted and fined under the Comstock Law. Rulings made during the appeals process helped to chip away at the Comstock Law.[18]

GROWING ACCEPTANCE OF BIRTH CONTROL
AND THE END OF THE COMSTOCK ERA

In the 1920s, birth control had growing acceptance in the United States, and family planning became common practice. The Comstock Law remained in effect, however, and there was still work to be done.

Sanger organized the first American Birth Control Conference in New York City in November 1921. During the conference, supporters established the American Birth Control League (which later became the Planned Parenthood Federation of America). At the close of the conference, as Sanger prepared to speak, the meeting was raided by police and Sanger was arrested. She was released soon afterward.

On January 2, 1923, Sanger opened the Clinical Research Bureau, a birth control clinic staffed by doctors to comply with the new interpretation of the New York State Law made during the 1918 appeal of Sanger's conviction for the first clinic. To avoid confrontation with law enforcement, the clinic worked with married women and stated that its primary mission was scientific research. The success of the Clinical Research Bureau, without interference from police, paved the way for clinics to open around the state and the country.

In 1932, a shipment of contraceptive supplies sent to Sanger was intercepted by United States Customs. At her lawyer's urging, Sanger had the shipment resent to Dr. Hannah Stone. The resulting trial, *United States v. One Package Containing 120, More or Less, Rubber Pessaries to Prevent Conception* established that the Comstock Law could not prevent the mailing of such materials to be used by medical professionals in a ruling in 1936.

Margaret Sanger appearing before Congress, photograph, 1932.

Sanger worked tirelessly to make safe and effective birth control legal and to bring it into the American mainstream. This work included numerous testimonies before Congress and other bodies, presenting evidence of the strain too many children placed on poor families and the ill health effects on mothers. Courtesy of the Sophia Smith Collection, Margaret Sanger Papers, Smith College.

A New Baby Is Born, brochure, ca. 1930–1940.

This brochure focuses on the way in which advocates of the birth control movement believed birth control could help strengthen families by avoiding poverty, malnutrition, and illness. The third panel, depicting the Gray family, is a mirror of Sanger's own family history, as her mother died from complications of tuberculosis, and Sanger herself contracted the disease. Courtesy of the Sophia Smith Collection, Margaret Sanger Research Bureau, Smith College.

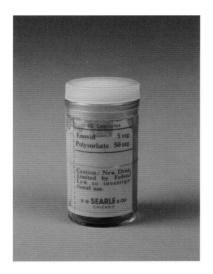

Enovid 5 Milligram Oral Contraceptive, G. D. Searle and Company, ca. 1957–1958.

Throughout her career, Margaret Sanger dreamed of a family planning option that would be highly effective, affordable, and convenient for women to use. Beginning in 1951, she partnered with Katharine Dexter McCormick, a former suffragist, to fund and drive the research of Gregory Pincus, John Rock, and M. C. Chang at the Worcester Foundation of Experimental Biology. The first oral steroid pills were approved for contraceptive use by the US Food and Drug Administration on May 9, 1960 (Enovid had originally been submitted to the FDA in 1957 and approved for use in treating menstrual disorders, making it widely available prior to 1960). Courtesy of the Division of Science and Medicine, National Museum of American History, Smithsonian Institution.

After several years of debate and study, the American Medical Association endorsed birth control within marriage. The organization urged greater scientific study, introduction of the topic into medical schools, and clarification of the law as it related to physicians.

While 1936 represented significant gains legally for the birth control movement, it was not until 1970 that the language of the Comstock laws was revised and contraception was no longer considered obscene.[19] Margaret Sanger devoted the rest of her life to ensuring that all women had access to the information they needed to plan their families. Countless other advocates continue to carry on her work.

THE MODERN FIRST LADY: ELEANOR ROOSEVELT

In the early 1920s when Franklin Roosevelt was beginning his political career in New York State politics, his wife, Eleanor Roosevelt (1884–1962), became involved with the Women's City Club, the National Consumers League, the Women's Division of the Democratic State Committee, the New York chapters of the League of Women Voters, and the Women's Trade Union League since she could not think of anything worse than attending teas and playing hostess.[20] In 1922, Roosevelt and her political friends Nancy Cook, Marion Dickerman, and Caroline O'Day traveled throughout the state to encourage the formation of Democratic women's clubs. Roosevelt was not a politician, but she was political. By 1924, she was nominated as the chair of the women's delegation at the Democratic National Convention, worked to get Al Smith

Eleanor Roosevelt at desk, photograph, 1932.

Eleanor Roosevelt opposed the ERA because she felt that its passage would undermine the progressive legislation for women workers that she helped to create. Courtesy of the Library of Congress.

NEW YORK STATE

WOMEN'S DEMOCRATIC NEWS

INCORPORATED

| VOL. I | ❦ | JULY, 1925 | ❦ | No. 3 |

To the Women of New York State, Regardless of Party

A MESSAGE FROM MRS. DANIEL O'DAY

WE women sought the vote in order that we might bring a more balanced viewpoint into government affairs. We felt that we could emphasize the importance of human rights, which we felt were often being lost sight of by our law makers in their efforts to protect property rights. We thought that we could aid in bringing about better laws concerning humanitarian measures; such as the health and education of children, the protection of our working women, the safeguarding of public morals and finally that we might eventually end the political boss system and the grafting that follows in its wake.

We vindicated this belief when we voted by hundreds of thousands, regardless of party, for Gov. Smith last fall, because he stood honestly and aggressively for definite measures of this kind.

When the Republican candidates for the Legislature hastened to assure us that they also stood with the Governor on all such matters it was further proof of the silent power of the women's vote.

With a Democratic Governor and a Republican Legislature, both pledged to support the measures that interested us most, the women of the State looked forward to a better day.

What happened?

Gov. Smith kept the faith. The Republican Legislature betrayed us at every point. Why? Because Gov. Smith might share in the credit for any such legislation passed. This is known in modern political circles as the "Mid-Victorian or President Arthur-Mark Hanna" school of thought.

All winter the bosses of the majority party cracked their whips and led their followers up hill and down, around and around and around to—NOWHERE. They were not skillful in the betrayal of their party pledges to the women of the State. Contrasted to their petty subterfuges the figure of the Governor, who kept his word, loomed greater than before. Every Republican legislator went home, fearful of the Assembly Elections this fall, and the laughing stock of the State.

With fine indifference to partisanship, which he has always shown when the welfare of the State was at stake, Governor Smith proposed to put the great question of public parks in the hands of an expert commission. This commission is composed of men of the highest standing and incidentally is overwhelmingly Republican. Last fall the people voted by a large majority a liberal appropriation for the further acquisition and development of State Parks, for they felt that under these Commissioners their money would be well and wisely spent.

But these men are not "politicians" and this was a matter of serious concern to Republican bosses, since it killed all chances for the customary spending of public funds to build up political fences. They had already suffered a similar loss of patronage when the Governor reorganized the Department of Public Works.

A suggested remedy, however, was found when a frantic wail went up from a few very rich men on Long Island who saw the privacy of their golf courses threatened. This remedy was to take from the eminent Commissioners, who were after all only able and conscientious men, who controlled no votes in their own districts, the spending of the money appropriated. The spending of the money was then to be placed with the elected Republican State Officials, whose renomination and re-election depends on their subserviency to the party bosses. The "cohesive power of public plunder" united the Lowmans and McGinnises, the Knights and the Hewitts, and all their ilk. Their bill was passed. It was vetoed by the Governor, who called an extra session, and many of the State Republican Legislators having talked with their constituents, announced that the Governor was right.

It looked to the alarmed Republican bosses like another victory for the Governor. Something must be done. The powers in Washington selected Senator Wadsworth for the vacant throne of Platt. New York was to have a BOSS. To Senator Wadsworth a bossless State was something new, and he has always been against anything new, including women's right to vote.

(Continued on page following)

New York State Women's Democratic News, newspaper, July 1925.

Roosevelt began this newspaper in 1925 with close friends Elinor Morgenthau and Caroline O'Day. The newspaper provided Roosevelt and her political friends an avenue to discuss the politics happening in Albany and to disseminate information to women across the state since county chairpersons reported updates on a monthly basis to the newspaper. Courtesy of the Cook-Dickerman Collection, Eleanor Roosevelt National Historic Site, National Park Service, US Department of the Interior.

Caroline O'Day, Nancy Cook, Eleanor Roosevelt, and Marion Dickerman, (*left to right*), Campobello Island, Canada, photograph, July 1926.

Eleanor Roosevelt had long-lasting friendships with this group of progressive and political women. Caroline O'Day was elected to Congress in New York, Nancy Cook was executive secretary of the women's division of the State Democratic Committee, and Marion Dickerman was vice president of the Todhunter School in New York City. These women served as Roosevelt's confidants and inspiration as she became involved in her own political activities. Courtesy of Alamy Stock Photos.

elected as governor of New York State, and, subsequently, worked on his presidential campaign in 1928.

By the time Franklin Roosevelt was elected governor of New York State, Eleanor Roosevelt had become a political force within the Democratic Party. Since she was now New York's first lady, she had to scale back her political agenda, but continued meaningful work at Val-Kill (a Colonial Revival furniture industry in Hyde Park that Roosevelt and her friends established to give local immigrant artisans work) and Todhunter School (a private school for girls in New York City where Roosevelt taught literature).[21] She also continued her work with the Women's Democratic Committee and was an advisor to her husband, especially in regard to progressive protective labor legislation and workers' rights. This work stopped when Franklin Roosevelt and Eleanor Roosevelt moved into the White House in 1933.[22]

While in the White House, Roosevelt set out to redefine the role of the First Lady. She held weekly press conferences with female reporters to discuss "women's issues," traveled and lectured widely across the United States, and wrote a popular syndicated newspaper column called *My Day*—all firsts for a First Lady. Roosevelt also championed the civil rights of African Americans when this was unpopular and was the president's information source about the conditions that average Americans faced during the Depression. Even after she left the role of First Lady, she continued political work and international human rights work as a member of the United Nations.

SHE SHE SHE CAMPS

Shortly after Franklin Roosevelt took the presidential office in 1933, Congress appropriated $500 million for relief of the needy and the unemployed. It created the Civilian Conservation Corps (CCC) to provide jobs in flood control, reforestation, and other conservation projects for men between the ages of eighteen and twenty-five. The CCC was one of the most popular New Deal programs, lasting through 1942, giving three million young men work, shelter, clothing, and food. However, Eleanor Roosevelt, who was all too aware that half of the American poor were women, was troubled by the male-only focus of the CCC, so she and Frances Perkins set out to remedy the situation.[23] Their major focus was to develop a CCC camp for women. The first camp TERA (Temporary Emergency Relief Assistance) was established in New York's Bear Mountain State Park in June 1933 with seventeen young women participants. Other nationwide camps were slow to start, but the program soon gathered momentum; ninety camps were ultimately established that helped 8,500 women during the worst years of the Depression.

Eleanor Roosevelt at Camp TERA, Bear Mountain, New York, photograph, August 7, 1933.

Courtesy of the Franklin D. Roosevelt Presidential Library and Museum.

EARLY PIONEERS IN NEW YORK STATE GOVERNMENT

Ruth Baker Pratt, photograph, ca.1930.

Ruth Baker Pratt (1877–1965) first held office in 1925 on the New York City Board of Aldermen. Not only was she the first woman elected to this position, she was outspoken against the Tammany-run mayor's office, claiming, "I cannot for the life of me see why New York City spends over $500,000 to support the Board of Aldermen. We are mere automatons moved at the will of that powerful organization, Tammany Hall." As a staunch Republican, she became a member of the Republican National Committee between 1929 and 1943, serving as a delegate several times at both the state and national conventions. In 1929 Pratt was the first woman from New York to be elected to Congress. She served for two terms. "Mrs. Ruth Baker Pratt Dies; State's First Woman in House," *New York Times*, 24 August 1965. Courtesy of the Library of Congress.

"Ruth Baker Pratt," political cartoon, ca. 1930.

This political cartoon reads: "Anyway there're worse places than New York." While Pratt was in New York City, she was an outspoken objector (female politician, Republican, and anti-Tammany), but in Washington, DC, her uniqueness was diminished because she was part of a group of female legislators within a Republican majority. She had a good record in Congress, but she was defeated in 1932 when the Democrats swept New York governor Franklin Roosevelt into the White House along with his supporters. United States House of Representatives, http://history.house.gov/People/Detail/19904. Courtesy of the Collection of Ronnie Lapinsky Sax.

Group of pins for Ruth Baker Pratt elections, 1928–1930.

Courtesy of the Collection of Ronnie Lapinsky Sax.

The G.O.P. Is the Only Party to Elect Women to State Offices, fan, 1928.

As soon as women won the vote, political parties began work for their support. This fan encourages women to vote for the Republican ticket in 1928, "Think of Your Home—Your Family. Then Vote the G.O.P. Ticket." Courtesy of the Collection of Ronnie Lapinsky Sax.

BETTY FRIEDAN AND PAULI MURRAY CREATE AN NAACP FOR WOMEN

Betty Friedan, a writer and activist, and Pauli Murray, a civil rights and women's issues activist, encouraged establishment of a feminist civil rights organization when the federal Equal Employment Opportunity Commission (EEOC) refused to enforce Title VII of the 1964 Civil Rights Act that prohibited discrimination based on sex. Thus, three hundred women met in Washington, DC, in the fall of 1966. The outcome was the founding of the National Organization for Women (NOW) with Friedan as the group's first president. Its focus was "[t]o take action to bring women into full participation in the mainstream of American society now, exercising all privileges and responsibilities thereof in truly equal partnership with men." One of NOW's first priorities was passage of the Equal Rights Amendment. NOW also advocated for legislation surrounding child care, maternity leave, abortion rights, equal access to education, and pension rights for women. Today, NOW is the largest organization of women's rights activists in the United States, with chapters in each of the fifty states, and serves as a political action group, similar to the NAACP, by seeking change toward greater gender equality through lobbying, advocacy, education, and protest.

> The problem lay buried, unspoken, for many years in the minds of American women. It was a strange stirring, a sense of dissatisfaction, a yearning that women suffered in the middle of the twentieth century in the United States. Each suburban wife struggled with it alone. As she made the beds, shopped for groceries, matched slipcover material, ate peanut butter sandwiches with her children, chauffeured Cub Scouts and Brownies, lay beside her husband at night—she was afraid to ask even of herself the silent question—"Is this all?"
>
> —Opening passage of *The Feminine Mystique*, 1963, by Betty Friedan

CAROLINE O'DAY
DEMOCRATIC CANDIDATE FOR CONGRESS

has devoted years of service, in public office and in private effort, to the welfare of the people of the State.

Make a Representative Woman Your Representative

Caroline O'Day Democratic Candidate for Congress, handbill, ca. 1934.

Caroline O'Day (1875–1943) was the third woman and first Democrat to be elected to Congress from the state of New York, serving from 1935 to 1943. She was active in Democratic state politics and a huge supporter of the New Deal. Courtesy of the Cook-Dickerman Collection, Eleanor Roosevelt National Historic Site, National Park Service, US Department of the Interior.

Betty Friedan, photograph, 1960.

Betty Friedan (1921–2006) was a lifelong activist, feminist, and writer. In 1963, she wrote *The Feminine Mystique*, which was critical of the role that suburban homemakers played in society during that era. Historians believe this best-selling book led to the second wave of the women's movement in the 1960s. Courtesy of the Library of Congress.

NOW-NY Banner, ca. 1975.

NOW-NYS was established in 1974 and today is the largest women's political organization in New York State. The NOW-NYS chapter is "dedicated to fighting for women's equality, and to improving the status of women in New York State." Courtesy of the New York State Museum, H-1976.94.1.

Support Affirmative Action, NOW, button, ca.1975.

Courtesy of the Collection of Ronnie Lapinsky Sax.

Brandeis University professor Dr. Pauli Murray poses for a portrait in Waltham, Massachusetts, on September 25, 1970, photograph.

Pauli Murray (1910–1985) was a civil rights advocate, feminist, lawyer, the first African American woman ordained as an Episcopal priest, and the first women to be awarded a JDS degree from Yale University. She was active in the civil rights movement and the women's movement and coined the term "Jane Crow" as a reminder that African American women faced both discrimination and sexism. Courtesy of Associated Press Images.

Rhoda Barney Jenkins at a NOW rally, photograph, ca. 1980.

Rhoda Barney Jenkins (1920–2007), standing on the left, was the great-granddaughter of Elizabeth Cady Stanton and a fourth-generation feminist. In addition to being a longtime supporter of NOW and an equal rights proponent, she was also an accomplished architect. Courtesy of Coline Jenkins, Elizabeth Cady Stanton Family.

NOW sign used by Rhoda Barney Jenkins, ca. 1980.

Courtesy of Coline Jenkins, Elizabeth Cady Stanton Family.

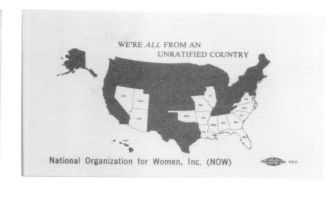

NOW business card with map, ca. 1975.

Courtesy of the Collection of Ronnie Lapinsky Sax.

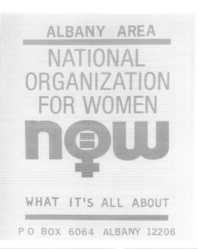

NOW Wonder Women, t-shirt, ca. 1975.

Courtesy of the New York State Museum,
H–1976.94.3

Assemblage of NOW materials, ca. 1975.

Courtesy of the New York State Museum,
H–1996.62.

PUBLISHING THE STORIES WOMEN *WANT* TO READ

Ms. MAGAZINE

The publishing world of twentieth-century New York City was dominated by men. Even in the offices of women's magazines, men served as editors, chose what type of articles were included, and solicited advertisers. Frustrated that women were not given the permission to write the type of articles they wanted to read, Gloria Steinem worked with Brenda Feigen to host meetings of female journalists in 1971 to discuss the possibility of a new type of women's publication. Out of the meetings came a long list of potential articles, and the goal of creating a glossy publication.

In August 1971, Clay Felker, editor of *New York* magazine, offered to launch the new magazine as an insert, and it appeared in December 1971 (although it was labeled as "Spring 1972," in case it lingered on newsstands). It sold out in eight days, and generated twenty-six thousand subscription orders. The first issue, with an image of a many-armed woman juggling a myriad of tasks on the cover, included stories on working conditions and equal pay, sexism in child-rearing, sisterhood, lesbianism, and "The Housewife's Moment of Truth," an article by Jane O'Reilly chronicling the instances when a woman realizes the unfairness of treatment of women.[24]

Selling advertising in the early years of the magazine was difficult, as the men who controlled advertising agencies often had set opinions regarding the type of advertisements that would be effective in a women's magazine. Gender stereotypes prevailed, as advertisers thought that women were not responsible for purchasing cars and thus would not buy automobile advertisements.

Founding editor Letty Cottin Pogrebin described the impact of the publication as the translation of "a movement into a magazine."[25] To some in the feminist movement, however, the magazine was not radical enough, and the message was "too watered down."[26] Many of the editors and contributors felt the need to strike a balance. Steinem explained, "I can understand if longtime feminists wanted more. But there needed to be articles that were for readers picking up a feminist magazine for the first or fifth or tenth time."[27]

GLORIA STEINEM

Following her studies at Smith College, Gloria Steinem (1934–) traveled in India, where her eyes were opened to political organizing and the importance of listening. Upon her return, she settled in New York City and began her career in journalism. Working as a freelance writer, Steinem received what she considered to be her "first serious assignment" to write "The Moral Disarmament of Betty Coed," on the changes to the social and professional lives of young women due to the birth

Ms. magazine, cover design by Miriam Wosk, Preview Issue, Spring 1972.

The first cover of *Ms.* magazine, which appeared on the preview issue, was designed by Miriam Wosk. It represents a modern version of the Hindu goddess Kali, chosen to represent the many tasks modern women juggle. Reprinted by permission of *Ms.* magazine, © 1972.

"Gloria Steinem and a Delegate," photograph, Diana Mara Henry, 1977.

Steinem served as a commissioner from New York State on the International Women's Year Commission committee. During the National Women's Conference in Houston, she kept up a tireless schedule as an organizer and served as a scribe for the minority caucus, helping to coalesce the diverse needs of the various minority groups into a cohesive resolution. Image © Diana Mara Henry.

Ms. magazine, July 1972.

Wonder Woman was chosen as the cover of the first full *Ms.* magazine, representing women's strength. *Ms.* covers have also featured real women of strength, from a variety of fields, as well as male feminist allies. Reprinted by permission of *Ms.* magazine, © 1972.

control pill.[28] Steinem's experience in the male-dominated publishing field led her to cofound *Ms.* magazine in 1972 as a forum for serious articles on women's issues generated by women editors and authors.

As an activist, Steinem has dedicated her life to travel to give talks, to promote feminist causes, including the ERA, and to facilitate discussions among diverse groups. In the 1960s and '70s, she traveled to colleges, community centers, and other venues, talking about women's liberation with speaking partners Dorothy Pitman Hughes, Margaret Sloan, and Florynce Kennedy.[29]

Steinem continues to promote women's rights and human rights through a variety of media. In 2013, President Obama awarded her with the Presidential Medal of Freedom, the highest civilian honor in the United States.

"FIGHTING SHIRLEY CHISHOLM—
UNBOUGHT AND UNBOSSED"

Shirley Chisholm campaign poster, 1972.

Courtesy of the New York State Museum, H-2010.41.1.

In 1968, Shirley Chisholm (1924–2005) became the first African American woman elected to the United States Congress. Prior to this, she served as the New York State assemblywoman from the Bushwick and Bedford-Stuyvesant areas of Brooklyn. Her major focus was improving conditions in her community. Chisholm ran against James Farmer Jr., director of the Congress on Racial Equality (CORE) and one of the most famous African American civil rights activists in the country. Her campaign platform included affordable housing, improved public education and daycare services, adequate hospital and nursing home facilities, and enforcement of anti-discrimination laws.[30] She won against Farmer by a two-to-one margin.

In Congress Chisolm represented two of the poorest urban communities in the country—Bedford Stuyvesant and Crown Heights, Brooklyn, where the population was predominately black and Puerto Rican. Despite this, the Democratic caucus assigned the freshman congresswoman from Brooklyn to the Rural Development and Forestry subcommittee. She protested the assignment and was reassigned to the Veterans Affairs Committee and, later, the Education and Employment Committees. At the time, Chisholm told reporters, "Apparently all they know here in Washington about Brooklyn is a tree grew here."[31]

Shirley Chisholm trading card, 1972.

Courtesy of the Collection of Ronnie Lapinsky Sax.

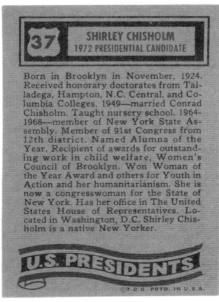

While in Congress, Chisholm publicly supported the ERA and brought the idea of women's equality to the House floor. "As a black person, I am no stranger to race prejudice. But the truth is that in the political world I have been far oftener discriminated against because I am a woman than because I am black. . . . Prejudice against women is still acceptable."[32] Chisholm, along with nationally prominent women, including Bella Abzug, Gloria Steinem, and Betty Friedan, founded the National Women's Political Caucus (NWPC) in 1971. She worked diligently to include black women and their issues in this organization and was somewhat successful.

In 1972, Chisholm, seeing herself a champion for the rights of all women, people of color, and the poor, decided to run for the office of president of the United States. She campaigned across the country and succeeded in getting her name on twelve primary ballots. At the Democratic National Convention, she received 152 delegate votes, or 10 percent of the total. While she did not win any primaries, Chisholm believed that her campaign for president was a "catalyst for change."[33]

> When I ran for the Congress, when I ran for president, I met more discrimination as a woman than for being black.
> —Shirley Chisholm to an AP reporter in December 1982

BATTLING BELLA ABZUG

Bella Abzug (1920–1998) was a longtime activist and proponent of equal rights for women. She grew up in New York City and became an attorney in the 1940s when few women entered this profession. In the 1960s, she became an anti-war activist, which led to a run for political office in New York City. In 1971, she made her first run and win for Congress on the Democratic ticket. Abzug was a huge supporter of the ERA, gay rights, and a founder of the National Women's Political Caucus.

Bella Running for Congress, photograph, 1976.

Bella Abzug giving a speech. Courtesy of the Museum of the City of New York, photograph by Diana Mara Henry, 2002.1.1.60.

Bella Abzug's hat and day dress with floral print, 1970–1979.

Abzug was well known for her hats and was often quoted as saying: "It's what's under the hat that counts!" Courtesy of the Museum of the City of New York, 99.33.5 and 99.33.12.

"Look Closely. There's Something Missing. Bella Abzug/Democrat for The Senate," handbill, ca. 1974.

Courtesy of the Sophia Smith Collection, Smith College.

While a congresswoman from New York, in the early 1970s, Abzug applied for a credit card and was refused. As a result, Abzug wrote and introduced legislation that would make this discrimination illegal. Single women were less likely than men to get credit, creditors were unlikely to give a married women credit in her own name, creditors were unwilling to count the wife's income when a married woman applied for credit, and women who were divorced or widowed had trouble establishing credit.[34] In short, women could rarely start a small business, get a credit card, or buy a house without being married. The Equal Credit Opportunity Act was passed by Congress in 1974, thus opening many doors to women.

> There are those who say I'm impatient, impetuous, uppity, rude, profane, brash, overbearing. Whether I'm any of these things or all of them, you can decide for yourself. But whatever I am—and this ought to be made very clear at the outset—I am a very serious woman.
>
> —Bella Abzug, *New York Times*, April 1, 1998

Look Closely.
There's Something Missing.

This is a picture of the U.S. Senate. Look closely. It has 100 members . . . you'll notice they're all men. In this 200th anniversary of American democracy, not even one woman serves in our highest lawmaking body.

There's something else missing from the Senate . . . strong, effective representation for *all* the people of New York State.

Incumbent Senator James Buckley has sided with President Ford *against* New York. He's voted *against* jobs, *against* social security increases, *against* consumer protection, *against* health and education programs, *against* child care, *against* the minimum wage.

He has voted for action that would raise gas and oil prices $40 billion a year. And he has spoken out for reckless international policies that could involve us in a war over Angola

and the Panama Canal. The people of New York want better representation than that. More and more of them are supporting Congresswoman Bella Abzug for the Senate.

In her three terms in Congress, Bella Abzug has provided strong effective leadership . . . her colleagues recently voted her the third "most influential" member of the House. (U.S. News & World Report, April 19).

House Majority Leader Thomas P. ("Tip") O'Neill says "she'd make the greatest Senator New York has ever seen."

Congressman Jonathan Bingham says "she has compiled an outstanding record of legislative achievements for New York State and for the Country as a whole." (Bella's work in Congress has brought more than $5 billion additional Federal aid to our state.)

We all need Bella as our Senator.

Help her get there. She'll be *more* than one in a hundred.

Bella Abzug/Democrat for The Senate
Primary Day, September 14

Bella Abzug for Senator Committee
130 East 40th Street, New York, N.Y. 10016

A copy of our report is filed with the Federal Election Commission, and is available for purchase from the Federal Election Commission, Washington, D.C.

Campaign buttons for Shirley Chisholm and Bella Abzug, ca. 1970.

Courtesy of the Collection of Ronnie Lapinsky Sax.

THE YEAR OF THE WOMAN

The United Nations declared 1975 "The Year of the Woman," and later, 1976 to 1985 was named the "United Nations Decade for Women." In January of 1975, Congress passed Public Law 94-167, drafted by Congresswoman Bella Abzug and Representative Patsy Mink.[35] It designated the "National Commission on the Observance of International Women's Year" and funded a plan to "convene a National Women's Conference."[36] Congress allocated five million dollars for the national conference and fifty-six state and territory meetings, all held in 1977.

In the state and territory meetings, planners were directed to specifically reach out to women who did not normally attend meetings, and funds were set aside for transportation for those who could not afford it.[37] Attendees elected delegates to the national meeting. They also voted on sixteen resolutions based on the National Commission's 1976 report, "To Form a More Perfect Union," and developed policies, called planks, for potential inclusion in a national plan of action. This was not without controversy and argument in many states, as meetings included women from groups opposed to measures suggested in the resolutions.[38] Ultimately, the state and territory meetings produced 4,500 resolutions, in addition to the sixteen suggested by the National Commission.[39]

International Women's Year, pin, ca. 1975.

Courtesy of the Collection of Ronnie Lapinsky Sax.

United Nations Decade for Women, button, ca. 1976.

Courtesy of the Collection of Ronnie Lapinsky Sax.

Focus on Women, button, ca. 1975.

Courtesy of the Collection of Ronnie Lapinsky Sax.

A Worldwide Sisterhood for Equality, button, ca. 1975.

Courtesy of the Collection of Ronnie Lapinsky Sax.

This collection of buttons and pins were worn during events celebrating the Year of the Woman and the Decade for Women. The logo for these efforts features a peace dove, with a Venus symbol representing women.

THE FIRST NEW YORK STATE WOMEN'S MEETING

The first New York State Women's Meeting was held at the Empire State Plaza in Albany, July 8–10, 1977. The primary goals for the meeting were to "assess the status of women in our social, political and economic institutions, identify any barriers to full and equal participation and recommend positive action to eliminate those barriers," and to elect delegates to the national meeting.[40]

The meeting, as well as the federal commission, also sought to "highlight the achievements of women." The opening show, *Celebrating Women*, was produced by Madeline Gilford and featured prominent actresses, a Hispanic dance troupe, and an African American rock group. Workshops were held for convention attendees on a variety of topics, including family, health, public life, employment, education, and consumerism. Cultural programming also took place around the plaza. Exhibitions featured the work of women artists, photographs by Alice Austen, images of New York State Women, "early artifacts from the women's suffrage movement" on loan from the Smithsonian, and art from what was then Bedford Women's Prison. "Television by and

New York State Women's Meeting handouts, 1977.

The official packet handed out to participants at the New York State Women's Meeting included workshop listings, maps of downtown Albany, flyers from governmental agencies on issues pertaining to women, and the "International Women's Year Poem," by Judith Cody. Courtesy of the New York State Museum, H-1984.18.24.

"Waiting to Speak at the Outdoor Session of the New York State Women's Meeting, Empire State Plaza, Albany," photograph, Diana Mara Henry, 1977.

The New York State Women's Meeting took over many of the indoor and outdoor spaces of the Empire State Plaza with workshops, plenary sessions, voting stations, and information and cultural displays. Image © Diana Mara Henry.

"New York State Basket Weaver at the New York State Women's Meeting, Empire State Plaza, Albany," photograph, Diana Mara Henry, 1977.

In many states, including New York, displays relating to cultural heritage and works by women artists and performers were featured. Image © Diana Mara Henry.

for women" was shown in a continuous loop. An oral history project worked to collect "the impressions, values and opinions" of the women attending the meeting.[41]

Meeting planners expected three thousand attendees. Actual attendance at the meeting was significantly larger, with reports stating anywhere from seven thousand to eleven thousand attendees. Gloria Steinem, who worked at the meeting as an International Women's Year commissioner, remembered:

> In Albany, the capital of New York State, more than eleven thousand women—four times more than we planned for—lined up outside government buildings in the sweltering July heat, then waited most of the night in an airless basement to cast ballots for delegates and issues. I'd stopped in Albany for the opening ceremony—and then I was going home to write and make a living, but I ended up staying for two days and two nights without bed or toothbrush, helping with the voting lines.[42]

New York State voted to adopt all sixteen of the nationally suggested resolutions and elected eighty-eight delegates to send to the national conference in Houston.[43]

MARY ANNE KRUPSAK (1932–)

Born in Schenectady, New York, Mary Anne Krupsak worked for women's rights in several capacities within New York State government. She served in the New York State Assembly from 1968 to 1972 and then in the New York State Senate from 1972 to 1974. As a senator, she sponsored

Carey Krupsak Team, button, ca. 1974.
Carey/Krupsak, necklace, ca. 1974.
Mary Anne Krupsak for Lt. Gov., button, ca. 1974.

These campaign materials supported Krupsak's 1974 run for lieutenant governor, with Hugh Carey running for governor. Courtesy of the New York State Museum, H-1976.224.175, H-2006.71.1585, H-1976.224.174.

"Krupsak. She's Not Just One of the Boys." political pamphlet, ca. 1974.

Courtesy of the New York State Museum, H-1976.224.266.

legislation to remove corroboration requirements for rape trials.

Krupsak served as the first female lieutenant governor of New York State under Governor Hugh Carey, from 1975 to 1978. In this role, she set a new precedent for the position, traveling extensively across the state meeting with constituents. She was appointed honorary co-chair of the President's National Commission on Observance of International Women's Year, alongside Bella Abzug.

In June of 1978, Krupsak withdrew her bid for reelection as lieutenant governor to challenge Carey for the Democratic nomination for governor. She lost in the primary.[44]

THE NATIONAL WOMEN'S CONFERENCE, HOUSTON

Over twenty thousand attendees gathered in Houston, Texas, for the National Women's Conference, held November 18–21, 1977. The conference was a diverse gathering and presented minority women with an important stage to voice their concerns.

The primary goal for the meeting was to develop a national plan of action for gender equality. In her opening address, Chairwoman Bella Abzug explained:

> The law directs us to examine the past and the present. It directs us to examine the status of American women, our needs, our problems, and the diversity of our lives. It directs us to seek change and improvements in the lives of women who have been held back by discriminatory practices.[45]

Twenty-six planks, or resolutions, were brought to the conference out of discussion and voting at the state meetings. Topics included child care, education, the Equal Rights Amendment, health, and reproductive freedom. One plank, promoting equal credit, passed unanimously, while seventeen others passed with majorities. Other topics inspired fierce debate, especially protections for sexual choice, which promoted protection of lesbian rights. Opponents were concerned with linking the feminist movement with lesbian rights, as "lesbian" was already used as a taunt at feminists. Supporters declared that protection for lesbian women was a women's issue, and some, including Gloria Steinem, believed that "any rebellious woman will be called a lesbian until the word 'lesbian' becomes as honorable a word as any other."[46] Ultimately, the resolution passed.

Mary Anne Krupsak for Governor, button, 1978.

Courtesy of the Collection of Ronnie Lapinsky Sax.

"May the Force Be with Us, Houston '77," t-shirt, 1977.

Courtesy of the New York State Museum, H-1991.99.1.

National Women's Conference, button, 1977.

Courtesy of the Collection of Ronnie Lapinsky Sax.

ERA Yes, League of Women Voters, IWY Houston 1977, button, 1977.

Courtesy of the Collection of Ronnie Lapinsky Sax.

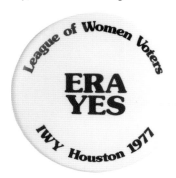

"Last Mile of the First National Women's conference," photograph, Diana Mara Henry, 1977.

"The torch of freedom has been handed from
generation to generation of women, and the torch
we see here today is a symbol of our past victories
and our hopes for the future." —Bella Abzug,
speech at first plenary session at the National
Women's Conference

The National Women's conference in Houston
was kicked off by a torch relay, which began in
Seneca Falls. Over one thousand women carried
the torch across fourteen states. The relay began on
September 29, 1977, when Millicent Brady Moore,
descendant of 1848 convention attendee Susan
Quinn Brown, handed the torch off to Kathrine
Switzer, first woman to officially compete in the
Boston Marathon.

The runners also carried a handwritten scroll
that contained Maya Angelou's 1977 revision of
the Declaration of Sentiments, a poem called "To
Form a More Perfect Union." The poem was read
the night before the relay began in Seneca Falls,
and again at the opening of the convention. Image
© Diana Mara Henry.

Women who formed the minority caucus at the conference were "drawn together by double discrimination."[47] Latinas, Native Americans, Asian Americans, and African Americans made up about one-quarter of the total delegates of the conference. The caucus decided to rewrite the minority plank that had been suggested by the National Commission. As the different minority groups discussed issues they faced, overarching themes emerged, and they were able to draft a statement. Each of the smaller groups also attached an amendment that addressed specialized concerns of their own communities. Coretta Scott King declared, "Let this message go forth from Houston, and spread all over this land. There is a new force, a new understanding, a new sisterhood against all injustice that has been born here. We will not be divided and defeated again."[48]

With twenty-six planks recognizing the need for federal involvement to improve equality, the plan for action was passed on to Congress and President Jimmy Carter. It led to the creation of the National Advisory Committee for Women. Additionally, the Senate granted a three-year extension for ratification of the Equal Rights Amendment. The meeting also served to raise awareness of women's issues and started conversations. Steinem later described the impact of the conference: "In 1977 . . . we were in the first stage, a necessary stage, of a social justice movement which is change of consciousness. You can't create change until you have the imagination of change and the Houston conference really created a majority change of consciousness."[49]

OPPOSITION

During the conference, a separate opposition meeting was also held at the Astro Arena in Houston, headed up by Phyllis Schlafly and Congressman Robert Dornan. Anti-feminist protesters considered the national conference and the plan for action "anti-family," and Schlafly called the International Women's Year Commission "a costly mistake at the taxpayer's expense."[50]

Opposition was present at the main conference as well. At some state meetings, delegates were chosen from opposition groups, including the Ku Klux Klan, even though these groups did not always match the majority opinion of the states they represented.[51]

CREATIVE WOMEN'S COLLECTIVE

The arts have been often used to communicate ideas and disseminate messages about the women's cause. In the twentieth century, some feminists took to the art of silk-screening, getting their message out through t-shirts and posters. In New York City, the Collective Graphics Workshop, founded in 1970 to create anti-war materials, transitioned into the Creative Women's Collective, "a non-profit organization of women artists: painters, sculptors, graphic artists, photographers, and others—who share a commitment to issues of concern to women and social change."[52] The collective's artists created original designs and did screen printing on posters and t-shirts for feminist groups and programs. Studio space was available for rent to artists. A diverse offering of classes helped members grow artistically, gain the skills needed to set up their own studios, and to use their talents to promote a cause. Courses included "silk screening for grass-roots fundraising," "flyer preparation," and even "basic

"Creative Women's Collective," poster, ca. 1975.

This poster, created to advertise the Creative Women's Collective, uses images taken in the collective's studios of women at work on silk-screening projects. Courtesy of the New York State Museum, H-1991.99.270.

"International Women's Day," poster, Creative Women's Collective, ca. 1975.

International Women's Day grew out of the women's labor movement in the beginning of the twentieth century and was first celebrated in 1911. The United Nations recognized the day in 1975, when the organization also celebrated the year of the woman. Courtesy of the New York State Museum, H-1991.99.266A.

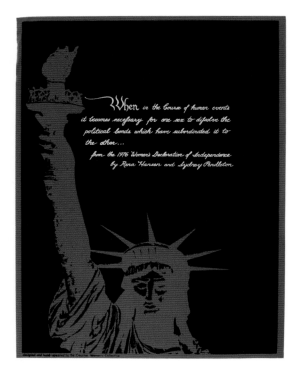

"Women's Declaration of Independence," poster, designed and silk-screened by Jacqueline Skiles, ca. 1977.

The Statue of Liberty and the Declaration of Independence were both frequently used as symbols in the fight for women's rights. In the 1970s, Rena Hansen and Sydney Pendleton penned the "Women's Declaration of Independence." The Creative Women's Collective designed and printed this poster as a fundraiser to help cover the costs of printing and distributing the new declaration. Courtesy of the New York State Museum, H-1991.99.280.

plumbing and electricity."[53] Located in an ethnically diverse neighborhood with a poor employment outlook for low-income youth, the collective offered a training program for young women, designed to teach them skills such as graphic design and silk-screening, that they could use to gain a job in the arts.[54]

PRESERVING MEMORIES AND CARRYING FORWARD THE MESSAGE

In the late nineteenth century, Susan B. Anthony, Elizabeth Cady Stanton, and Matilda Joslyn Gage set out to write the *History of Woman Suffrage*, a task that eventually generated six volumes. The publication wasn't completed until after all three women had died and additional authors joined in writing and editing. The effort was one of preservation, but it was also political: putting the history of the movement down on paper was a marketing tool that helped the cause. In the twentieth century, saving the history of the movement took on many forms, including art and historic preservation.

Sites dedicated to the history of the women's rights movement serve to remind us not only of the women who fought for the cause, but also the struggles they faced. These sites and memorials can serve as reminders of just how far we have come, and of the work left to be done.

The Portrait Monument

The Portrait Monument, originally titled *The Woman Movement*, depicts Lucretia Mott, Elizabeth Cady Stanton, and Susan B. Anthony, as well as unfinished sections representing rights yet to be won. Adelaide Johnson was commissioned to create the work, and the portraits are copies of her busts of the three women originally created for display at the Court of Honor in the Women's Building at the 1893 World's Columbian Exposition.[55]

Presented as a gift to the US Capitol by the National Woman's Party, *The Portrait Monument* was intended for display in the Rotunda. When congressional committees declared it "too heavy" and "not of adequate artistic merit," the National Woman's Party had it delivered to the Capitol anyway and announced an unveiling on February 15, 1921, Susan B. Anthony's 101st birthday.

Following the ceremony, the monument was quickly moved downstairs to the crypt. The placement hid Johnson's inscription on the back, which at that point had only been penciled on. Soon after, the inscription was painted over.[56]

After years of demands that the sculpture be moved back to the Rotunda, legislation to move it finally passed the Senate in 1995 but was killed in the House of Representatives. A year later, legislation was passed, but without funding. After almost $75,000 of private funds were raised, the work was finally moved. New York representative Carolyn Maloney commented:

It took 72 years for women to get the vote and 76 years to get the statue moved. They said the statue was too ugly to stand in the Rotunda. Have you looked at Abraham Lincoln lately? He wasn't placed in the Rotunda because of his good looks and neither were these women. They are placed here because of their accomplishments.[57]

Final movement of the sculpture was not without controversy or question. Objecting to the way that Johnson's work effectively wrote the contributions of African American women out of the history of the suffrage movement, the National Congress of Black Women worked to

The Portrait Monument to Lucretia Mott, Elizabeth Cady Stanton, and Susan B. Anthony, Adelaide Johnson, 1921, marble, photographed by Harris & Ewing, ca. 1921.

The sculpture depicts three leaders of the women's rights movement in the nineteenth century, Elizabeth Cady Stanton, Susan B. Anthony, and Lucretia Mott. The unfinished pillar represented work yet to be accomplished. Courtesy of the Library of Congress.

Delivery of *The Portrait Monument* to the Capitol, photograph, 1921.

Sculptor Adelaide Johnson looked on as *The Portrait Monument* was delivered to the Capitol. Courtesy of the Library of Congress.

The Portrait Monument in the Crypt of the Capitol, photograph, 1929.

The women in this photograph are displaying the National Woman's Party flag and laying a wreath at the portrait monument. At the time, the sculpture was displayed downstairs, in the crypt of the Capitol. The location was hardly a place of honor, as it was cramped, dark, and adjacent to the bathrooms. Courtesy of the Library of Congress.

block the move. After a movement for Sojourner Truth to be carved into the unfinished section failed in 2004, a bronze bust of Truth was accepted in 2006 and was unveiled in 2009 in Emancipation Hall.[58]

THE SUSAN B. ANTHONY HOUSE, ROCHESTER, NEW YORK

Susan B. Anthony's House, at 17 Madison Street in Rochester, New York, was already a place of pilgrimage for suffrage leaders before Anthony's death. By 1894, rooms in the first floor served as public offices for the cause, while mail was sorted upstairs in the bedrooms. In 1895, Anthony added a third story to the house, to accommodate a workroom. The space quickly filled with writings collected for the *History of Woman Suffrage.*

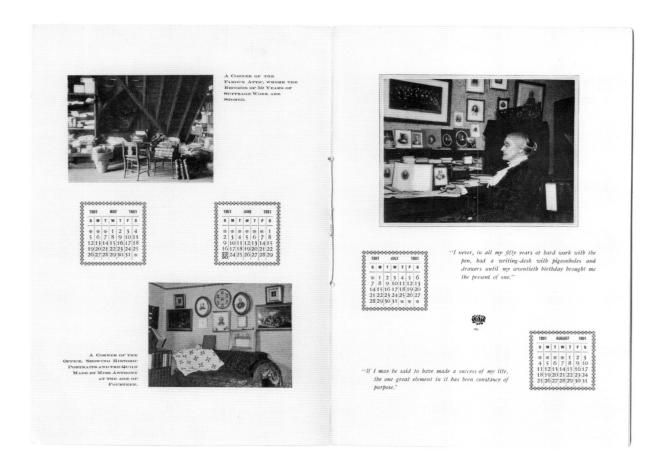

After the deaths of Susan B. Anthony in 1906 and her sister Mary Anthony in 1907, the house went through a series of private owners. In 1944, the Rochester Federation of Women's Clubs placed a historic marker outside, sparking discussion about turning the house into a museum.[59] On August 25, 1945, Eleanor Roosevelt reported in her *My Day* column:

> I am told by the president of the Rochester, N. Y. Federation of Women's Clubs that they have formed a Susan B. Anthony memorial fund for the purpose of raising $10,000 to buy the house in which Miss Anthony lived. It will be possible for women in the future to draw courage and inspiration by renewing their memories of this courageous and self-sacrificing woman.[60]

The Anthony Home Calendar, 1900.

Published while Susan B. Anthony was still alive, The Anthony Home Calendar highlighted quotes by Anthony and images of her home. There was an emphasis on spaces used for suffrage work, including the attic workroom, where Anthony and her colleagues worked on organizing papers for the *History of Woman Suffrage*. The image of Anthony seated at her desk shows her collection of photographs of women who were friends and colleagues in the suffrage movement. Courtesy of the Department of Rare Books and Special Collections, University of Rochester Libraries.

Sign, ca. 1907.

This sign was used to mark the Anthony house shortly after Susan and Mary's deaths in 1906 and 1907, ten years before women gained suffrage in New York State. The site was given great importance by the suffragists who kept up the fight. Courtesy of the National Susan B. Anthony Museum & House.

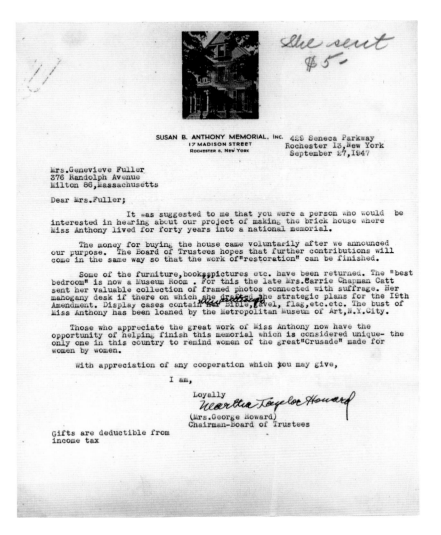

Letter, Mrs. George Howard to
Mrs. Genevieve Fuller, September 27, 1947.

Organizers from the Rochester Federation of
Women's Clubs sent out hundreds of written
appeals to women across the country, asking
for donations to support purchase of the house
to turn it into a memorial. Another round of
fundraising followed, raising money for the
restoration of the house to open it to the public.
Copies of these letters, with notations of the
donations that were sent, are still in the collection of the Susan B. Anthony House. Courtesy of
the National Susan B. Anthony Museum & House.

The campaign was successful, and the house
was purchased. The donations included one
from Roosevelt herself.

Susan and Mary's belongings were split
among friends after their deaths, so their fur-
nishings and personal items had to be sought
out for the museum. Carrie Chapman Catt
put together a collection of photographs
depicting the history of the women's rights
movement and its leaders, to be displayed in
the house.

Women's Rights National Historic Park, Seneca Falls, New York

Seneca Falls lacked a site devoted to remem-
bering women's rights well into the twentieth
century, despite the importance the 1848 Seneca Falls convention had to the movement. In
1871, the Wesleyan Congregation built a new
church and sold the chapel where the convention took place.[61] In the ensuing years,
the building was buried under additions and
served as several different businesses, including a car dealership, a movie theater, and a
laundromat.[62] Stanton and her family moved
to New York City in 1862, and their house
went through a procession of private owners
as well.[63]

The village became a site of pilgrimage. In
1908, during the sixtieth-anniversary celebra-
tion meetings, a memorial plaque sculpted by Elizabeth St. John Matthews was placed on the side of the building that had been the Wesleyan
Chapel.[64] In 1923, the ERA was launched by Alice Paul from Seneca Falls
during celebrations for the seventy-fifth anniversary of the 1848 convention. In 1932, a New York State Historic Marker was erected, which
soon became the site of petition drives supporting the development of
a National Historic Site.

In 1978, feminists succeeded in getting the National Park Service to
consider development of a national historic park focused on women's
rights. After a site visit, the National Parks Service made a recommen-
dation to Congress in favor of creation of a new park, and legislation
was announced March 8, 1980, at the beginning of women's history
month. The law passed and was signed by President Carter, but it did
not include funding. The start of the Reagan administration and new
funding freezes further imperiled founding of the park.

The Elizabeth Cady Stanton Foundation stepped in to raise funds
to purchase Stanton's home, and with a major last-minute contribution

Seventy-fifth anniversary commemorations in Seneca Falls, photograph, 1923.

The seventy-fifth anniversary of the 1848 women's rights convention was commemorated with speeches, music, and pageantry on the lawn of Trinity Episcopal Church in Seneca Falls. Alice Paul used the occasion to announce the Equal Rights Amendment. Courtesy of the Seneca Falls Historical Society.

Unveiling a commemorative plaque at the Wesleyan Chapel, photograph, 1908.

During a 1908 meeting commemorating the sixtieth anniversary of the Seneca Falls convention, hosted by Harriot Stanton Blatch and the Equality League of Self-Supporting Women, a commemorative bronze plaque was unveiled on the former Wesleyan Chapel. The bas-relief, sculpted by Elizabeth St. John Matthews, read, "On this spot stood the Wesleyan Chapel where the first Woman's Rights Convention in the world's history was held, July 19 and 20, 1848. At that meeting Elizabeth Cady Stanton moved the following resolution, which was seconded by Frederick Douglass: Resolved, That it is the duty of the women of this country to secure to themselves the sacred right to the elective franchise" (Wellman, *The Road to Seneca Falls*, 229–230). Courtesy of the Seneca Falls Historical Society.

The former Wesleyan Chapel, Seneca Falls, New York, photograph, ca. 1970.

After the Wesleyan Church moved to a new building, the former chapel that was the site of the 1848 women's rights convention served as several different private businesses, including a laundromat, as shown in this photograph. The building was unrecognizable due to a series of additions, save for the 1908 commemorative plaque and 1932 New York State Historic Marker. Courtesy of the Seneca Falls Historical Society.

New York State Historic Marker, 1948.

The New York State Education Department placed this marker at the Susan B. Anthony House in 1948. In 1966, the site was also designated as a National Historic Landmark. Courtesy of the National Susan B. Anthony Museum & House.

Women's Rights Centennial Committee ribbon, 1948, and Amelia Bloomer commemorative card, 1948.

In 1948, the village of Seneca Falls held a celebration commemorating the 100th anniversary of the Seneca Falls convention. Focus of the celebrations was on the early leaders of the women's rights movement, even those, like Amelia Bloomer, who had not been present at the 1848 convention. Courtesy of the Seneca Falls Historical Society.

from actor and activist Alan Alda, the house was saved. The park opened on July 17, 1982.[65] The event was both celebratory and political, with many protesters present calling for another effort to pass the Equal Rights Amendment. Alda served as the keynote speaker at the event and was originally told he could not speak about the ERA, at which point he declined to attend. When the National Parks Service changed its mind, Alda said, "What beat us is hatred of women. People don't care about equality, because they don't care about women."[66]

The National Parks Service purchased the Wesleyan Chapel in 1985 and first undertook the process of peeling off all the later additions. There was little original fabric left, and the building was stabilized and partially enclosed with a pavilion roof. In 2009, rehabilitation work began on the building once more. Missing walls were replaced, and the building was made to look like it would have in 1848.[67] The park was also able to acquire the M'Clintock House, which is currently open as a museum, and the Hunt House, which is under restoration.

THE FUTURE

The stories of the women who fought for equality and of those who made important contributions to American society are told more and more in museums, at historic sites, in history books, in movies, and on the currency . . . but women's representation in history continues to lag far behind men's. Still, victories are being made.

In June 2016, after months of heated debate, the United States Treasury Department announced that a new slate of women would grace one side of several denominations of paper bills. While allegorical females appeared on United States currency on numerous occasions, there have been few instances of real women doing so. Martha Washington appeared on a $1 silver certificate in the nineteenth century, a silver dollar honoring Susan B. Anthony was released in 1979, and Sacagawea was depicted on a gold dollar coin in 2000. The new bills will feature a slate of women who influenced the women's rights movement, many with New York State ties: Harriet Tubman on the $20 bill; Lucretia Mott, Sojourner Truth, Susan B. Anthony, Elizabeth Cady Stanton, and Alice Paul on the $10 bill; and Marian Anderson and Eleanor Roosevelt (as well as Martin Luther King Jr.) on the $5 bill.[68]

An effort is underway to place a statue of Elizabeth Cady Stanton and Susan B. Anthony in New York City's Central Park. When completed, the sculpture will be the first to represent real women from history in the park.[69] Supporters of the project cite examples from cities around the world, where women are being inserted into the historical narrative in public spaces, through efforts such as the renaming of streets and transportation stops. The project received conceptual approval from New York City Parks commissioner Mitchell J. Silver and is now in the process of fundraising.[70] The project has drawn support from diverse donors, including the donation of $1,920 from Girl Scout Troop 3484 in Manhattan, raised through cookie sales.

Bring Women of History—Out of the Dark and into the Park, bracelet, 2016.

After learning about the Central Park women's monument project, students at Fiorello H. LaGuardia High School of Music & Art and Performing Arts decided to sell bracelets as a fundraiser. The slogan they created, "out of the dark and into the park," echoes the suffragist rallying call, "Forward, out of error, Leave behind the night, Forward through the darkness, Forward into Light." Courtesy of the New York State Museum, Pam Elam Collection, H-2016.32.

CONCLUSION

The *Votes for Women: Celebrating New York's Suffrage Centennial* exhibition provides an opportunity to reexamine the efforts of the state's women and men who worked for the vote and the subsequent push for equality. However, this endeavor does not end after the centennial celebration; historians across the state continue working to document this important movement, and the New York State Museum is actively collecting artifacts related to women's history—most recently, artifacts connected to the 2017 Women's March on Washington, DC, and associated New York State marches. As the struggle for women's equality continues, how will you help preserve this vital story?

Susan B. Anthony's gravesite, Rochester, New York, Election Day 2016, photograph.

On November 8, 2016, over ten thousand people visited Susan B. Anthony's gravesite at Mount Hope Cemetery to pay homage to one of the leaders of the suffrage movement. With the Democratic Party's nomination, Hillary Rodham Clinton ran as the first female presidential candidate backed by a major political party. Clinton won the popular vote but lost the electoral vote. Courtesy of the City of Rochester Communications Bureau.

NOTES

INTRODUCTION

1. "Women Adopt Form for Equal Rights," *New York Times*, July 22, 1923.

2. Lauren Gambino, "Hillary Clinton's Rise Earns Place of Honor in Birthplace of US Women's Suffrage," *The Guardian*, 18 June 2016. https://www.theguardian.com/us-news/2016/jun/18/hillary-clinton-seneca-falls-women-rights-history (accessed on 30 June 2016).

SECTION 1. AGITATE! AGITATE!, 1776–1890

1. Abigail Adams to John Adams, 31 March 1776.

2. Abigail Adams to John Adams, 14 August 1776.

3. Abigail Adams to John Adams, 7 May 1776.

4. Elizabeth Ann Bartlett, *Liberty, Equality, Sorority: The Origins and Interpretation of American Feminist Thought: Frances Wright, Sarah Grimke, and Margaret Fuller* (Brooklyn: Carlson, 1994), 26.

5. Elizabeth Cady Stanton, Susan B. Anthony, and Matilda Joslyn Gage, eds., *History of Woman Suffrage*, Vol. 1 (New York: Fowler and Wells, 1881), 35.

6. Megan Marshall, *Margaret Fuller: A New American Life* (New York: Houghton Mifflin Harcourt, 2013), 132–135.

7. Phyllis Cole, "Stanton, Fuller, and the Grammar of Romanticism," *The New England Quarterly*, Vol. 73, No. 4 (December 2000): 533–559.

8. Elisha P. Hurlbut, *Essays on Human Rights and Their Political Guaranties* (New York: Greeley and McElrath, 1845).

9. Jeffrey Dunnington, "A Study of the Journal of Elisha P. Hurlbut, American Social Reformer, 1858–1887" (master's thesis, Virginia Commonwealth University, 2014), 14.

10. William G. Bishop and William H. Attree, *Report of the Debates and Proceedings of the Convention for the Revision of the Constitution of the State of New-York, 1846* (Albany: Evening Atlas, 1846), 646.

11. Laura E. Free, *Suffrage Reconstructed: Gender, Race, and Voting Rights in the Civil War Era* (Ithaca: Cornell University Press, 2015), 33.

12. Judith Wellman, *The Road to Seneca Falls: Elizabeth Cady Stanton and the First Woman's Rights Convention* (Urbana: University of Illinois Press, 2004), 146–152.

13. Robert Owen, quoted in Yuri Suhl, *Ernestine L. Rose and the Battle for Human Rights* (New York: Reynal, 1959), 28.

14. Ernestine Rose, quoted in Suhl, *Ernestine L. Rose and the Battle for Human Rights*, 65.

15. Speech to the 1851 Women's Rights Convention, Ernestine Rose Society, Brandeis University, http://www.brandeis.edu/wsrc/affiliates/ernestinerose/1851speech.html (accessed 20 June 2016).

16. "About Ernestine Rose," Ernestine Rose Society, Brandeis University, https://www.brandeis.edu/wsrc/affiliates/ernestinerose/shortbio.html (accessed 31 May 2016).

17. "A Feminist Pioneer," Ernestine Rose Society, Brandeis University, http://www.brandeis.edu/wsrc/affiliates/ernestinerose/ (accessed 20 June 2016).

18. Ira V. Brown, "'Am I Not a Woman and a Sister?' The Anti-Slavery Convention of American Women, 1837–1839," *Pennsylvania History: A Journal of Mid-Atlantic Studies*, Vol. 50, No. 1 (January 1983): 1–19.

19. William Lloyd Garrison, *Liberator*, 14 July 1832, in Brown, "'Am I Not a Woman and a Sister?'"

20. Brown, "'Am I Not a Woman and a Sister?'"

21. Gerda Lerner, *The Grimké Sisters of South Carolina: Rebels Against Slavery* (Boston: Houghton Mifflin, 1967), 165–204.

22. Sarah Grimké, "Letters on the Equality of the Sexes and the Condition of Woman," *New England Spectator*, 1838.

23. Sherry H. Penney and James D. Livingston, *A Very Dangerous Woman: Martha Wright and Women's Rights* (Boston and Amherst: University of Massachusetts Press, 2004), 68–69.

24. Stanton, Anthony, and Gage, *History of Woman Suffrage*, 1:62.

25. *Seneca County Courier*, July 11, 1848, reprinted in Stanton, Anthony, and Gage, *History of Woman Suffrage*, 1:67.

26. Wellman, *The Road to Seneca Falls*, 191–193.

27. *Report of the Woman's Rights Convention, Held at Seneca Falls, N.Y., July 19th and 20th, 1848* (Rochester: John Dick, The North Star Office, 1848).

28. Wellman, *The Road to Seneca Falls*, 195.

29. Stanton, Anthony, and Gage, *History of Woman Suffrage*, 1:73.

30. Stanton, Anthony, and Gage, *History of Woman Suffrage*, 1:75.

31. Stanton, Anthony, and Gage, *History of Woman Suffrage*, 1:78–81.

32. Stanton, Anthony, and Gage, *History of Woman Suffrage*, 1:86–87.

33. Stanton, Anthony, and Gage, *History of Woman Suffrage*, 1:87.

34. Free, *Suffrage Reconstructed*, 43.

35. Penney and Livingston, *A Very Dangerous Woman*, 37.

36. Wellman, *The Road to Seneca Falls*, 61.

37. Lucretia Mott, *Discourse on Woman, by Lucretia Mott. Delivered at the Assembly Buildings, December 17, 1849. Being a full photographic report, revised by the author.* (Philadelphia: T.B. Peterson, 1850), 3; from Library of Congress, National American Woman Suffrage Association Collection, http://memory.loc.gov/cgi-bin/query/h?ammem/nawbib:@field(NUMBER+@band(rbnawsa+n2748)) (accessed 31 May 2016).

38. Mott, *Discourse on Woman*, 7.

39. "Hints for Wives," in Penney and Livingston, *A Very Dangerous Woman*, 78–79.

40. Martha Coffin Wright to Lucretia Mott, 16 October 1848, in Penney and Livingston, *A Very Dangerous Woman*, 81.

41. Martha Coffin Wright to Lucretia Mott, 13 May 1846, in Penney and Livingston, *A Very Dangerous Woman*, 70–71.

42. Martha Coffin Wright to Elizabeth M'Clintock, 8 January 1850, Garrison Family Papers, Sophia Smith Collection, Smith College.

43. Amy Kesselman, "The 'Freedom Suit': Feminism and Dress Reform in the United States, 1848–1875," *Gender and Society*, Vol. 5, No. 4 (December 1991): 495–510.

44. *History of Woman Suffrage*, 1:459.

45. Eleanor Flexner and Ellen Fitzpatrick, *Century of Struggle: The Woman's Rights Movement in the United States* (Cambridge: The Belknap Press of Harvard University Press, 1996), 80–81.

46. Ann D. Gordon, ed., *The Selected Papers of Elizabeth Cady Stanton and Susan B. Anthony: In the School of Anti-Slavery, 1840–1866* (New Brunswick: Rutgers University Press, 2001), 1:40.

47. Sarah Flick interview on C-Span, *Matilda Joslyn Gage Home*, 21 September 2015, http://www.c-span.org/video/?328400-1/matilda-joslyn-gage-home. Speech to the National Women's Rights Convention, 1852, http://www.matildajoslyngage.org/gage-home/womens-rights-room/gages-writing/national-womans-rights-convention-1852/ (accessed 27 May 2015).

48. Matilda Joslyn Gage to "My dear Helen," 11 December 1893, Gage Collection, Schlesinger Library, Radcliffe College, in Sally Roesch Wagner, *Sisters in Spirit: Haudenosaunee (Iroquois) Influence on Early American Feminists* (Summertown: Native Voices, 2001), 32.

49. Wagner, *Sisters in Spirit*.

50. "Sojourner Truth," Women's Rights National Historical Park, National Park Service, https://www.nps.gov/wori/learn/historyculture/sojourner-truth.htm (accessed 22 June 2016).

51. "Sojourner Truth."

52. Frances Ellen Watkins Harper, "We Are All Bound Up Together," in *Proceedings of the Eleventh Women's Rights Convention* (New York: Robert J. Johnston, 1866).

53. Parker Pillsbury to Elizabeth Cady Stanton, May(?) 1860, in Gordon, *The Selected Papers of Elizabeth Cady Stanton and Susan B. Anthony: In the School of Anti-Slavery, 1840–1866*, 1:433.

54. Gordon, *The Selected Papers of Elizabeth Cady Stanton and Susan B. Anthony: In the School of Anti-Slavery, 1840–1866*, 1:429.

55. "Equal Rights Convention," *The Argus* (Albany, NY), 21 November 1866.

56. Flexner and Fitzpatrick, *Century of Struggle*, 139; "Equal Rights Convention," *The Argus* (Albany, NY), 21 November 1866; "Albany: Equal Rights Convention—Opposition to the Constitutional Amendment—An Address from Miss Anthony on the Rights of Working Women," *New York Times*, 22 November 1866.

57. Lisa Tetrault, *The Myth of Seneca Falls: Memory and the Women's Suffrage Movement, 1848–1898* (Chapel Hill: University of North Carolina Press, 2014), 19–22.

58. Tetrault, *The Myth of Seneca Falls*, 24–25.

59. Flexner and Fitzpatrick, *Century of Struggle*, 138.

60. Elizabeth Cady Stanton, Susan B. Anthony, and Matilda Joslyn Gage, eds., *History of Woman Suffrage*, Vol. 2 (New York: Fowler & Wells, 1882), 270.

61. Stanton, Anthony, and Gage, *History of Woman Suffrage*, 2:270–282.

62. Ann D. Gordon, ed., *The Selected Papers of Elizabeth Cady Stanton and Susan B. Anthony: Against an Aristocracy of Sex, 1866–1873* (New Brunswick: Rutgers University Press, 2001), 2:73.

63. Stanton, Anthony, and Gage, *History of Woman Suffrage*, 2:284.

64. Gordon, *The Selected Papers of Elizabeth Cady Stanton and Susan B. Anthony: Against an Aristocracy of Sex, 1866–1873*, 2:75–76.

65. Stanton, Anthony, and Gage, *History of Woman Suffrage*, 2:284.

66. Stanton, Anthony, and Gage, *History of Woman Suffrage*, 2:287–304.

67. Tetrault, *The Myth of Seneca Falls*, 28.

68. Flexner and Fitzpatrick, *Century of Struggle*, 138.

69. Tetrault, *The Myth of Seneca Falls*, 31.

70. Tetrault, *The Myth of Seneca Falls*, 31–32.

71. Tetrault, *The Myth of Seneca Falls*, 33.

72. Flexner and Fitzpatrick, *Century of Struggle*, 161.

73. Flexner and Fitzpatrick, *Century of Struggle*, 158–159.

74. Flexner and Fitzpatrick, *Century of Struggle*, 159–160; *An Account of the Proceedings of the Trial of Susan B. Anthony on the Charge of Illegal Voting, at the Presidential Election in Nov., 1872* (Rochester: Daily Democrat and Chronicle Book Print, 1874), New York State Library Special Collections.

75. Lois Beachy Underhill, *The Woman Who Ran for President* (Bridgehampton: Bridge Works, 1995), 66.

76. Underhill, *The Woman Who Ran for President*, 68.

77. *New York Herald*, 2 April 1870, in Underhill, *The Woman Who Ran for President*, 77–78.

78. Underhill, *The Woman Who Ran for President*, 94–101.

79. Julia Davis, "Belva Ann Lockwood: Remover of Mountains," *American Bar Association Journal*, Vol. 65, No. 2 (1 June 1979): 924.

80. Davis, "Belva Ann Lockwood," 925–927.

81. Kenneth Florey, *Women's Suffrage Memorabilia: An Illustrated Historical Study* (Jefferson: McFarland, 2013), 22–25; Davis, "Belva Ann Lockwood," 928; Jill Norgren, "I Cannot Vote, But Can Be Voted For!," *American History*, Vol. 43, No. 2 (June 2008): 38–43.

82. Tetrault, *The Myth of Seneca Falls*, 126–137, 214.

83. Elizabeth Cady Stanton to Clara Colby, 8 December 1892, in Lori D. Ginzberg, *Elizabeth Cady Stanton: An American Life* (New York: Hill and Wang, 2010), 165.

84. Elizabeth Cady Stanton to William Lloyd Garrison Jr., 6 January 1896, in Ginzberg, *Elizabeth Cady Stanton*, 172.

85. Ginzberg, *Elizabeth Cady Stanton*, 176.

SECTION 2. WINNING THE VOTE, 1890–1920

1. The National American Woman Suffrage Association, http://www.brynmawr.edu/library/exhibits/suffrage/nawsa.html (accessed 17 May 2016).

2. Blake McKelvey, "Women's Rights in Rochester: A Century of Progress," *Rochester History*, Vol. 10, Nos. 2 and 3 (July 1948): 15–17.

3. McKelvey, "Women's Rights in Rochester"; Lillian S. Williams, *Strangers in the Land of Paradise: The Creation of an African American Community, Buffalo, New York, 1900–1940* (Bloomington: Indiana University Press, 1999), 154–155, 182–184.

4. "History of Empire State Federation of Women's Clubs, 1952," Series 6: ESFWC Subject Files, 1952–1991. M. E. Grenander Department of Special Collections and Archives.

5. Robert A. Huff, "Anne Miller and the Geneva Political Equality Club, 1897–1912," *New York History*, Vol. 65, No. 4 (October 1984): 325–348.

6. Carolyn Zogg, "Fossenvue: Summers' Memories in the Late Eighteen Hundreds," written for Seneca County's bicentennial year in 2004.

7. Anne Fitzhugh Miller, *Embers of Fossenvue*, self-published, 1901, located at Geneva Historical Society, Geneva, New York.

8. Hilda R. Watrous, *Harriet May Mills, 1857–1935: A Biography* (Syracuse: New York State Fair in honor of the 50th anniversary of the Harriet May Mills Women's Building, 1984).

9. Stanton, Anthony, and Gage, *History of Woman Suffrage*, 1:675.

10. Kerry Segrave, *Women and Capital Punishment in America, 1840–1899* (McFarland: London, 2008), 128–140.

11. "Horrible Crime of Mrs. Druse," *Chicago Tribune*, 23 December 1886, 1.

12. Segrave, *Women and Capital Punishment in America*, 130.

13. Annulla Linders and Alana Van Gundy-Yoder, "Gall, Gallantry, and the Gallows: Capital Punishment and the Social Construction of Gender, 1840–1920," *Gender and Society*, Vol. 22, No. 3 (June 2008): 324–348.

14. "The Hanging of Mrs. Druse," *Chicago Tribune*, February 26, 1887, 14.

15. Frances Graham, *Sixty Years of Action, 1874–1934: A History of Sixty Years of Work of the Woman's Christian Temperance Union of the State of New York* (Lockport: 1935), 12.

16. David Kevin McDonald, "Organizing Womanhood: Women's Culture and the Politics of Woman Suffrage in New York State, 1865–1917," PhD dissertation, State University of New York at Stony Brook, 1987, 60.

17. Susan B. Anthony and Ida Husted Harper, eds., *History of Woman Suffrage*, Vol. 4: 1883–1900 (Hollenbeck Press: Indianapolis, 1902), 848–854.

18. Anthony and Harper, *History of Woman Suffrage*, 4:850.

19. Anthony and Harper, *History of Woman Suffrage*, 4:94.

20. Lillian Wald, *The House on Henry Street* (New York: Henry Holt, 1915), 266–267.

21. Frances Perkins Center, francesperkinscenter.org (accessed on 7 July 2016).

22. Frances Perkins Center, francesperkinscenter.org.

23. Robert Cooney, *Winning the Vote: The Triumph of the American Woman Suffrage Movement* (Santa Cruz: American Graphics Press, 2005), 121.

24. Ellen Carol Dubois, *Harriot Stanton Blatch and the Winning of Woman Suffrage* (New Haven: Yale University Press, 1997), 102–103.

25. "Suffrage Parade Has Police Guard: Strong Force Out to Keep Order," *New York Times*, 22 May 1910.

26. Ida Husted Harper, ed., *History of Woman Suffrage*, Vol. 6: 1900–1920 (New York: National American Woman Suffrage Association, 1922), 452–453.

27. Betsy Fahlman, *Sculptor and Suffrage: The Art and Life of Alice Morgan Wright* (Albany: Albany Institute of History and Art, 1978), 6.

28. Florey, *Women's Suffrage Memorabilia*, 68–69.

29. Dubois, *Harriot Stanton Blatch*, 187.

30. Jo Freeman, "How 'Sex' Got into Title VII: Persistent Opportunism as a Maker of Public Policy," *Law and Inequality: A Journal of Theory and Practice*, Vol. 9, No. 2 (March 1991): 163–184.

31. Susan Goodier, *No Votes for Women: The New York State Anti-Suffrage Movement* (Urbana: University of Illinois Press, 2013), 11.

32. Harper, *History of Woman Suffrage*, 6:468; "Women Win Assemblymen: Sixty-three Sign Petition to Take Up Suffrage Bill To-day," *New York Times*, 28 March 1912.

33. Judith Wellman, *National Register Nomination for Sherwood Equal Rights District*, no date.

34. Harper, *History of Woman Suffrage*, 6:468–472.

35. Doris Daniels, "Building a Winning Coalition: The Suffrage Fight in New York State," *New York History*, Vol. 60, No. 1 (January 1979): 77–78.

36. Flexner and Fitzpatrick, *Century of Struggle*, 266–268.

37. Flexner and Fitzpatrick, *Century of Struggle*, 274.

38. Christine Stansell, "A Forgotten Fight for Suffrage," *New York Times*, 24 August 2010.

39. Woodrow Wilson, State of the Union address, 2 December 1918.

SECTION 3. THE CONTINUING FIGHT FOR EQUAL RIGHTS, 1920–PRESENT

1. Alice Paul, original ERA language.

2. Katherine Kraft, "ERA: History and Status, Sixty Years of Struggle: From 1923–1982," *Radcliff Quarterly*, Vol. 68, No. 1 (March 1982): 2–6.

3. http://www.equalrightsamendment.org/history.htm (accessed on 7 July 2016).

4. Pam Elam, "The Militant State of Mind: Organizing the Congressional Union, Inc.," *Women's Studies International Forum*, Vol. 12, No.1 (1989): 101.

5. Elam, "The Militant State of Mind," 102–103.

6. Ellen Chesler, *Woman of Valor: Margaret Sanger and the Birth Control Movement in America* (New York: Simon and Schuster, 1992), 34.

7. "A Century of Lawmaking for a New Nation: U.S. Congressional Documents and Debates, 1774–1875," Statues at Large, the Library of Congress, American Memory, https://memory.loc.gov/cgi-bin/ampage?collId=llsl&fileName=017/llsl017.db&recNum=639 (accessed 2 June 2016).

8. Margaret Sanger, *My Fight for Birth Control* (New York: Farrar and Reinhart, 1931), in Linda K. Kerber and Jane Sherron De Hart, eds., *Women's America: Refocusing the Past*, 4th ed. (New York: Oxford University Press, 1995), 337.

9. Sanger, *My Fight for Birth Control*, in Kerber and De Hart, 340.

10. Chesler, *Woman of Valor*, 65.

11. Chesler, *Woman of Valor*, 97–99.

12. Chesler, *Woman of Valor*, 102–103.

13. Chesler, *Woman of Valor*, 105.

14. Chesler, *Woman of Valor*, 140.

15. Sanger, *My Fight for Birth Control*, in Kerber and De Hart, 340–341.

16. Chesler, *Woman of Valor*, 151–154.

17. Chesler, *Woman of Valor*, 156–160.

18. "Papers of Mary Ware Dennett, 1874–1944: A Finding Aid," Arthur and Elizabeth Schlesinger Library on the History of Women in America, Radcliffe Institute for Advanced Study, Harvard University, http://oasis.lib.harvard.edu/oasis/deliver/~sch00058 (accessed 7 June 2016).

19. Chesler, *Woman of Valor*, 372–376, 430; Armond Fields, *Katharine Dexter McCormick: Pioneer for Women's Rights* (Westport: Praeger, 2003), 261–263; Suzanne White Junod and Laura Marks, "Women's Trials: The Approval of the First Oral Contraceptive Pill in the United States and Great Britain," *Journal of the History of Medicine and Allied Sciences*, Vol. 57, No. 2 (April 2002): 117–160.

20. https://www.gwu.edu/~erpapers/abouteleanor/erbiography.cfm.

21. John T. McGuire, "Making the Democratic Party a Partner: Eleanor Roosevelt, The Women's Joint Conference, and the Women's Division of the New York State Democratic Party, 1921–1927," *Hudson River Valley Review*, Vol. 18, No. 2 (September 2001): 37–39.

22. McGuire, "Making the Democratic Party a Partner."

23. https://www.gwu.edu/~erpapers/teachinger/glossary/she-she-she-camps.cfm (accessed 25 July 2016).

24. Abigail Pogrebin, "How Do You Spell Ms.," *New York Magazine*, 30 October 2011, http://nymag.com/news/features/ms-magazine-2011-11/ (accessed 11 April 2016).

25. "About," *Ms.* Magazine Blog, http://msmagazine.com/blog/about/ (accessed 27 June 2016).

26. Vivan Gronick, quoted in Pogrebin, "How Do You Spell Ms."

27. Gloria Steinem, quoted in Pogrebin, "How Do You Spell Ms."

28. Dennis McLellan, "Innovative Editor of New York Magazine," *Los Angeles Times*, 2 July 2008, http://articles.latimes.com/2008/jul/02/local/me-felker2 (accessed 29 June 2016); Gloria Steinem, "The Moral Disarmament of Betty Coed," *Esquire*, September 1962.

29. Gloria Steinem, *My Life on the Road* (New York: Random House, 2015), 48–49.

30. Julie Gallagher, "Waging 'The Good Fight': The Political Career of Shirley Chisholm, 1953–1982," *The Journal of African American History*, Vol. 92, No. 3 (Summer 2007): 400.

31. James Barron, "Shirley Chisholm, 80, Dies; 'Unbossed' Pioneer in Congress and Presidential Candidate," *New York Times*, 4 January 2005.

32. *Congressional Record*, 21 May 1969, Extension Remarks, 91st Congress/1st session, p. 13380.

33. Barron, "Shirley Chisholm, 80, Dies."

34. Gail R. Reizenstein, "A Fresh Look at the Equal Credit Opportunity Act," *Akron Law Review*, Vol. 14, No. 2 (Fall 1980): 215–250.

35. Gloria Steinem, "Houston and History," *Outrageous Acts and Everyday Rebellions* (New York: Holt, Rinehart and Winston, 1983), 280.

36. Program, *1st New York State Women's Meeting, Empire State Plaza, Albany, NY, July 8–10, 1977*.

37. *The Spirit of Houston: The First National Women's Conference, an Official Report to the President, the Congress and the People of the United States*, National Commission on the Observance of International Women's Year, 1978, 105

38. *The Spirit of Houston*, 109.

39. *The Spirit of Houston*, 111.

40. Program, *1st New York State Women's Meeting*, 3.

41. Program, *1st New York State Women's Meeting*, 42.

42. Steinem, *My Life on the Road*, 56.

43. *The Spirit of Houston*, 115.

44. "Mary Anne Krupsak Papers," University of Rochester, River Campus Libraries, Manuscript and Special Collections, http://rbscp.lib.rochester.edu/4001 (accessed 18 May 2016).

45. Bella Abzug, Speech to the First Plenary Session, November 19, 1977, National Women's Conference, in *The Spirit of Houston*, 218.

46. *Sisters of '77*, directed by Cynthia Salzman Mondell and Allen Mondell (Dallas: Media Projects, 2005).

47. *The Spirit of Houston*, 156.

48. *The Spirit of Houston*, 156–157.

49. Steinem, in *Sisters of '77*.

50. Steinem, in *Sisters of '77*.

51. Steinem, *Outrageous Acts and Everyday Rebellions*, 280.

52. Emerson Schwartzkopf, "Collective Promotes Women, T-Shirts," *The Press*, Section 2, Vol. 1, No. 6 (October 1979): 33, 39.

53. Course offering flyers, New York State Museum Accession files, H-1991.99.

54. Schwartzkopf, "Collective Promotes Women, T-Shirts," 39.

55. "Portrait Monument to Lucretia Mott, Elizabeth Cady Stanton and Susan B. Anthony," Architect of the Capitol, http://www.aoc.gov/capitol-hill/other-statues/portrait-monument (accessed 6 June 2018).

56. Tetrault, *The Myth of Seneca Falls*, 188–190.

57. Tetrault, *The Myth of Seneca Falls*, 197.

58. Tetrault, *The Myth of Seneca Falls*, 197.

59. "Her Home" timeline, National Susan B. Anthony Museum and House, http://susanbanthonyhouse.org/blog/her-home/ (accessed 13 June 2016).

60. Eleanor Roosevelt, "My Day," 25 August 1945, from the Eleanor Roosevelt Papers Project, George Washington University, https://www.gwu.edu/~erpapers/myday/displaydoc.cfm?_y=1945&_f=md000113 (accessed 13 June 2016).

61. "Wesleyan Chapel," Women's Rights National Historical Park, National Park Service, https://www.nps.gov/wori/learn/historyculture/wesleyan-chapel.htm (accessed 13 June 2016).

62. Photographic archives, Seneca Falls Historical Society, Seneca Falls, New York.

63. "Elizabeth Cady Stanton House," Women's Rights National Historical Park, National Park Service, https://www.nps.gov/wori/learn/historyculture/elizabeth-cady-stanton-house.htm (accessed 13 June 2016).

64. Wellman, *The Road to Seneca Falls*, 230.

65. Tetrault, *The Myth of Seneca Falls*, 195–196.

66. "Women's Rights Park Opens Upstate," *New York Times*, 19 July 1982.

67. "Wesleyan Chapel Rehabilitation Project," Women's Rights National Historical Park, National Park Service, https://www.nps.gov/wori/learn/historyculture/wesleyan-chapel-rehabilitation-project.htm (accessed 13 June 2016).

68. "Modern Money," US Department of the Treasury, US Bureau of Engraving and Printing, https://modernmoney.treasury.gov/ (accessed 16 June 2016).

69. Chadwick Moore, "Fighting to Bring Women in History to Central Park," *New York Times*, 12 July 2015.

70. Elizabeth Cady Stanton and Susan B. Anthony Statue Fund, http://www.centralparkwherearethewomen.org/ (accessed 16 June 2016).

INDEX

Note: *Italicized* page numbers indicate material in captions separate from text of book.